Interviews with **Betty Friedan**

Conversations with Public Intellectuals Series
Douglas Brinkley and David Oshinsky, General Editors

Interviews with

Betty Friedan

Edited by
Janann Sherman

University Press of Mississippi
Jackson

Books by Betty Friedan

The Feminine Mystique. New York: W. W. Norton & Company, 1963.
It Changed My Life: Writings on the Women's Movement. Cambridge: Harvard University Press, 1976.
The Second Stage. New York: Simon & Schuster, 1981.
The Fountain of Age. New York: Simon & Schuster, 1993.
Beyond Gender: The Real Politics of Work and Family. Brigid O'Farrell, ed. Baltimore: Johns Hopkins University Press, 1997.
Life So Far: A Memoir. New York: Simon & Schuster, 2000.

www.upress.state.ms.us

Photograph on page iii: © 2002 Nancy Crampton

10 09 08 07 06 05 04 03 02   4 3 2 1
∞
Library of Congress Cataloging-in-Publication Data

Interviews with Betty Friedan / edited by Janann Sherman.
    p. cm.—(Conversations with public intellectuals series)
    Includes index.
    ISBN 1-57806-479-1 (cloth : alk. paper)—ISBN 1-57806-480-5 (pbk. : alk. paper)
    1. Friedan, Betty—Interviews.   2. Feminists—United States—Interviews.   3.
Feminism—United States—History.   4. United States—Social conditions—1960–1980.   5.
United States—Social conditions—1980–   I. Sherman, Janann.   II. Series.
HQ1413.F75 I58   2002
305.42'0973—dc21   2002022718

British Library Cataloging-in-Publication Data available

Contents

v

Introduction

Writer, teacher, and public intellectual, Betty Friedan has been in the spotlight almost continuously since the publication of her landmark book, *The Feminine Mystique*, in 1963. In the conversations that follow, this complicated and intense woman speaks frankly and with considerable passion to a host of journalists and academics. This collection of twenty-two interviews spans thirty-six years and publications as diverse as the *New York Times*, *Working Woman*, and *Playboy*. Although the interviews are inevitably shaped by the views of the interviewers and the publications in which they appear, the nature of the genre requires that interrogators step aside and let her speak for herself. While Friedan's extensive body of published work spells out her positions on a host of important public matters, the immediacy of these public conversations captures her passion and her wit, her candor and contradictions. The logic of her arguments for equity and fairness, and the remarkable consistency of her views about men, women, and the American family, provide a rich resource for scholarly research, while the nature of the format raises important questions about the role of the media in the personification of complex ideas and the limits that imposes on both the person and the ideas.

No one recognized women's oppression in fifties America, not even the women themselves, until Betty Friedan and *The Feminine Mystique* named the phenomenon and made a coherent argument about its causes. Postwar prosperity had provided women with a life of ease their mothers hadn't imagined and a standard of living that was the envy of the world. At the same time, women were assailed by a public discourse that contended they could find true happiness only in domesticity. Any discomfort with the limits of their assigned domestic vocations was experienced as a personal failing. Friedan was alerted to the dissonance between the ideal of the contented suburban housewife and the reality of discontent—what she called "the problem that had no name"—by the results of a survey she circulated for the fifteenth anniversary of her Smith College class, reinforced by her own difficulties in balancing motherhood and a writing career. For her book, she interviewed hundreds of housewives, analyzed the embedded messages about gender roles in women's magazines, advice columns, movies, and advertising, and dissected assertions from experts in scientific and psychological circles. Friedan uncovered a noticeable shift against women's autonomy after World War II. Women who had experienced independence and cultural validation for their contributions to the war effort faced intense pressures—economic, cultural, and psychological—after the war to make homemaking their primary career. These women had become victims, Friedan said, of the patriarchal ideology of "the feminine mystique." The problems women experienced as personal, she wrote, were instead a reflection of a culture that did not "permit women to accept or gratify their basic need to grow and fulfill their potentialities as human beings." In prose saturated with indignation and passion, Friedan called for nothing less than "a drastic reshaping of the cultural image of femininity that will permit women to reach maturity, identity, [and] completeness of self" through a fulfilling career. "The only way for a woman, as for a man, to find herself, to know herself as a person," Friedan wrote, "is by creative work of her own. There is no other way."

Friedan expected, and perhaps even hoped, that her book would be controversial. Earlier efforts to publish articles based on her findings had been soundly rejected, even though she had amiable working relationships with a host of women's magazines. No one, it seemed, wanted to print something with which, as *Redbook* indicated, "only the most neurotic housewife could possibly identify." Her publisher cautiously printed only 3,000 copies. This perhaps partially explains why Friedan, in her conversation with Jane Howard just after the book was published, comes out swinging. The subtitle to the interview, "Angry Battler for Her Sex," seems an apt description of a pugnacious Friedan who drew a sharp dichotomy between "women" and herself. Women, in her estimation, were frivolous, evaded using their intellect, and generally took the easy way out by marrying young. They were guilty, she implied, of colluding in their own oppression. These women, sold the bill of goods she called the feminine mystique, felt dissatisfied but helpless. She exhorted women to wake up: "Don't be an appliance, a vegetable, or a service station," she said. "As for me, I'm very unbored. I'm nasty, I'm bitchy, I get mad, but by God, I'm absorbed in what I'm doing." All this rhetoric seems overly combative and defensive, especially in light of the enormous popularity of her book. Still, at the time, she couldn't know that it would be a success; she apparently assumed that a controversial book by an unconventional author might earn the publicity to make it so. *The Feminine Mystique* became an instant bestseller. Mainstream women to whom the book was addressed would remember where they were when they first read *The Feminine Mystique* and frequently remarked to her, as she relates in numerous interviews, that "it changed my life." Ultimately the book set off a movement that virtually redefined the role of women in American society.

Throughout the 1960s, Friedan granted few interviews. Preferring to disseminate her views unmediated, she wrote her own articles. This seems a wise choice, given that those who wrote about her seemed to focus at least as much on her physical characteristics, her life story, and her personality as they did on what she had to say. The leader of any movement sets its tone, and for the nascent women's movement, Betty Friedan was the message. Hers was the face of feminism, as numerous interviewers indicate. Physical descriptions abound in these interviews, many of them unflattering. They emphasize her big nose, her "droopy, basset-hound eyes," her tendency to pudginess, her flamboyance, her profanity, her drinking.

Similarly, these writers mine Friedan's biography for clues to her psyche and produce a handful of well-honed parables: her early experience with anti-Semitism, her mother's disappointment at sacrificing career for family, her decision to decline a prestigious fellowship because of the disapproval of a boyfriend, her romance with leftist politics, the job she lost because she requested a second maternity leave, her confinement in suburbia where she hid her writing from family and friends "like drinking in the morning," her violent marriage.

This effort to achieve the essence of Betty Friedan and, by extension, the women's movement she launched turns most tellingly on discussions of her personality. All who interviewed her had strong feelings about her, many of them negative. They provide a veritable litany of liabilities: she is messy, imperious, self-serving, aggressive, demanding, temperamental, rude. What everyone seemed to find fascinating was how unladylike she was.

Although one person's imperiousness is another's charisma, close associates admitted Friedan was difficult, at best. Nonetheless, many recognized her enormous contributions to feminism. "She is a terror to deal with and there is an overpowering ego at work," NOW activist Jacqui Ceballos told interviewer Paul Wilkes. "But this is the first person who awakened women to their oppression and for that alone we should pay homage."

Betty Friedan was the most radical woman in America in 1966 when she founded the National Organization for Women "to take action to bring women into full participation in the mainstream of American society NOW." Ironically, within less than a decade, she would represent the conservative, even reactionary, wing of the feminist movement. NOW was organized by the kind of women who responded to the message of *The Feminine Mystique*— white, middle-class, highly educated women who had embraced liberal individualism, with its emphasis on independence, equality before the law, and personal development. These liberal feminists defined women's rights largely in material terms: equal pay for equal work, equal job opportunity, affordable childcare. Friedan's plan for NOW was to employ political pressure, litigation, and public mobilization to change laws and public policies limiting women.

NOW membership quadrupled in the first year, and before long, Friedan found herself embroiled in conflict. As Marilyn French points out, it was "exceedingly difficult to unify women" whose "common cause is obscured by the clashing of classes, races, religious and ethnic categories, and subcultures." Moreover, Betty Friedan's outsize personality sold her book and her ideas, built her reputation, and launched a movement, but it was also her undoing as leader of that movement. Her abrasive personality undercut her message and her rigid adherence to her vision of a gradualist political agenda denied the movement a critical flexibility. Friedan was pushed aside by younger, more radical feminists, whose agenda went well beyond Friedan's call for self-realization in a career to a full-fledged assault on sexism in all of its forms. These feminists, schooled in the crucible of civil rights and New Left movements, were committed to social transformation. They called their movement "women's liberation" and contended that the gut issues of women's oppression could not be legislated away. To them, the Equal Rights Amendment, considered by liberal feminists the pinnacle of social change, was inadequate and beside the point. Impatient with evolution, they sought revolution.

Central to this new radicalism was a focus on sexual politics, a term that encompassed everything from rape to abortion to pornography to sexual identity. Friedan saw this shift as wrong-headed and self-defeating, a costly diversion from economic equality issues. Through forums provided by interviewers, Friedan savagely attacked her radical sisters as the "bra-burning, anti-man, politics of orgasm school," and warned women not to be seduced by their divisive rhetoric. Perhaps the most devastating split in the movement, as far as Friedan was concerned, was over the issue of lesbianism. When radicals in the movement argued that lesbianism was the only fully feminist position, Friedan's response to what she termed the "lavender menace" was both personal and political. She was both shocked by this public declaration of sexuality, she told Marilyn French, and concerned that it endangered her campaign "to gain rights for women without alienating men." She believed, rightly as it turned out, that this focus would fuel a media circus, alienate mainstream women, and divert attention from avenues of meaningful change in the status of women.

Though Friedan remained synonymous in the minds of millions of American women with the women's movement, she had lost control. She was hurt and angry. She turned to teaching, writing, and getting even. Believing that "nothing is taken seriously unless it is written in a book," as she told Mary Walton, she pulled together *It Changed My Life: Writings on the Women's Movement*, a compilation of old and new writings, a catalog of slights, and a self-serving recital of power struggles. Friedan poured out her fury and frustration that her movement had been stolen from her by a pro-lesbian, man-bashing cabal.

She had bones to pick with a host of individuals and groups, especially Gloria Steinem, a younger and more photogenic feminist, who had become a media darling. Their dispute was political and it was personal. "I was really opposed to the radical chic, anti-man politics she espoused," Friedan told David Sheff. What made her angriest, though, was that the press seemed unaware that Steinem was merely a "public relations person" while she was the "founder." During many of these conversations, Friedan persists in claiming sole credit for both launching the movement and for sustaining it. "If Betty Friedan weren't alive," she asserted to Paul Wilkes, "she'd have to be invented to see the movement through." The movement was foundering, she makes it clear, because feminists stubbornly resisted her counsel.

Her movement was about equality, she said, not, as the word liberation implied, about rejecting men and marriage for some abstract notion of freedom. While radicals indicted men and the sexual double standard, with

Steinem calling marriage a form of prostitution, Friedan indicted sex roles rather than men. Blaming men, Friedan told Denise Watson, was a "perversion of feminism," one she found to be "ideologically and politically and actually fallacious." She had very intentionally named it the National Organization *for* Women, not *of* Women. "It wasn't going to be women against men," she said. Men had to be included in negotiations for women's equality. Man was not the enemy, she maintained, but a fellow victim. Friedan drew a compelling parallel between the feminine mystique and the "masculine mystique." It was surely no accident that men, as Friedan reiterated in numerous interviews, who were forced to stifle their emotions and under intense pressure to be the sole provider, died much younger than women. Just as women should be free to express ambition and intelligence, Friedan believed that men should be free to express nurturance and sensitivity. True women's liberation would liberate both sexes from oppressive gender roles.

As the movement matured and the battle for the ERA was abandoned, Betty Friedan began to formulate what seemed to her to be the next logical stage of the women's movement. Feminism needed to evolve, she said, with changing realities. The first stage had been to break into man's world. *The Second Stage,* as she called her 1981 book, should be to construct a shared world with men. Without this second stage, Friedan presciently told Paula Gottlieb, "women could be stuck halfway through, and there might be a real reaction against the women's movement in the next generation." Younger women in the 1980s "had a whole new set of problems" related to trying to sustain work and family. "What is needed," said Friedan, "is an integration of the two." Unfortunately, radical feminists, she told Gottlieb, were still locked into first-stage thinking which had overlooked, indeed denigrated, the important biological and psychological blessings of motherhood and family. In place of the feminine mystique, they had espoused a "feminist mystique," a preoccupation with women's individualistic needs at the expense of more traditional sources of women's identity. To be sure, this was a mystique she had helped create, but she had modified her position, as she tells Mary Walton, in light of a new generation of young women who had absorbed the message of women's liberation and believed that they could have it all. What they were finding, however, was that women's career opportunities had been merely added to women's responsibilities in the home, resulting in a "superwoman syndrome" that, far from liberating women, doubly oppressed them.

Over the years and in countless interviews, Friedan maintained that feminism had always been about choice. And that choice must include a woman's right to choose the traditional role of wife and mother. "No feminism that was opposed to family," Friedan told Sheff, could be embraced by "the great majority of women." If family duties continued "to stifle women's autonomy," Friedan wrote in *The Second Stage*, "the solution is not the break with family—as radical feminists would have it—but the reorganization of it." She elaborated on that idea in her conversation with Bettyann Kevles, describing "a basic remodeling of American society" into one in which "women and men could have equal access to both family and career." For Friedan, who never wavered from her belief that the solution to women's oppression lay in economic justice, such an overhaul required not only fathers sharing parenting but also national policies to support women with paid maternity leaves, flexible work hours, job-sharing, and state-supported childcare. Parenting must now, she told Gottlieb, "be shared between the mother, the father and the government."

Such a possibility may have seemed reasonable when Friedan published *The Second Stage* in 1981, but the rise of the conservative right, and the presidencies of Ronald Reagan and George Bush, moved public policy in the opposite direction. Conversations with Gottlieb and Curt Suplee in the early eighties reveal an optimistic Friedan, certain that her "critical mass theory" would work. Women were close to 50 percent of the workforce, more than half the registered voters, and feminism, she said, had become mainstream. Women would soon harness their own political power to turn the tide. But her optimism faded as conservatives set about dismantling the machinery to enforce sex discrimination laws, undoing equal pay for comparable work, and crusading against a woman's right to choose. And women failed to respond in an organized way to these developments.

Characteristically, Friedan cast the blame widely. The message and the attainments of feminism, she claimed in several interviews, were being distorted by an unholy coalition of radical feminists and the conservative right, leaving mainstream women stranded. "The language of rage and sexual politics" rendered the movement vulnerable to attacks from the right as anti-family, making it easy, she told Mary Walton, "for the so-called Moral Majority to lump ERA with homosexual rights and abortion into one explosive package of licentious, family-threatening sex." Moreover, the hollow rhetoric of family values was being cynically employed to reinvigorate the feminine mystique, suggesting that any woman who assumed a non-conventional role, regardless of necessity, was responsible for neglecting her family. The terms may be social, but Friedan saw the source as economic. "I think family values are very important," she told Robert Selle, "but we have to reframe them in terms of new economic and demographic realities." Feminists need to embrace the family and take the rhetorical high ground away from conservatives who deny that women must work. When she looked at American society, Friedan said to Nathan Gardels, she saw "a big, stagnant pond covered by the green scum of materialism." Women and minorities were being scapegoated in order to shift attention and blame from a skewed economic system that favored the wealthy. "If the kids are suffering," she told Sheff, "it's society's fault for not making accommodations for working mothers and fathers who put in twelve hour days." These were issues she would return to again and again.

In the early 1990s, Friedan took a respite from feminism and its discontents to turn yet another personal challenge into a public crusade. As with the feminine mystique, she found the catalyst for this new project in her own experience. The springboard was her sixtieth birthday party in 1981. Dispirited by the prospect of facing her old age in a youth-obsessed culture, in typical Friedan fashion, she decided to plunge into research. At gerontological conferences and meetings at Harvard, she reported to Brian Lamb and Alice Luddington, she heard "a definition of age only in terms of deterioration and decline." Depressed, she mined popular culture for positive images of age and came up empty. So she turned to a favorite research tool and began interviewing active seniors like herself. That's when, she told Lamb, she "began to realize that I was dealing with another mystique."

The resulting book, *The Fountain of Age,* a compendium of scientific studies, anecdotal evidence, and personal experiences, sought to explode the myths of age just as, thirty years before, she exploded the myths of the contented housewife. The "mystique of age" she contended, was "more pernicious and pervasive" than the feminine mystique, because it became a self-fulfilling prophecy. People who believed the rhetoric prematurely gave up on life. In the interviews that followed the publication of her book, Friedan laments the wasted wisdom and experience of lives cut short by hasty retirement, early preparation for death, and withdrawal from society into "manicured age ghettos," a term that echoed her critique of the "comfortable concentration camps" of 1950s suburbia.

Many of the themes of *The Fountain of Age* reflect similarities to *The Feminine Mystique*. Both women and the aged are culturally defined as weak and helpless. And Friedan's solutions for both groups are similar. In her conversations, she emphasizes that it is largely a question of mind over matter; "changing the very way you think about yourself could have an effect on the aging process." But positive thinking only goes so far; change requires individual action. Both groups—the aged and women—she asserts, must find ways to enrich their own lives by finding purpose and projects, and by taking control of their own lives. "When people give up control over their lives and have no purpose to their days," she tells Alice Luddington in 1993, much as she told interviewers in 1963, "it is a dehumanizing experience." Just as she redefined the feminine mystique to liberate afflicted women, she redefines old age as an adventure, a liberation from the concerns and problems of the first two-thirds of life, a period of growth and "generativity." And just like with the feminine mystique, Friedan predicts a "paradigm shift" in America's response to aging which she, of course, will lead.

Betty Friedan's model for a vital old age, like her model for overcoming the feminine mystique, was herself. And perhaps the chief beneficiary of her new way of thinking was, in both cases, also herself. In writing *The Feminine Mystique*, she told interviewers, she had liberated not only other women, but also herself from that patriarchal ideology. And in the process of writing *The Fountain of Age*, she told Lamb, "I've liberated myself. [I've] moved from this denial and dread of age to an affirmation of where I am now."

As the century turned, Friedan was still living the vital life she championed, directing a million-dollar, four-year project based at Cornell University to design a "New Paradigm: Women, Work, Family and Public Policy," to transfer her feminist principles into a broad societal agenda for the twenty-first century. Once again, as Linda Myers puts it, "she aims to transform the world."

This brief discussion of Betty Friedan's life and work traces the development of her ideas as a public intellectual as presented in the following interviews. In many respects, Betty Friedan was her own worst enemy. As Paul Wilkes noted in 1970, "Betty has offended, at one time or another, virtually everyone she has worked closely with." From the accompanying commentaries, that group included those who wrote about her. It is ironic that the genre she resented for misrepresenting her serves so well in this volume in letting her speak for herself. The juxtaposition between her ideas and writers' perceptions of her make this collection a rich source for the analysis not only of Friedan and her work, but also for myriad other topics concerning the role of media in politics, public perceptions, and social movements.

The interviews here have been selected to represent a wide range of publication venues and a broad array of Betty Friedan's views and commentary. They are arranged chronologically for easy reference and presented unedited so as to be of maximum value to scholars. Naturally there is a certain amount of repetition, which often functions to reveal the importance of a particular subject to both Friedan and her interviewers and, in some cases, how her attitudes and ideas have changed over time.

This collection could not have happened without the cooperation of the many interviewers and publishers who granted their permission to reprint the selected interviews. I wish to thank Rhonda Charnes for her persistence in helping me locate interviews, Paula Casey for her encouragement, and Seetha Srinivasan, director of the University Press of Mississippi, for her patience and support in seeing this manuscript through to production. And finally, I'd like to extend my abundant gratitude to my chief collaborator and gentlest critic, Charles Sherman.

Chronology

1921   Born on February 4 in Peoria, Illinois, to Harry Goldstein and Miriam Horwitz Goldstein. Bettye Naomi Goldstein is oldest of three children (sister Amy and brother Harry).

1927–33   Attends Whittier School in Peoria.

1933–35   Attends Roosevelt Junior High School in Peoria; writes for the school paper, *The Reflector*.

1935–38   Attends Central High School in Peoria; on staff of the school newspaper, *Opinion*, and founds a literary magazine, *Tide*; graduates June 9, 1938, one of six valedictorians of her class.

1939–42   Attends Smith College, psychology major; studies with gestalt psychologist Kurt Koffka; writes for and later edits the student newspaper, *The Smith College Associated News (SCAN)*; Phi Beta Kappa, junior year; graduates summa cum laude.

1943–44   Attends the University of California at Berkeley on scholarship; studies with Erik Erikson; declines fellowship for Ph.D.

1944–45   Moves to New York City; employed as assistant news editor for the *Federated Press*, a left-wing news service.

1945   June, loses job to returning veteran.

1946–52   Reporter for *UE News*, newspaper of the United Electrical, Radio and Machine Workers of America.

1947   Marries Carl Friedan on June 12.

1948   Gives birth to son, Daniel, on October 3.

1952   Gives birth to son, Jonathan, on November 27; fired from job at *UE News* after claiming second maternity leave.

1952–62   Freelance writer for mainstream women's magazines and stay-at-home mom.

1956   Gives birth to daughter, Emily, on May 23.

1957   Fifteen-year Smith college reunion; circulates questionnaire to Smith graduates concerning their lives as wives and mothers.

1963   Publishes *The Feminine Mystique.*

1966   Co-founds the National Organization for Women.

1966–70   President of the National Organization for Women.

1969   Divorces Carl Friedan after twenty-two-year stormy marriage; co-founds the National Association for the Repeal of Abortion Laws (NARAL—later called the National Abortion Rights Action League).

1970   Leaves presidency of NOW; leads Women's Strike for Equality, August 26.

1971   Co-founds National Women's Political Caucus (NWPC).

1972–75   Holds numerous visiting professorships to discuss gender and public policy.

1973   Organizes the first International Feminist Conference.

1975   Receives honorary doctorate from Smith College; attends the first International Women's Year Conference in Mexico.

1976   Publishes *It Changed My Life: Writings on the Women's Movement.*

1977   Attends International Women's Conference in Houston.

1978   Senior research associate at Columbia University's Center for Social Sciences.

1980   Fellow at Harvard's Institute for Politics at the John F. Kennedy School of Government.

1981   Publishes *Second Stage.*

1984   Democratic Party delegate at nomination of Geraldine Ferraro for vice president.

1985   Chair of the American Jewish Congress's Commission on the Status of Women.

1986–93   Fellow at University of Southern California's Andrus Gerontology Center in the fall; teaches at New York University in the spring.

1993   Open heart surgery; publishes *The Fountain of Age.*

1994   Fellow at the Woodrow Wilson International Center for Scholars.

1995   Attends Fourth United Nations' Conference on Women in Beijing, China.

1997   Publishes *Beyond Gender: The Real Politics of Work and Family.*

1998   Receives million-dollar Ford Foundation grant to conduct conferences on her New Paradigm: Gender, Work and Public Policy at Cornell University.

2000   Publishes *Life So Far: A Memoir*.

Interviews with **Betty Friedan**

Betty Friedan's Pet Pique: *The Feminine Mystique*—Angry Battler for Her Sex

Jane Howard / 1963

From *Life* magazine, (1 November 1963),
84–88. © 1963 Time Inc. Reprinted by
permission.

"This whole society could erupt in one great big wave of boredom, just because we've been conned into expecting more joys from our little houses than they can possibly give us," says Betty Friedan. "As for me, I'm very unbored. I'm nasty, I'm bitchy, I get mad, but by God, I'm absorbed in what I'm doing."

Mrs. Friedan, an impassioned New York suburbanite, was never really bored in her life. A native of Peoria, *summa cum laude* graduate of Smith, graduate fellow in psychology, mother of three, free-lance writer, she never had time to be. But she discovered the many homemakers she talked to were oddly dissatisfied with their lot when according to the script they have been following they should have been deliriously happy. She looked into the matter and came up with an angry book called *The Feminine Mystique*. In it she indicts educators, psychiatrists, anthropologists and all others who since World War II have preached Freud's dictum—a "mystique" she has called it—that a woman can only "fulfill" herself as a wife and mother. The book was an overnight best seller, as disruptive of cocktail party conversation and women's clubs discussions as a tear-gas bomb. Its author has been vilified and praised in about equal quantities. "What I say seems to arouse violent emotions," says Betty Friedan

3

cheerily. "But if I can put across the idea that a woman is first of all a person, not a mommy, not a sex object, not an unpaid dishwasher—that she needn't choose between house and career but have both—it'll all be worth it."

In conversations with *Life*'s Jane Howard, Betty Friedan aired her views on the feminine mystique and related controversies:

- Being born a woman with a brain in America today can seem a handicap. You feel like a freak. I used to think I might have enjoyed life more if I'd been born a Frenchwoman in the time of Mme. de Stael, a bluestocking with salons and lovers and lots of good talk. I've changed my mind. Now I think now is fine, now is great. When I was doing the housewife bit, though, I thought it was awful.

- Women aren't brought up to think well enough to talk. It's a revelation for a man to find a woman he can really talk to. I began to realize a while back that many of my best friends were men.

- A good woman is one who loves passionately, has guts, seriousness and passionate convictions, takes responsibility and shapes society. Doing these things is every bit as important as being a good mother and making men happy. I'm horrified by the word "cool." Coolness is an evasion of life. Being cool isn't it at all. What I think you're supposed to be is passionate, fanatic and crusading. I'd rather be hot and wrong. I'd rather be committed than detached.

- I guess a lot of women don't like my book because they probably feel they're threatened by it. Perhaps it's because they don't take themselves seriously, won't work to the limit of their ability. For them it's easier—they can always say what a great actress or writer they could have been if only they'd kept at it, but of course they gave it up to make a home. They don't subject themselves to the decisions and actions it takes to get started.

- I don't like this self-pitying, trapped housewife bit. I think women who have been victims of the feminine mystique should do something about it, should attack the things they used to take for granted, should grow. Growth is what human beings are made for. If we don't grow, we die.

- "Career woman" has been made an ooky phrase. The feminine mystique created it and we've got to think of something to replace "career." "Vocation" maybe. "Career woman" made me think that if I'd stayed in the academic world I'd have had to be celibate.

- Capital C Career Women seem to resent my book, maybe because I say that all women should try to do what the Career Women are already doing. Maybe they're finding that they're not so special. Maybe they don't want others muscling into the act.

- You don't have to choose a joyless celibacy if you want to use your brain. You needn't make huge decisions, you have to make the right little ones—like studying for the exam instead of going to the movies and writing in the morning instead of getting an early start for the beach.

- There's so much unnecessary martyrdom. I'm not sure it wouldn't be better to have a lot of eccentric old maids and scarlet women around than all these dreary, dreary virtuous housewives. Not that plenty of women with husbands and children and homes aren't terrific people themselves. I know some, and I think soon there will be many more, but they won't call themselves housewives.
- Women are like Negroes in that both got their rights on paper long before they did in reality. Women achieved equality on paper the year before I was born, but it won't become a reality until enough women choose to use their rights. It's happening, it's going to happen more and more.
- Masculine mystique? Sure there've been a lot of jokes. My husband was the first to crack one. There's some truth in it. Why should men be all that strong? This man's-world-woman's-world bit is for the birds. Men aren't barred from growing as women are. Yet men are victims of the feminine mystique too because it keeps them from knowing women as human beings.
- Can women who've been stifled for long years by the mystique come out from under? Some can learn to, but women who don't have the discipline, won't make the effort or are simply afraid to be tested may turn out to be the displaced persons of our time. They'll be no more alive than their green stamps and grandchildren's snapshots can make them feel.
- Today a girl evades her identity crisis by getting married to a boy who doesn't know who or what he is either. Love is so over-glorified as a solution to all problems in America. It's wonderful but it isn't everything. One of the things I most enjoy is good talk, deep communication, and it's absurd to think as alleged, that you can only have this with a husband or lover. There can be a whole rich diversity of love and communication of which sexual love, long may it live, is only one.
- Many boys never get any sense of purpose or identity because they're brought up in the bedroom suburbs with their mothers and no men around except the garbage man, milkman and TV repairman.
- Community work can be an internship for women if they take themselves seriously. I'm all for politics, for example—it's one of the great passions. Women should do more, though, than lick envelopes. I've never been much more than a passive Democrat because I don't want to collect furniture for auctions, I want to make policy. To a real politician politics is never boring—to envelope-lickers it is. I was an assistant den mother a while and I was never so bored in all my life. Even my son was bored. We both quit.
- I like revolutions. Revolutionaries are my kind of heroes. I don't even mind Joan of Arc. What we need in America is more heroines. We have sex objects and unreal creatures in love stories but nobody to model ourselves after. But the delayed revolution, the real sexual revolution, the emergence of women as people, will happen.
- Children don't need all that mommyness. It doesn't matter to them who waxes

the floor. You don't need to make them your profession. They need not be your jewels. The mom, the nagging, domineering mother, the castrative wife, is the mother who lives through her husband and children.

- Some people think I'm saying, "Women of the world unite—you have nothing to lose but your men." It's not true. You have nothing to lose but your vacuum cleaners.

- I've always been the opposite of what the feminine mystique says a good mother should be because I don't find name tapes and car pools all that great. I don't live through my kids. They're separate beings, apart from me, who continually surprise and delight me.

- Don't be an appliance, a vegetable or a service station. How will you get a man? If you find yourself first you won't need any trickery. He'll find you, and he'll have plenty of competition.

- Lincoln is my oldest hero, partly because I'm from Illinois where nobody can grow up without being aware of him, partly because I'm passionate about any kind of emancipation.

Mother Superior to Women's Lib

Paul Wilkes / 1970

From the *New York Times Magazine,* (29 November
1970), 27–29, 140–43, 149–50, 157. Reprinted
by permission of The New York Times.

Her eyes glistening with tears, Betty Naomi Goldstein watched the sun set
dozens of times from a lonesome perch by the weed-filled, abandoned cemetery in Peoria, Ill. Betty wasn't an attractive girl—her long nose had already
drawn the crude comments of the boys in school. On top of that, she was
doubly cursed for a young girl growing up in the late-1930s Midwest: she was
intelligent and a Jew. Her friends overlooked her appearance and brains, but
when it came time for the pubescent savagery of sorority-pledging at Peoria
High School, ethnics could no longer be forgotten. Lumped with the blacks
and girls from poor families, Betty Goldstein was not asked to join a sorority,
thus effectively banishing her from even the most meager social life. While
her classmates bubbled on to each other in the late afternoons, the outcast
looked out over the cemetery and vowed, "If they don't like me, some day
they'll learn to respect me."

Young Betty composed a simple prayer to see her through those days of
rejection: "I want a boy who will like me best, and I want a work to do." A
stormy twenty-year marriage to Carl Friedan, an advertising executive, that
ended in divorce over a year ago never quite fulfilled her first request, but the
second has surely been answered.

Betty Friedan (rhymes with "sedan"), starting with her book in 1963, *The
Feminine Mystique,* has presided as mother superior over the women's liberation

7

movement. Although women's lib groups may number 100 in New York alone, she started the first one, NOW, the National Organization for Women. It was Betty Friedan who almost single-handedly held the shaky coalition of women's groups together for the strike last Aug. 26 that saw thousands of women across the country protesting their sexual bondage, and who preserved the coalition that is now planning another strike for Dec. 12. For the past seven years it has been Betty Friedan, protesting at all-male bars, prodding the consciences of women (and men) in dozens of speeches each year, badgering Congressmen to pass laws and enforce those on the books that give women the parity they now lack.

It is mid-afternoon, and the mother superior is making preparations for a trip to the provinces to talk to novices and drum up further recruits, in this instance at male-dominated and -oriented Wake Forest University. She lives in one of a string of brownstones on West 93rd Street just off Central Park West that were collectively renovated and painted a vibrant shade of olive. The scene is typical: Betty is late, she can't find what she needs (a copy of *Communitas* by Paul and Percival Goodman), her clothing is in disarray (baggy white panty-hose, two buttons undone on her dress) and there are further complications (the family poodle has vomited twice on the oriental rug, and the cat has just given birth to three kittens on fourteen-year-old Emily Friedan's bunk bed).

"*Omygawd,*" Betty hollers down to Jane, her Haitian maid, in a gravelly voice, "Mervin's made a mess." At forty-nine, she is a vision of somebody's eccentric, middle-aged aunt, her hair a swirl of cowlicks, her face deeply lined, her chin double, her brown eyes coursing back and forth. Then, mumbling to herself as she steps over piles of papers that have spilled off the mound on her office desk, "Where the hell is that book? Did I lend it to somebody? No, no. I've got to sound like I know something in Washington tomorrow. Where the hell is that book?"

Communitas, found on the top shelf of a bookcase, is stuffed, together with plane tickets and various papers into a "Carl Friedan Advertising" blue-plastic carrying case and a leather purse the size and shape of a horse's feedbag. In a cab a few minutes later, she digs down into the bag to find a crumpled check-book and some overdue bills, including one from New York Telephone for $132, that have to be paid. Blithely, she writes out the checks without entering anything on the stub. "Oh, I have a girl who is sympathetic to the movement at the bank," she says. "She calls me when my balance is down."

Stanley Aronson, a Brooklyn-raised and -accented cab driver, turns around and without any preliminaries says, "You're *her*, ain't ya? Well, you're the cause of all my troubles, I just want you to know. My wife, she'd join the movement in a minute, she would. She was O.K. till she started believing all that equality. . . ."

"But why isn't she equal?" comes the gravelly voice from the back seat. "Slavery was outlawed a hundred years ago. *Uhmm*. What airport are we going to anyway—La Guardia, right?"

At the Winston-Salem, N.C., airport, Betty is met by four girls who sheepishly admit they are about all Wake Forest has in the way of a women's liberation movement. They apologize in advance for the scanty crowd they expect for tonight's speech. "I'm afraid the awareness level is about zero around here," says one of the girls, dressed in a stylish midi and high, brown, laced boots. During the half-hour ride to the campus, in between absent-minded rummagings through the plastic portfolio and the leather feedbag, Betty asks questions, but does not seem to hear the answers.

"Hours, do you have the same house hours as men? How available are birth-control pills? What kind of punishment do you get if they catch you in a boy's room? Who administers the discipline system anyhow?"

During a dinner arranged by the coterie of women's lib advocates, Betty, seated at a table of twenty people, is a target of questions. Some she doesn't answer at all, others she smiles at, some she answers with a few terse sentences, as often off the subject as on.

The mother superior's mind is somewhere else, and the four girls who picked her up at the airport hope it will also arrive in Winston-Salem shortly. "She looks so different—I've seen her on TV before," whispers one of the girls. "Her hair looks like Phyllis Diller's. I hope they won't start throwing stones when she talks."

The lecture agency that scheduled Betty at Wake Forest at a fee of $750 had told her to expect to speak before 600 people. The four girls said they would be happy if 300 showed. Amid twitters from the males, a few catcalls and a hush from the girls who are seeing Women's Liberation Herself in the flesh for the first time, Betty is presented a few minutes later to a crowd of 1,700 people, the largest any speaker has ever drawn at Wake Forest.

For a Southern audience, usually silent after the speaker is introduced and courteously applauded, the Wake Forest gathering is noisy. The organizers of the Friedan speech look around nervously, wondering if one of them should say something as the speaker stands silently at the microphone and calmly runs her eyes over the audience.

There is no need to worry. Like some great Shakespearean performer, the seemingly disoriented Betty lowers the gravelly voice an octave and says, "Many people think men are the enemy in the movement I represent. Man is not the enemy. He is the fellow victim." The impish grins leave male faces, and there is silence. The mother superior knows her audience, and if there is an enemy out there she knows well how to blunt his attack.

With the deep lines on her face washed out by television lights, and with long tongues of hair that look like sideburns swaying lazily as she speaks, Betty works in slowly. "Why should men die ten years earlier? . . . Why should man be saddled with his masculine mystique, his image as tight-lipped, brutal, crew-cut—not able to cry out for help? . . . And women: are they only castrating monsters, or Lolita sex objects, or morons whose greatest quest in life is to have their kitchen sinks and husband's shirts as white as snow?"

The tempo builds and soon the Jewish girl from Peoria is doing justice to the pulpit at Wait Chapel at Wake Forest, a pulpit complete with a green cloth bearing the IHS emblem, a pulpit that has been beaten and caressed by the hands of Baptist preachers who have come here to harangue students on more cosmic problems than liberation of the female sex. "We have the rights on paper, but what does that mean? . . . What does your university think of you girls when they demand that you be in your rooms when the boys are still free? . . . Obviously you aren't able to control your own conduct, that's what they are saying. . . . We are tired of being in political movements and looking up the zip codes. . . . We are tired of being in religious organizations and making dolls out of dish clothes. . . . We are tired of being treated—and all those discriminatory rules at Wake Forest say this—as sex objects.

"This is a two-sex revolution, and when it is completed we will have new and honest patterns of life and profession, where ability and not gender count." The voice goes low again. "And that man who is strong enough to be gentle, yes, strong enough, will be strong enough to march with the woman who is leaving behind her ruffles and her rage." A standing ovation, male and female.

Buoyed by the reception, Betty continues to teach and preach the movement in the car going back to the motel with her reception committee. "Don't be frivolous," she says in response to a question about Ti-Grace Atkinson, a radical NOW member who split with Betty over ideology. "Don't get into the bra-burning, anti-man, politics-of-orgasm school like Ti-Grace did. Confront the Administration, demand the same rights as the boys, go door to door when Sam Ervin [the North Carolina Senator who opposed the Equal Rights Amendment] comes up for election and get him out." It is so much like Yves Montand in *"La Guerre est Fini,"* complete with flashes of oncoming headlights—the monologue of a tormented leader and the reassuring nods of cell members.

Coming down from the euphoria of the moment, one of the girls confronts Betty with a sobering question: "But will it be different now that you've been here? Or will they all forget tomorrow?" Visions of the mother superior arranging the folds of her flowing robe and taking the novice's head to lay it on her knee. Betty Friedan smiles confidently, "Oh yes, my dear, it always is different after."

At the motel bar, she plops into a chair and orders a double-gin-and-tonic. "No mixed drinks?" she looks up in shock at the waitress. Against the law, the waitress explains, but she'll be happy to provide the mix if Betty has the essence in a brown paper bag. "Wine?" asks Betty. Nothing but beer without a food order. She gives the menu a hurried once-over. "Egg rolls and . . . you have champagne? Good, a bottle of champagne."

The next morning Betty is scheduled to testify before the Senate Select Committee on Nutrition and Human Needs on women's requirements in new housing. "Not dishwashers and garbage disposals," she laughs shortly after 7 A.M., still having the Oriental look of the recently arisen. "I mean the captivity of high rises and the isolation of suburbs. Women are trapped and new housing has to free them to do something besides raise children."

On the flight to Washington, her conversation is sparse as she reads hurriedly through *Communitas,* marking dozens of pages with snippets of paper. Then on to *The Feminine Mystique,* and a few more markers. "I can see why they asked me to appear," she says as the cab pulls up in front of the New Senate Office Building. "I can see why." She smiles slyly, but does not explain.

As experts are paraded before the committee, Betty is still at work, reading, putting in more pieces of paper and refining her presentation outline. Television cameramen train on each witness; then, a few minutes into each persentation, sensing that the worn professionalese will only make the pile on the cutting-room floor, they turn their attention to each other or to styrofoam cups of coffee. Two committee members, Senators George McGovern, the chairman, and Charles Percy, show a remarkable amount of interest in the testimony and ask incisive questions of each witness.

When Betty Friedan is introduced, television crews leap to their positions as if The Event were about to occur. The soft whir of camera motors indicates Betty is being recorded from the start. "I am here speaking for the silent majority, the truly silent majority," she begins. A smile crosses the face of Republican Percy.

The books and outline Betty had laid out before her are ignored. The preparation turns out to be for nought, as the rhetoric of the movement takes over. The whir of the motors continues through much of the first twenty minutes of her testimony, which builds until she is gasping for breath between sentences: "It is immoral for housing to be ruled over by men, old men mostly. . . . The women of this country are tired of being prisoners. . . . The image is of the moronic housewife whose sole aspiration in life is to have kitchen sink and husband's shirts. . . ." The committee reporter, used to the drone of experts, has a look of panic in her eyes as she tries frantically to keep up. As Betty's voice goes higher in pitch—to a point where it sounds about to break—Senator Percy becomes more restless.

In making pertinent points, Betty instinctively turns to her left, toward the cameras and away from Percy and McGovern. "We have sexual ghettos all over this country. . . . What we are saying is that the American woman's time is worth nothing. . . . That her talents need not be utilized. . . . We are polarizing male from female. . . . The violence in our cities, in the war in Vietnam, is just another manifestation of that basic polarization. . . ."

"Mrs. Friedan," Senator Percy interjects.

"A few more minutes, Senator, and I'll be finished," she returns, and picks up the last half of a sentence and goes on for another ten minutes.

At the end of her testimony, Percy asks a three-part question. Betty takes eight minutes to answer the first third, and the Senator is not about to pursue the remaining two-thirds. After he succeeds in gently stopping her with a series of thank-yous, Percy is asked his impressions of her testimony. "The Niagara Falls effect of it all! I just couldn't pick out the important parts. Some men have the same problem, like Hubert Humphrey. He was Vice President, but don't forget he never made President."

In the cab on the way to the airport, Betty's mood moves between guilt and self-patronization. "I went on and on, didn't I?" she asks. "I panicked. All my hangups from being the little girl from Illinois came through. I didn't have a Ph.D. like the other witnesses. I am a woman of self-destruction at times; the culture has built that in. All the preparation. And I gave them the old speech, didn't I? But I don't dwell on my failures the way I used to," she says with a raised eyebrow and a tone of self-assurance. "As a matter of fact, it's a good thing I testified at all. If they were listening. I said some important things."

This little girl from Illinois was born in Peoria in 1921 to Harry Goldstein, owner of the fine jewelry shop on Jefferson Street, and his wife, Miriam. Miriam was eighteen years Harry's junior and a former society editor for the local newspaper, who, as custom required, put aside her professional life to become mother and housewife. Just as her daughter was to be a misfit as a homemaker some twenty years later, Miriam Goldstein did not enjoy her new role either. "It took me until college to sort this out," Betty recalls, "but it was obvious she belittled, cut down my father because she had no place to channel her terrific energies. It's a typical female disorder that I call impotent rage."

It was not an unhappy home life, yet there was a degree of tension present, with Betty wondering when the next flareup would occur. At school, she was a hyperactive girl, bright, talkative, better able to make friends with girls than boys. Describing her adolescent years, Betty closes her eyes so tightly the lids show heavy folds and the words are punctuated by long periods of silence: "Those were . . . such . . . painful . . . painful years."

Her small circle of friends abruptly went their separate ways when the sorority selections were made at Peoria High School and Betty plunged into a loneliness that she attempted to conquer by writing poetry and reading voraciously. Trying to keep some balance in her daughter's life, Harry Goldstein prohibited her from borrowing more than five library books at a time. She thought this cruel punishment. "When I had dates, and it wasn't that often, they were the rejects, misfits just like me. I guess Peoria is where my awareness of injustices in minority groups and a passionate concern for them was born. My father often told me that the people friendly to him in business wouldn't speak to him after sundown."

In retaliation for being snubbed socially, Betty joined with two boys and started Tide, a school literary magazine. Harriet Parkhurst, who met Betty in high school and went through Smith College with her, and who is now the mother of six children in Peoria, remembers that "she was very intense in those days, everything she did had to be the best. Tide had to be the best literary magazine every produced anywhere and at any time. She made the dramatic honor society with a walk-through in Jane Eyre. It was evident even then that she was drawn to a higher calling. Her intellectual abilities won her some admiration, but so precious few of us cared about brains back then."

Betty was independent on the surface but, when she felt her girlishness would not be rejected, played the typical schoolgirl. A brilliant physics student, she pretended that laboratory experiments were too difficult so that athletes would work them for her. After her graduation as valedictorian of the class of 1938, she went East to Smith and there moped through the first year, continuing the heartbreaking, virtually dateless life of a young girl who would have happily traded thirty points on the I.Q. scale for a modicum of good looks and popularity.

In her last three years of college, however, Betty found herself becoming more and more comfortable with her surroundings, the group of friends she was making, and professors like Kurt Koffka, who thought she was brilliant. "For the first time," she recalls, "I wasn't a freak for having brains." She wrote biting editorials for the Smith newspaper *SCAN*, in one article warning the wealthy Smithies not to feign martyrdom for the small sacrifices they were asked to make in the early stages of World War II (like walking instead of riding with their Ivy League dates, who had to cut back on gas consumption). The girl in the messy Braemar sweaters and tweed skirts, who might have a corner of her slip caught in the zipper, went on to election to Phi Beta Kappa in her junior year and graduation at the top of her class, *summa cum laude.*

She won a fellowship in psychology to study at Berkeley, greeting it initially with squeals of joy. Nights of moroseness followed. "I was that girl with all As and I wanted boys worse than anything." When Betty tells about Berkeley, as when she tells about other landmarks in her life, the sentences never quite get finished. "I fell in love with a guy that . . . I was so much in the mood for love then . . . with all the brilliance, I saw myself becoming the old maid college teacher."

There were idyllic picnics with cucumber sandwiches and wine, and, for the first time in Betty Goldstein's life, love. At the end of her first year, after studying under men like Erik Erikson, she was offered a larger fellowship that would have supported her through a doctorate. Her boy friend, whose name she guards, but who she says went on to become a scientist, confronted her with a choice that altered her life: "You can take that fellowship, but you know I'll never get one like it. You know what it will do to us."

The discord that characterized her adult life was at its polarizing best that day. "It was the kind of either-or situation that is my constant burden in life; either I pursue my career or I sublimate my wishes to a man's."

She turned down the fellowship and probably planted the seed of discontent that would bloom as a book almost two decades later. The romance didn't last, even after her sacrifice, and Betty came to Greenwich Village to live and to work for a news service and then for labor newspapers. Several times she applied for a researcher's job at Time-Life, but never followed through. "I knew the men got the bylines, and women got the coffee."

She met Carl Friedan through a journalist friend and the attraction was immediate. Carl, who was staging summer stock and little theater works, moved into her apartment two months after their first date and they married seven months later. For Betty, it was the end of a haunting loneliness that had only a brief respite at Berkeley. For the Friedans, it was the start of a marriage that would be stormy almost from its beginning and would end in violence. (When they went out socially, the Friedans would as often fight as not. On one occasion, Carl threw a bowl full of sugar in his wife's face. He carries an oversized and scarred knuckle on his left ring-finger from stopping a mirror thrown by Betty.)

After their second child was born, Betty left full-time work and divided her time between family and freelancing four or five articles a year, usually for women's magazines. On the census form, she made a new entry under "Occupation" that confronted her with reality: "Housewife." For the second time in her life, she was afflicted with serious asthma attacks. The first time was at Berkeley, and there she had gone into analysis and "found that my deep-seated hostilities toward my mother were boiling inside me and had to be released." This second time, the problem was more apparent, yet harder to resolve: Betty Friedan was being forced into a role she detested.

When she began to dedicate more time to freelancing and less to dishes and dusting, she was able to discontinue her visits to the analyst. Yet, a vague feeling of emptiness often welled up in her. "Carl's vision of a wife was one who stayed home and cooked and played with the children. And one who didn't compete. I was not that wife. In some of those early years, I made more money a week than he did, and I took to doing stupid things like losing my purse so we wouldn't have a fight." Her freelance income allowed the Friedans to hire help at their home, at the time a sprawling, gingerbread house in Rockland County. "My trips into the real world to do the interviews and visit editors in New York was the difference between Betty Friedan in a mental institution or out."

Then came the fateful fifteen-year reunion of the Smith class of 1942. Betty was assigned the typical class survey, the results of which were to be delivered at the reunion dinner. Thinking she could get a magazine story out of it, she skillfully made up a questionnaire that plumbed the depths beneath the tranquil surface of her classmates' lives. She thought it would show that education did not prevent women from adapting to their roles as housewives. Betty Friedan wanted to believe that herself, to stop the gnawing in the back of her own mind.

Instead she discovered, as she first called it, "the problem that has no name." These suburban housewives had husbands climbing up the success ladder, children in good schools, a daughter in ballet, a son in Scouts, modern appliances and dozens of magazines that extolled the virtues of being wife and mother. Betty Friedan found her educated classmates were asking: "Is this all? Is there nothing more to my life?"

She wrote her article and presented it to *McCall's*. Rejected. *Ladies' Home Journal* rewrote it and gave it an opposite slant. She withdrew the article. *Redbook* told her it wouldn't run an article about "a few neurotic housewives." A year had gone by and she had no sale, W. W. Norton and Company had wanted her to expand a story she had done for *Harper's Magazine* on the coming ice age (her only scientific magazine piece and one that has been included in anthologies), but she convinced them she was on to something more important. She was given $1,000 to begin a book about this problem that had no name.

In 1963, Norton published 3,000 copies of what Betty Friedan had labeled *The Feminine Mystique*, a book she had spent five years researching and writing, a book that encompassed the experiences of hundreds of suburban housewives she had interviewed. It was an indictment of the popularizers and translators of Freud's male-oriented views, the mass media and advertising agencies that she said had combined to portray the ideal American woman as a brainless,

blissful homemaker, content to have men rule the world—and her. Throughout thirteen repetitive and often bludgeoning chapters she drove home well-
researched points that had the cumulative effect of making the U.S. housewife, who had been idolized in her starched cotton dress and gently chided
for her dishpan hands, feel she had been sold a bill of goods by conspirators
who were depriving her of the opportunity to use her own abilities and education. As Betty wrote in the book: "There was a strange discrepancy between
the reality of our lives as women and the image to which we were trying to
conform, the image I came to call 'the feminine mystique.' "

By the time the book came out, the Norton people were frankly tired of
this overbearing woman who was already years late in delivering her manuscript. They hoped that with publication, they could be rid of her, and
expected to mark off a small loss for the book. "But I knew I had something,"
she says. "I knew it was big but the book had to be promoted." Betty eventually
browbeat Norton into paying a freelance publicist, Tania Grossinger, to
devote a few weeks to the book.

Miss Grossinger, now with Stein and Day, recalls: "The book probably
would have died on the shelves; it wasn't a subject people wanted to hear
about in those days. At first, Betty's enthusiasm was her worst enemy; she
would talk so fast nobody could understand. My pitch to the stations was that
she had an important book but that she had to be shut up. She was willing to
take some direction then, but now I see her on television and shudder at this
all-knowing monster I created. There were few stations that asked her back
because she was a tough interview. I can remember her confronting Virginia
Graham on 'Girl Talk' and screaming, 'If you don't let me have my say, I'm
going to say orgasm ten times.' "

The book did take off and eventually sold over 60,000 hard-bound copies.
There are now 1,500,000 copies of the paperback version in print and over
the years Betty Friedan has made about $100,000 from the work. After *The
Feminine Mystique* became a best seller, Random House offered Betty a $30,000
advance for her second book. This prompted a call from Norton president
George Brockway for a luncheon meeting to bring his newly successful author
back into the fold. "I remember him pleading with me," Betty looks back, "and
I remember looking him right in the eye and saying, 'George, you made me
feel Jewish for trying to sell that book. Go——yourself!' "

While the book brought her prominence in the public eye, it brought her grief in her private life. "I probably appeared on more talk shows with black eyes than without," she says. "Carl hated my success and he would throw my schedules, my notes all over the house." Natalie Gittelson, the stunningly attractive special projects editor at *Harper's Bazaar*, who has known Betty for years, says: "The book was a catharsis for Betty. She was trying to work out the problems in her own marriage through it and then the success in a perverse way came to haunt that marriage."

Hundreds of those who read the book wrote to its author. Many women said that Betty had told them the sad story of their own lives and now they were about to change them. Still others were hostile. "Betty was more threatening to women than men then," says Mrs. Gittelson, "because she created doubts in their minds that many didn't want to confront." Betty responded by defining the ideal woman in her own image: "A woman who is passionate, fanatic and crusading. I'd rather she be hot than wrong, rather she be committed than detached."

Betty soon began her speaking tours, gathering material in the meanwhile for a second book, which at various times was called *The Unfinished Revolution* and *The New Woman*. She found instead that there was no book to be done on the transition in progress in American womanhood.

"The trend just wasn't yet there," she explains. "What was needed was a movement. So, I guess I started it."

With the enactment of the Civil Rights Act of 1964, race and sex discrimination in employment were banned. From the start, the Equal Employment Opportunity Commission, empowered to enforce the act, made it clear it would concentrate on racial discrimination, leaving women's rights for another, less troubled day. When the state EEOC heads met in Washington in 1966 to discuss the act's application to women, Betty Friedan, writer and reporter, was there. A vocal minority in the EEOC, including Aileen Hernandez, the current NOW president, and Kay Clarenbach, decided that a resolution should be passed asking the Government to begin the fight against sexually discriminatory hiring practices. "But the Aunt Toms were on the Government's side," Betty says. "Mary Keyserling, head of the Women's Bureau [in the Labor Department], and Esther Peterson, Assistant Secretary for Labor Standards, notified us that the group had no authority to pass anything. In other words, they should generate their report and go home."

The incident that spurred Betty Friedan to found NOW took place when a female EEOC lawyer closed her office door and broke down in tears: "Mrs. Friedan," she said, "you're the only one who can do it. You have to start an NAACP for women." Betty recalls her thoughts at the time: "I've never even been a member of women's groups. I have no patience for that kind of thing." Nevertheless, the National Organization for Women was begun, and Betty Friedan was elected its first president.

NOW's credo, which sounded so radical in those days, was ". . . to take action to bring women into full participation in the mainstream of American society now, exercising all the privileges and responsibilities thereof in truly equal partnership with men." And for Betty Friedan, implementing that statement and leading a movement that was to gain the name women's liberation became a full-time occupation. "I think she was driven by something she believed in," notes one writer friend, "but she kept her life in a frenzy to counteract the marriage and the fact that she was a blocked writer who felt guilty about it."

Betty Friedan, already known as an author, became known as the activist. She sent letters to President Johnson asking for legislation to help women elevate themselves to first-class citizenship. Protesting against paperpushing at the New York office of the Equal Employment Opportunity Commission, she walked into the office carrying bundles of newspapers wrapped in red tape, emblazoned with: "Title Seven [of the Civil Rights Act] has no teeth, EEOC has no guts." She sat in at the Oak Room of the Plaza Hotel during the lunch hour, a time reserved for males for the past 61 years. NOW protested against ads that exploited women, against political groups that refused to write women's rights into their platforms and against textbook publishers who underplayed the role of women in history.

The Friedan marriage worsened. "I was ridden with guilty from the beginning of the movement, but if I didn't keep things moving in those days, our programs would have died." Looking back over the ten years he has known Carl and Betty Friedan, psychologist Harold Greenwald says: "Her transition was much like the blacks, from masochism to activism. The blacks used to wail, 'Nobody knows the trouble I see,' and it got them nowhere. Betty realized that the choice she had made wasn't working, her self-destruction to keep a marriage together was dragging her down further, so she became an activist. And her audience, like the blacks, was ready to listen to anyone who said they didn't have to be victims. Publicly, I guess she's been very successful; yet there is so much in her personal life that she would have otherwise."

NOW and the women's liberation movement stumbled along during the early months with sometimes only the strong and uncompromising presence of Betty Friedan to keep factions from destroying one another. Jacqui Michot Ceballos, active in NOW since 1967, says: "Betty's greatest strength—her aggressiveness—is also her greatest weakness. In those days it was needed; Betty was needed to completely dominate meetings, to get something accomplished. And, as for consciousness-raising, there is no one close to her in that department. She's spoken hundreds of times, and NOW chapters have sprung up after she inspired an audience."

In her quest to keep the movement alive, Betty has offended, at one time or another, virtually everyone she has worked closely with. A typical Friedanism is related by Luci Kamisar, a vice president of NOW: "Betty wanted to issue a press release so she called me at home to tell me—*tell me,* that is, to get over to her house immediately and do it. She had the typewriter, she had the facilities for reproducing it at hand, and I told her that she could get it done just as easily by herself and that I had something else to do. The tirade that followed was interrupted when I hung up on her. The woman needs to be brought under control. Her resignation speech from the presidency of NOW took three hours [Betty admits to two]. Structurally, administratively, things weren't getting done in NOW, and now they can be. There just isn't a place for her in an ongoing organization like ours. She has been appointed to a new position as chairwoman of the advisory committee. And there is no advisory committee."

Betty's swan song to the group she helped start was the Aug. 26 Women's Strike for Equality. Conversations with a number of women in and out of NOW show that Betty was locked in a bitter struggle with a faction, some of them Lesbians, who wanted to move NOW toward a more militant, anti-man posture. Betty was ready to step down from the presidency, but she felt some dramatic action was needed before she left "to put the group back on the right path, toward a positive end, toward a pro-life stand and not one that would feed the fires of impotent rage. I didn't work for the past three years to see the movement suddenly begin a rapid descent to its own demise."

Throughout the six months of preparations for strike day, the iron hand of Betty Friedan was present—as it had been present in the movement at large—

and was, many women will agree, needed. Ruthann Miller, a young socialist who believes Betty's attempts at changing the system are ill-fated and that a total revolution is needed, fought with her over everything from tactics to the parade route. Radical elements within the broad-based coalition of women's groups that joined to stage the strike wanted street theater and massive confrontations. More conservative elements wanted a dignified march and that was all. The mother superior, not so much reconciling as bulldozing, prevailed.

"And let's face it," says Susan Brownmiller, the journalist and radical feminist, "if any other woman had called a strike press conference, she would have been talking to herself. Without the name of Betty Friedan, the strike would never have happened."

On Aug. 26, thousands of women filled New York's Fifth Avenue, curb to curb, and marched. In Boston, Baltimore, San Francisco and Miami other women marched, shattered teacups, dumped babies on the laps of wide-eyed city officials. The scale that Betty Friedan had hoped for—with secretaries abandoning their typewriters and homemakers leaving ther stoves—had not been realized, but she and the women's liberation movement made the point that anyone who thought their intentions frivolous was mistaken.

Betty Friedan looks back on it all—the book, the movement, the strike— and says dryly, "I've been at work trying to liberate every woman in this country, and I'm not yet liberated, I've not fulfilled myself." One of her oldest friends, Columbia sociology professor William Goode, comments: "There is a quality to this woman that takes a while to understand. She is essentially a selfless person; she genuinely believes that she must do certain things to accomplish good or defeat evil, even at expense to her own life. What shows is Betty's enthusiasm, her indefatigability. What doesn't show is that this woman, who could seemingly do without the love and tenderness of a man, is crying out for these qualities all the more loudly."

With Professor Goode, writer Arthur Herzog and Betty Rollin, a senior editor at *Look* magazine, Betty lived this past summer in what she enjoys calling a commune. The rented house in East Hampton was more "a halfway house for unattached people rented by us old groupies," says Professor Goode. "She is interested in far more than the women's thing; she wants to explore different life styles, life styles that somehow guarantee that people are going to care and continue caring about each other. She had a very successful time with group encounter in California and was going to do a book on that before the movement took over her life. Betty looks back on her life, as many of us do, and says there have to be better ways to live. And she's the type to do something about it."

Gloria Steinem, the writer, who worked with Betty on the Aug. 26 strike says, "She found that love between unequals can never succeed and she has undertaken the immense job of bringing up the status of women so that love can succeed. Hopefully, so that her own emotional needs as a woman can eventually be fulfilled."

To radical feminists, Betty Friedan is the albatross they would like to shed. Sally Kempton puts it this way: "She misrepresents the case for feminism by making people believe that reform is the answer. The problem is more fundamental, the entire society has to be upended. And on top of that, she projects the star image, the elitist, which is totally out of whack with what we believe. And there she goes, in sexually suggestive clothing, saying she is the spokesman for the movement. She is not the movement mother; that is Simone de Beauvoir."

Jacqui Ceballos won't gloss over Betty's faults: "She's a terror to deal with and there is an overpowering ego at work. But this is the first person who awakened women to their oppression and for that alone we should pay her homage." Susan Brownmiller says: "Many younger women are horrified that Betty can talk to the Establishment, that she has a black maid, that she is a celebrity. There is a serious generation gap. For me, personally, this woman changed my life. I read *The Feminine Mystique* when I was twenty-eight and a researcher at *Newsweek* worrying myself to death that I should be aspiring to suburban wifehood."

It has been more than a year since Betty was divorced. Friends claim she is never at a loss for male companions and Betty herself says, "In the last two years I've somehow become more attractive to men. They say power is sexy, and that is a worrisome thing. Is someone dating you for your name?" She knows she is often the brunt of jokes or talk behind her back because of her flamboyance, her drinking—heavy, but not as heavy as it was in the waning years of her marriage—and her use of profanity. "Still, Betty has three kids who really know who their mother is," says Mrs. Gittelson. "In the fashion business I'm surrounded by women who make a point of being women. Betty has that marvelous quality—like Diana Vreeland of *Vogue*—of transcending all that."

When she is with friends like Mrs. Gittelson and Ruth Greenwald, Harold's wife, Betty is no proselytizer for the movement. "She introduces me as 'a friend despite her ideological weaknesses,' " says Mrs. Gittelson, who is not a women's lib advocate. "She might spend the evening talking about her children, confiding sorrowfully that Jonathan wasn't accepted at Princeton [as his brother Daniel was at age 15] because she is a revolutionary." Mrs. Greenwald often gets calls from Betty before a party. "There is an unsure little girl inside her. She'll call me to see what she should wear."

Her friends often wonder how Betty manages financially. The royalties from *The Feminine Mystique* and Random House's advance are long gone, and the movement work has been nonpaying. School bills for her children, the cost of a maid and an apartment, coupled with her own heedlessness about money, keep her constantly on the verge of being broke. Her livelihood is earned largely through her talks (which lately have been bringing as much as $2,000 an appearance—although one-third is deducted as an agency commission and she must sometimes pay her own expenses) and is supplemented by $100 a week from her ex-husband, who has since married a former model.

On a recent day, from early afternoon until late into evening, Betty Friedan talked about what she wants out of a life that she admits has been controlling her more than she it. Braless in black blouse, reptile-patterned pants and vest, she sat on a brightly patterned Victorian couch in her apartment and spoke, sometimes huskily with eyes closed, but most often animatedly, with flailing arms and in a voice that broke when the excitement level got too high:

"Amazingly, I've never had self-doubts about the book I wrote or the movement, although my personal life is a study in indecision. I wouldn't say that I started the movement; it surely is a product of historical forces, but if Betty Friedan weren't alive, she'd have to be invented to see the movement through. Seven years ago I was considered the most radical woman in America; now the radicals in women's lib call me hopelessly bourgeois and all that. For instance, it drove them crazy when I was photographed in a low-cut dress at Ethel Scull's party that helped raise money for the strike. I don't like my boobs all over the newspapers either, but I do like to look feminine and the fact is that I had a women's lib button on the front of the dress and it pulled it down somehow. Now I double-tie the top so that won't happen again.

"If anything were to be said about me when the history of the movement is written, I'd like it to read, 'She was the one who said women were people, she organized them and taught them to spell their own names.' [James Baldwin in a letter to his nephew said the white man had taught the blacks to spell their names, and until the black man could learn to spell his own name he would never be free.] And I guess it will have to read, 'She was the country's most guilt-ridden writer.' That bothers me a lot that I haven't written, because my conscience is basically a writer's, and when I feel something strongly I have to put it down on paper. Writing is so much harder than being an activist. I really will get to work now, I promise, and do a book that synthesizes what I've been saying in my speeches. I will call it 'Human-sex.' It will not be another *Feminine Mystique.* I've resigned myself to that.

"Right now, my biggest desire is to slow down, to stop being the prime example of the either-or kind of life I oppose, the career-or-love choice. I want both. Of course, there are things to get done. The next step in the movement is to have marriage, divorce, families, communities re-evaluated so we can somehow construct new life styles for groups of people. The nuclear family—mommy, daddy, brother and sister—isn't meeting the needs of millions of people.

"As for me, I don't know what my role in the women's liberation movement will be. I would like to weld together a coalition of women, blacks and students. Thus far we have announced a permanent coalition of the women's groups who put on the August strike. Our next act is a strike on Dec. 12. In New York, we'll march on Governor Rockefeller's office to demand free, easy abortions and to protest the people who are trying to sabotage the state's abortion laws. Then, on to Gracie Mansion to let the Mayor know we must have 24-hours-a-day, seven-day-a-week child care centers. We're going to march down Fifth Avenue just like we did in August, and I hope women in every major city will also be marching.

"But I think my own direction will be political. And I think the year will be 1972. I've done enough fighting *against;* it's time I did more fighting *for,* I've helped and freed a lot of women, and I think I would have their vote; in fact, I don't think there is another woman in America who could muster more votes. And I'd love to be in the Senate. I don't want to sound corny about it, but . . . well, you know about Joan of Arc and the voices that guided her? I think I hear voices sometimes, too. It is no more than your own sixth sense telling you what is best; but it's like hearing voices. I certainly don't want that burning-at-the-stake bit. No either-or any more. I want a juicy personal life. I don't want to go to bed alone until the revolution is over."

The Liberation of Betty Friedan

Lyn Tornabene / 1971

From *McCall's* magazine (May 1971), 84,
136–40, 142, 146. Reprinted by permission of
Lyn Tornabene.

The handsome, young president of Ohio's Denison University walks jaun-
tily to the podium of the crowded auditorium to introduce the evening's lec-
turer who will speak on women's rights. He makes a Women's Lib joke or two,
and then presents Betty Friedan, "one of the most formidable women in
America . . ."; the students giggle.

The speaker steps to the podium. Alas, the podium is so tall and she so
petite that she cannot be seen, so she steps out from behind it and stands
center stage. She runs a hand through her hair, pulls back her shoulders, and
to the shiny young man, growls in a voice that is Tallulah Bankhead with a
cold: "I am the serious leader of a serious movement. If I were Malcolm X, you
wouldn't *dare* make jokes. . . . If there are any more jokes, I shall walk out of
this auditorium."

That is only the beginning. By the time she has finished her speech, she
has vivisected the hapless president and left his remains for his startled,
affronted student body to reassemble.

Same speaker. Next night. Same subject: Women's Lib. Augsburg College,
Minnesota. One hour before her lecture, she learns that a man she has loved
has died in a New York hospital, despite transfusions of eighty quarts of blood
which she had solicited. She sobs with grief and with guilt; she hadn't said
good-bye, she hadn't done enough. She takes a deep breath and a quick drink;

it is almost time to go on. In the car on the way to the auditorium, she deposits her despair with the committee that has come to escort her. She is able to do this, to take total strangers intimately into her life.

Her audience this night numbers nearly 2,000, and she faces them quickly, with an almost whispered plea, not for the liberation of women, but for the liberation of men. She rambles through visions of an emotional Utopia wherein men and women will be free to love one another on an equal, lofty plane, where no one will die lonely and unfulfilled. People in the audience— male and female—weep off and on as she speaks, and when she finishes with a husky call to make love not war, they applaud for seven minutes.

Same speaker. She is at a party in Manhattan wearing a pretty chiffon midi. She is soft, happy, and outgoing; she likes parties. At this one she is the celebrity. Guests come to pay her homage. A bearded man follows her around, moonstruck. She doesn't notice. She has eyes only for the other celebrity who has just arrived: king of the male chauvinists, Norman Mailer. They talk. She attacks his attitude toward women, but she is sending off strange, familiar vibes. She leaves the party visibly atwitter. "Norman Mailer has never *known* a woman like me."

Meet Betty Naomi Goldstein Friedan, author of *The Feminine Mystique,* founder of the National Organization for Women and the Women's Strike for Equality, spiritual leader of the new feminism, and America's first Jewish folk heroine.

"I am—and you will learn from the people you talk to—an ordinary, fallible woman," she says at our first encounter. She turns out to be only half right. Fallible, yes. Ordinary, no. She has the energy of ten preschoolers, more resilience than Richard Nixon. She is abrupt, fierce, and her manners are often so bad they have become famous. She has friends so loyal they defend her excessively and enemies so hostile they won't even discuss her.

"Betty is a star," says a writer friend, Betty Rollin. "Once you know that, everything else falls into place."

Certainly there are facets in the life of Betty Friedan that place her in the common sisterhood of women. She is fifty and would rather not be. She is recently divorced from a marriage of two decades and groping, not without pleasure, to find a new context for herself. She has raised three children: Danny, twenty-two, a Princeton graduate at eighteen; Jonathan, nineteen, a student at Columbia; Emily, fourteen, teeth in braces, the only one at home.

She houses a dog named Mervin and a cat named Penelope which has not been spayed. But these are the only suggestions of ordinariness in her life.

Sit next to her on an airplane, up front, in first class. She settles herself amidst hand luggage, reading matter, Manila folders, and takes out a large, plastic envelope in which she has stuffed a random selection of mail. She picks up a letter and holds it almost against her eyelashes, due to a difficult eye problem. She hasn't paid for her apartment in three months and her bill is nearly a thousand dollars. She makes out a check, seals it into an envelope, records it nowhere. Other assorted bills are older, unopened.

Betty is submerged in disorder. "Not a low-level mess," says Betty Rollin. "A high-level mess."

Walk around her duplex apartment on the unfashionable side of Central Park. The living room is done in Prince Valiant colors: rich, vibrant reds, blues, and purples. It has Victorian furniture Betty bought at auction when she lived in suburbia—no item over $35. In a hall there is a mammoth pirate's trunk filled with *The Feminine Mystique*—the full manuscript, notes, memos, research. In the bathroom, her panty hose dry over the tub. Next door, in a workroom, stacks of overstuffed folders sit on a small desk; she has finally been sent, by worried friends, a part-time secretary who has been able to organize at least the first level of work to be done.

The door to the next room barely wedges open. To get in you must step over boxes of papers and magazines, cartons of hate letters and fan mail, piles of urgent requests: Will you serve on our committee? Will you make an appearance at the meeting? Will you be on our TV show? Can you leave for Brazil to promote the publication of your book in Portuguese? Letters and clippings and research browning with age. Memorabilia of an activist with an odd sense of timing.

Who, after all, sent for her in this troubled decade to start more trouble? Women's *rights*? When all of us—her peers and such—were so comfortable and settled (or drained). She, who hates so much being put upon—did she have to start a revolution in the midst of a thousand revolutions? When we found out that our kids hated us, that our air was befouled, nature unbalanced, our cars unsafe—in the year we had to give up smoking, for God's sake—did we also have to be liberated?

Destiny is capricious about packaging heroes. She walks like a tipsy penguin, carrying herself belly forward like a woman in the third month of her first pregnancy. With her slim arms and legs, her pregnant posture, wearing her no-bra bra under clinging jerseys, she could be the fertility icon of a pagan tribe. It is, perhaps, a reflection of a mercurial personality that she never looks the same twice. At a lectern she is sometimes earth mother, sometimes bitch, sometimes child. People who admire her find her attractive. To her enemies she is all the witches from Macbeth.

She loves clothes and shopping, but she has no time, so she usually looks as if she were interrupted in the middle of dressing. She puts her makeup on in the taxi, rushing, late, to a fundraising party, and spills it on a startlingly red jersey dress. Fond as she is of décolletage, she curdled with embarrassment when a friend, writer Arthur Herzog, told her the dress was totally inappropriate. "Why the hell didn't you tell me earlier?" Photographers had a field day.

The *enfant terrible* was born at 4 A.M. in Peoria, Illinois, on February 4, 1921. Her father was a jeweler. Within five years, Betty had a sister, Amy, and a brother with curly hair.

Betty was a brilliant child who was remote from her siblings and had few friends. Books were her greatest, and perhaps only, joy. "It wasn't a question of rejection," her mother says, "but that other children her age recognized her brilliance and held her in awe." Betty would add that it was also because she was Jewish, not a glossy thing to be in Peoria then.

"Betty always excelled at everything, but she never felt she did well at anything," her mother says. "Her father was very proud of her. She used to come by the store on Saturdays, and her father would take her to lunch with him and other prominent businessmen. I think he sort of exploited her, really . . ."

"I hate the Middle West," Betty says today. Once she left it to go to Smith College, she returned as infrequently as possible. The only member of the Goldstein family left in Illinois is brother Harry, and he and Betty are estranged. Amy, who married a minister, is now divorced and lives in New York. Mr. Goldstein died in the 'forties after a long illness, and Betty's mother, widowed three times and still youthful and attractive at seventy-three, has settled in southern California.

It was at Smith that Betty realized her intellect, there that she became a radical (everyone did in those late Depression–early War years), there that she became a determined reporter, and there that she learned she had delicate health. In her freshman year she developed emphysema. Since then, under stress, she has been subject to asthma attacks.

In 1942 she graduated *summa cum laude* and went to the University of California at Berkeley with a research fellowship in psychology. At Berkeley she was a student of Gestalt therapy, and then, when her father died and her asthma became unbearable, a subject of it. Eventually she moved to New York, shared an apartment in Greenwich Village, and got a job with a now-defunct radical newspaper. She loved her work and the "newspaper guys who drank their lunch and then wrote great stories." One of the guys got her a blind date with a slim young man named Carl Friedan, who was just out of the Army and a producer of summer stock. They married in 1947 and stayed married through what, from all reports, must have been a sadomasochistic free-for-all. Did she fling the typewriters, or did he? Did she start the shouting, or did he? Was she the monster, or he the beast, and who made life a living hell? Such questions and answers were the core of their messy, expensive divorce two years ago. Carl is married now to a beautiful blond model whom he displays like an Olympic trophy. ("You see what I've got . . . you see?")

"It wasn't *all* bad," Betty says. "We made three beautiful children. We must have done something right." The happiest days, she says, were when her children were infants, and they lived in an apartment project in the rambling residential borough of New York called Queens. They were days of little writing, intensive child care, shoestring entertaining and anonymity. After Emily was born and Carl had established his own advertising-public-relations agency, the Friedans moved to the suburbs. From that time on, Betty had a soap-opera role: She was succeeding as a public figure and failing in her private life.

The house was an eleven-room jewel overlooking the Hudson River in a town called Grandview which is exactly one and four-fifths miles long. That is, it is *small*. The townsfolk still remember that though the Friedans had a full-time maid, Betty sold boxwood hedges to make money and Carl installed a pay phone because, for four dollars a month, it was the cheapest way to have a second phone in the house. They recall that Betty was a "typical career woman you wouldn't ask to borrow a cup of sugar"—that she wore extreme clothes, held what she termed an athiest Bar Mitzvah for her son, and was banned from all car pools because she wanted to send the children to school in a taxi.

In Grandview, Betty's horror of provincialism turned into an abhorrence of suburbia she flaunts today. Though she was active in her tiny community, she stayed remote from it, using as her excuse writing articles that were, as a former editor of *Redbook* puts it, "pretty close to things she wound up denouncing in her book." She felt freakish having a career, worried that she was neglecting her children, and was lonely because "Carl didn't like me very much and he didn't come home a lot." In general, she fretted, and she wondered if other women felt the way she did.

When she went to Smith for her fifteenth reunion, she took with her a questionnaire. The answers she got led her to believe that her fellow graduates were as unhappy as she. She tried, unsuccessfully, to sell an article based on the questionnaire and then continued researching, planning a book. In 1959 she signed a contract with W. W. Norton and Company, getting a $1,000 advance against royalties for a book to be called *The Togetherness Woman*. At that point, Betty was the only person on earth who thought the project was any more than a routine publishing venture.

"It was gut-writing," she says, "a transcending experience." And among other things, it helped her exorcise the conflicts she felt about her mother, whom she had always considered castrating and useless, a woman always busy with a new committee, a new cause. "I knew my mother was unhappy, but I didn't think of the woman thing until I was writing," she says. She says, furthermore, that her mother "lived out her fantasies through me," that because her mother is fastidious and neat, she isn't, and it is because her mother is "hypocritically" always polite that she is not.

Along with a copy of *The Feminine Mystique*, Betty sent her mother a note: "With all the troubles we have had, you gave me the power to break through the feminine mystique which will not, I think, be a problem any longer for Emily. I hope you accept the book for what it is, an affirmation of the values of your life and mine."

The book was, at first, the most talked about and least read of its time. To this date it has sold only 53,000 copies in hard cover. Repetitiously, it told women that they had been sold down the river by educators, Freud, Margaret Mead, and the media, and that they should get out of their cozy houses and do something with themselves. The message was years ahead of its time, but Betty promoted it relentlessly, and as more women got depressed watching their World War II babies leave home, more picked up *The Feminine Mystique*.

The paperback, published late in 1964, sold 1,300,000 copies in the first edition.

Everybody, including Betty's mother and Betty herself, declares now that the success of the book dealt the mortal blow to the Friedan marriage. Everybody, that is, except Carl who says, "The marriage was over long before 'sixty-three." The only change it made in their life together he says, is that "our expenses tripled. It brought her fame rather than fortune and she lived as though she had the fortune."

So be it. *The Feminine Mystique* obviously has been absorbed into American folklore and vocabulary, and women all over the world testify that it changed their lives. Young women, particularly, encircle Betty as she travels, telling her how much the book has meant to them. She is, surprisingly, the guru of newly emerging, nonmilitant, ambitious coeds who, like every generation gone before, want life to be different from their mothers'.

"You and I are the transitional women," Betty tells me. "For us . . . for most women raised the way we were . . . to make dynamic changes is very hard." On still another plane trip, for another lecture, she puts her head back and talks about destiny taking her out of herself, beyond herself. Like a figure in a Greek drama, she fears the gods are going to get her because she has strayed so far from her appointed role. She fears in her soul the celebrity she enjoys. She wonders if she has done the right thing with her life, but she's not sure she really has had full control over the options.

In the momentum of her book's success, Betty signed a fat-cat contract for a second book, getting an advance of $10,000 a year for three years. (The money is long gone and the book long overdue.) The Friedan house was sold, and the family moved into a cooperative apartment in Manhattan. They also bought a summer house in a community called Lonelyville on Fire Island which would make a tasty morsel for an analyst. And it had belonged to a family named Goldstein.

None of Betty's friends was aware that what was going on beyond her troubled household was the germination of the Women's Liberation movement. She never recruits among her friends, which pleases some and hurts others. Cornered at parties about "the woman thing," she would say, "I don't want to talk about it," and walk off. And so it appeared out of nowhere to Friedan-watchers that one day in 1966 an article in a New York newspaper announced Betty Friedan's National Organization for Women, "a new civil-

rights organization pledged to work actively to bring women into full participation in the mainstream of American society NOW, exercising all the privileges and responsibilities thereof in truly equal partnership with men."

Betty got her usual reaction. Men laughed. Women shuddered. Militants
called the conservative NOW the "NAACP," and they didn't mean it kindly.
Lesbian groups said it was for "the four Ms: middle-class, middle-aged, moderate matrons." None of it deterred Betty. She staged sit-ins, nudged legislators,
ignored the backbiting going in in NOW, and forged on.

Eventually the liberation movement surged forward with a passion only
history will be able to fathom. As it did so—as the bookworm from Peoria
found herself in a position of leadership and prominence beyond her fondest
dreams—the Friedan marriage finally died. Also dead was Betty's term of office
in NOW. She moved—or was pushed—into an honorary position that does
little more than keep her name on the group's stationery. The day she was
divorced, Betty says, "I went to a bar and sat and cried, not because I was
alone but for all the wasted years."

Upset and at loose ends, she went to Esalen Institute at Big Sur to participate in encounter groups. There, on the Technicolor cliffs above the angry
Pacific, her visions soared, and she began to dream of new life-styles and new
communities to house the brave new world.

The next move toward this brave new world was announced early in 1970
in a speech at the national conference of NOW. "I . . . propose that we accept
the responsibility of mobilizing the chain reaction we have helped release, for
instant revolution against sexual oppression in this year, 1970. I propose that
on Wednesday, August 26, we call a twenty-four-hour general strike, a resis-
tance both passive and active, of all women in America against the concrete
conditions of their oppression. . . .

"And when it begins to get dark, instead of cooking dinner or making love,
we will assemble, and we will carry candles symbolic of that flame of the
passionate journey down through history—relit anew in every city—to con-
verge the visible power of women at city hall—at the political arena where
the larger options of our life are decided. And by the time these twenty-four
hours are ended, our revolution will be a fact."

August 26, 1970, was, Betty says, "one of the happiest days of my life . . .
if not *the* happiest." The Women's Strike for Equality, which she envisioned in

an instant and bulldozed into reality, turned the tide of the liberation movement.

After that day, the fight for women's rights took on dignity. Betty, detached from the writhings within the movement since the strike, is particularly staying aloof from the lesbian elements supported publicly by younger feminists, such as Kate Millett and Gloria Steinem.

"I have transcended the woman thing," says the Mrs. Friedan who is, if not exactly a new woman since her divorce, certainly a different one. Among other things, her visions now have no mundane tethers. "What would you say if I ran against Javits in 1972?" she tossed into a conversation one night. It was pointed out to her that New York's senior Senator isn't up for reelection in 1972, but she was already off on a new idea.

"She is impossible, but we love her," Betty Rollin says. "She's such a vulnerable, open, unphony person. She's not careful, and you've got to love somebody who's not careful."

See Betty Friedan as I did on the last afternoon we worked together. I call to ask for a convenient time to stop by. *"No* time is convenient," she snaps. Then she says, "Oh, hell, wait a minute. Some woman from South America is coming over at four. You can come, too." Growl. Click.

"Some woman from South America" turns out to be Ana Cuadros, Colombia's Ambassador Extraordinary and Plenipotentiary to the United Nations. She has come to Betty to ask how to organize a Women's Liberation group in her country. Also present, wearing a Women-of-the-World-Unite button, is NOW leader Jacqui Ceballos, who had lived in Colombia many years and is acting as translator.

Betty has had a few drinks and is very cheerful. She curls on a couch, serves coffee, crackers, and cheese, and talks, rapid-fire, about the status of women. As always, her mind is racing so far ahead of her ability to communicate she never finishes a thought. "Within a year . . . this year . . . there will be a world meeting of the new feminists. It's a *world* movement now . . . women are not that different, you know, no matter where they . . . When I wrote my book, I thought I was some kind of freak, the way I felt, you know, because I wanted to work and . . . but I learned there were *millions* . . . *millions* . . . each one thought she was alone and a freak . . ."

"Yes, but how?" the Ambassadress keeps asking. She sits ramrod straight, holding one of her exquisitely manicured hands to her mouth, a square, diamond-set emerald glittering on her finger. She looks at the slouching, pants-clad ladies and appears baffled.

"When you get home," says Betty, "you call a meeting . . . some organization women and some *young* women . . . good fiery people . . . an actress . . . a writer . . . and . . . You move from here to there . . . You stick your neck out . . ." She pauses. She runs her fingers through her hair. She spreads a cracker with cheese, and starts it to her mouth, sets it down, and says: "Jacqui, you know what I've been thinking?" Jacqui seems to see an invisible balloon rising into the air.

"A *world* strike for women!" Betty says hoarsely. Jacqui jumps in her chair and claps her hands. Betty says, "Goose pimples . . . *goose* pimples," then laughs excitedly. "The meeting, th meeting . . . will be . . . a world planning meeting for a world strike . . ." She puts her head back against the couch and shuts her eyes for a second. Her skin actually takes on a sheen of excitement. "Yes, yes," she says, like Molly Bloom in *Ulysses*. "Yes." Then she dismisses the subject with two flicks of the back of her hand. She laughs: "And Ana will be our man at the U.N.," stuffs the cracker in her mouth, and talks on.

Later I ask a NOW member if she has heard about the world strike. She says she has, and wants to know how I know. I tell her I was there when the idea struck. She says, "You were watching history being made, you know."

I knew.

Should You Accept Alimony?
An Interview with Betty Friedan

Kathleen Brady / 1976

From *Harper's Bazaar* magazine, (July 1976),
45, 87, 94. Reprinted by permission of
Harper's Bazaar.

Alimony, rooted in the legal philosophy that the divorced, and therefore non-supported, woman would otherwise become a public charge, is certainly not something any self-respecting, independent woman would consider—but should she? In an interview with *Bazaar*, Betty Friedan, founder of America's contemporary feminist movement, holds that women are entitled to severance pay and even a pension at the breakup of a marriage.

"If we lived in complete equality, and women earned as much as men, we wouldn't need to consider alimony. But such is not the case. At least half the women have spent key years as housewives while men were advancing in careers. That's a reality you can't ignore. The work that a woman has been doing in the home, especially in the child-rearing years, is certainly of equal value to work most people do outside the home, and it is equal to her husband's in terms of their family's fortunes. The more enlightened people in the Women's Movement recognize that the next big issue is not the abolition of the family or marriage, but a *new approach* to both.

"In addition to equal opportunity and education for all working women, we must come to grips with the economic value of the work that women have been doing in the home. I don't like the word "alimony" because it somehow connotes taking advantage of sex. Nor do we feminists like the terms "maintenance," which assumes the woman is like an automobile, or "allowance," which assumes she's a child. So we've developed the concept of entitlement.

"Entitlement is the equivalent of severance pay for work done at home during the length of the marriage, and is a fee above and beyond child support. Entitlement also includes a pension for old age, since housewives who haven't developed marketable skills can find themselves destitute. This is not a question of taking advantage of their sex, but, rather, sheer justice after years of service to the family.

"In the early days of the Movement, we fell into a trap when we said, "No alimony!" because housewives who divorced were in terrible straits. We fell into another trap by accepting no-fault divorce without provision for mandatory economic settlement, distribution of property or entitlement, which left women in the lurch financially. We did force recognition of the concept of equality, but now we have to deal with the fact that equality is the ideal, not yet the reality.

"The Swedes have advanced to what I consider the next step after the Women's Movement. The philosophy behind their 1973 Family Reform Law admits that equality between the sexes requires a new approach to the man as well as to the woman and the institution of marriage. They say that when Greta and Otto marry and both decide to work, then both will contribute an equal or relatively equal amount to the care of their house. If by their mutual agreement one stays home to take full responsibility for the house, that spouse is entitled to some proportion of the other's earnings as his or her due.

"If both work, but she takes prime responsibility for the house, which is the case in most places in America today, then she is entitled to keep a larger amount of her pay for her own private use than he keeps, because she is contributing more labor to their joint life. This does away with the concept that the wife is automatically a servant simply because she's a woman. They mutually decide how their house will be cared for; if she's going to take full responsibility for the house and not earn money at a job, she is still performing work which has economic value. That's not paying wages to a housewife, or giving women a bonus for staying home; it's just recognizing that there are many ways of sharing and distributing the work of the home.

"A woman in the 25–40 age bracket is still young enough to start a career and be valued in the work force, but in her case, I still believe in the concept of money as a sort of severance and a retraining. Take the common example of a woman who puts her husband through school before they get divorced. She is not only entitled to severance and a pension based on his income and an equal distribution of whatever property they have, but she also deserves equivalent training. Today, judges are awarding this in some instances.

"Feminists agree that a young woman who has supported herself is not entitled to anything extra in the divorce just because she's a woman. But other women at 25 still deserve entitlement support to establish themselves. Amounts would vary because some emerge from marriage with no education and no employable skills.

"Such a woman has a special problem if there are children and she has custody of them. It's difficult today for any family to support itself on one income, and since child support isn't always enforced, she can be in a bad way. If the mother takes care of the children, then the father certainly has to provide financially. Similarly—and this is happening more often—if the father takes the children, and the mother makes a good income, she certainly should contribute financially. Unfortunately, in too many cases, the mother gives up custody of the children, not because she wants to, but because she has no other economic choice. I am for the equal right of the father to have custody, depending on what's good for the children, the mother and himself. But I deplore the necessity of too many women to give up the responsibility and joy of their children because they can't support themselves and the children.

"Even if a woman remarries, her entitlement funds—beyond child support—should probably continue, as this money is regarded as severance or pension pay. If you were laid off from a job at General Electric, you'd still be entitled to severance, even if you later joined Westinghouse.

"Experts say the woman having the most difficult time with all this is the one who is 40 or over. At this age, years of household service have probably rendered her unemployable, so her husband should provide her with funds to support her throughout her lifetime, especially if he's in a comfortable bracket.

"This is not a gold-digger, take-all-you-can-get approach, but merely a way of being self-protective and recognizing economic reality. This society is years away from complete equality. In today's economic situation, especially with inflation, everybody's standard of living is being reduced, so even if the man isn't resentful to start out with, he's going to try to protect himself as well. It would be better to work out entitlement in an automatically collectable way, say deducted from his pay. Or perhaps he could put up a bond to guarantee his appearance in court if he falls behind on payments as many men do. Otherwise you'll have to take up the matter with a lawyer and pay more money in legal fees than you can collect, and you'll subject yourself to continuing psychological rage.

"I wish that at the time of my divorce I had simply said that all the property we owned be sold and put in escrow for the education and support of the kids. Since I could support myself, I didn't ask for alimony, but I didn't realize the impossibility of collecting child support, no matter what the judge orders, and the cost of lawyer fees. Now my advice would be that a settlement is infinitely superior to monthly payment.

"After the confrontations of the last 10 years, the Women's Movement has a much more complex innovational job to do of restructuring the law and traditions of marriage. I think a man/woman relationship of real intimacy, a real mutual support in every sense of the word, infused by love and sexuality, is the best thing there is. I'm terribly intrigued by recent studies, especially one of the Common Market countries, which showed that the happiest people in Western society today are men and women living together, but not married. Not only does this mean they are much happier than people living alone; they are also happier than married couples. I think there is something still very wrong with marriage as it has been, with the way women and men have entered into it, with what has kept them together, and the hostilities built into it. And yet the emotional, human, psychological, sexual, even economic needs that make people want to live together are very real.

"When marriage can be achieved on a basis of independence within mutual interdependence, then I think it could be quite beautiful, and based on many bonds besides child rearing, because that only lasts a few years. In the future we may value intimacy and commitment even more than the excitement of changing partners. And this would be quite different from being locked by economic necessity into marriages that do not really produce joy or intimacy and that contain buried hostilities."

Once More to the Ramparts

Mary Walton / 1981

From *Chicago Tribune Magazine*, (25 October
1981), 12–14, 16, 18, 20. Reprinted by
permission of Mary Walton.

It is eighteen years since *The Feminine Mystique* was published and fifteen
years almost to the day since the National Organization of Women was
founded. The women's movement has made enormous strides in opening previously closed doors. But women still earn barely more than half as much as
men, and the Equal Rights Amendment appears doomed. Challenges from the
ultraconservative Right threaten to wipe out new gains. Comes now Betty
Friedan at age sixty with a new book, *The Second Stage*, which suggests the
movement abandon a misguided "feminist mystique" that cost it support and
made it vulnerable to charges of being "antifamily." Instead women—and
men—should support more family-oriented issues. She feels sure she is right,
based on her experiences and observations. She herself has reordered her priorities. The question is: Can the woman who raised consciousness once do it
again? Will anybody listen?

The taped voice is measured, cordial. "This is Betty Friedan. I am in Sag
Harbor. . . ."
Suddenly the tape is interrupted by Betty Friedan herself. "Hello, hello. I'm
here." Now there are two Friedans on the line, the live one impatiently trying
to override her prerecorded self. "Hello, hello."
The caller is paralyzed, wanting to answer but not knowing how to inter-
rupt. What if the live one hangs up?

The tape ends. The real Friedan stays on, but she is too busy to talk. "I have to make a very weighty decision about slipcovers," she pleads in that familiar, raspy voice. "And then I have to buy some fish."

Could this be the wrong number? Is this the Betty Friedan who wrote *The Feminine Mystique*, the revolutionary manifesto of women's liberation, as it was called back then? Betty Friedan, a founder of the National Organization for Women (NOW), who led 10,000 women down Fifth Avenue and presented Pope Paul VI with the cross-like symbol of the women's movement. (What *chutzpah!*) The Mother of Us All choosing slipcovers and buying fish?

Ah, well. Women's work is never done. There always was this side to Friedan, especially in the beginning. In the morning, she was covertly tapping out *The Feminine Mystique* like a hidden addiction; in the afternoon she was Mom, ferrying the kids around, shopping for Victorian bargains to fill the Victorian house with, to have a few people over for dinner.

Betty Friedan became one of the new class of Superwomen. *I can do it all!* Write books, lead movements, and still raise children. That sort of thing. But even as the public persona was crusading in a strident, demagogic, slightly mad fashion, the private persona was having a rough time. Friedan's marriage crumbled, she never cooked anymore, and the new apartment was a mess.

All the while, in fact, that Friedan was denouncing the American female's homebound way of life as a corporate conspiracy to sell more vacuum cleaners, she was cutting her own apron strings, living the very movement she was organizing.

But for Friedan, and for millions of women who translated liberation into jobs, things went wrong that still don't seem to be going right. It wasn't supposed to be this way. To be sure, women have entered the work force in droves. And some even have clawed their way to the top. But oddly enough, all the surveys show they still are doing most of the housework and taking care of the kids. Or they aren't having kids. Or they aren't even getting married. And those fat paychecks still go to the men, who earn on a national average 41 percent more than women. Fifty-nine crummy cents on the dollar and *still* fixing dinner. Meanwhile, the soldiers of the Far Right, the Dark Forces of Reaction, have slithered out from all their cobwebby little nooks and crannies and pounced on the fragile gains of the women's movement.

So here was Betty Friedan, who started it all eighteen years ago, and when the friends of her daughter, now grown and a Harvard medical student, came round, they were something less than grateful.

"What I sensed from them," Friedan says, was "a certain sullenness about feminism." Daughter Emily, twenty-five, recalls a cross-generational female gathering of women, single and attached, including herself and her famous mother. The mood was jocular enough, but there was an undercurrent of resentment. People were talking like victims, not winners. "Look what you did to us," they chorused to Betty Friedan. "You got us into this, and now you're going to get us out."

The Lone Ranger never had a clearer mandate. At first Friedan did nothing. Hadn't she been preaching moderation for years, denouncing "female chauvinists" who hated men, and refusing to support lesbian rights? Unfortunately no one was paying much attention anymore. Younger feminists regarded her as irrelevant, even eccentric. A reporter remembering her recent speeches noted that as she approached the mike, a wave of "collective eye-rolling" would wash over the audience, a sigh that wondered, "What is she going to say this time and how long is it going to take?" In 1977, she wasn't even elected one of 88 delegates from New York to a national women's conference.

In 1978, she and a dozen other current and former NOW leaders attempted to start an alternative organization. It was called Womansurge, an unfortunate name, and not even appropriate, since it surged nowhere. Although it was unlike Friedan to acknowledge it, she was down maybe, and even forgotten by some who didn't know who she was and how she had changed the lives of countless women. So many would tell her that very thing, hundreds upon hundreds, that she titled her second book *It Changed My Life*.

In the last few years, Friedan had become less visible, though never obscure. She bought a house on Long Island and took up a more literary life as she worked on a third book on the subject of women outliving men. Her priorities were changing.

You had to know something was up in 1977 when she wrote a story in the *New York Times* about cooking. She described making two dinners with her son in terms that approached religious experience. Clearly, she was a convert. "I am considering making soup from scratch next summer. . . ," she wrote. "I'll buy a big tureen and some large bowls. And then with bread and salad and cheese and wine, I could have people over to dinner again. It can't be that difficult running a blender. I used to be very creative with chef's salad and leftovers. It can't be that hard to make Caesar salad. Or lots of cold cooked vegetables."

But she couldn't help wondering about the movement. She perceived, as she would later write quite eloquently, "This uneasy sense of battles won, only to be fought over again, of battles that should have been won, according to all the rules, and yet are not, of battles that suddenly one does not really want to win, and the weariness of battle altogether—how many women feel it? What does it mean? This nervousness in the women's movement, this sense of enemies and dangers, ominipresent, unseen, of shadowboxing enemies who aren't there—are they paranoid phantoms, and if so, why do their enemies always win? This unarticulated malaise now within the women's move-ment—is something wonderful dulling, dwindling, tarnishing from going on too long, or coming to an end too soon, before it is really finished?"

It was not enough merely to talk about solutions. "Nothing is taken seri-ously until it's written as a book." She wrote the book in a year, with an eye to the June, 1982, expiration of the Equal Rights Amendment.

"I wrote with the feeling of a gun at my head," Friedan says. "I take very seriously the ERA deadline. It would take a miracle, of course. I wrote this book with one thought—that maybe it would help bring about that miracle, and if it doesn't, it will leave us in better shape not to go into another 50-year sleep if we lose the ERA, so we will be passing on the right questions. We must have the energy and commitment of the young."

Called *The Second Stage*, this book is a bold attempt to reshape the move-ment's priorities, a call to set aside the anger that has separated the men from the women and reaffirm the importance of the family.

The book holds that the feminine mystique that bound women to husband and home has been exchanged for a career-oriented "feminist mystique" that discounts both the pleasures and demands of childrearing and conjugal home maintenance. In short, she is talking about the sort of thing that is driving young couples up the wall these days. Like who quits work to take care of the baby and for how long. To Friedan's way of thinking, the failure to address such mundane family issues, combined with an overemphasis on abortion and lesbian rights, has worked to the detriment of the women's movement, pre-venting it from building broad-based support among both men and women and making it vulnerable to attacks by the Far Right that feminism is "anti-family."

Among many feminists, this position is going to make her only slightly more popular than Nancy Reagan. The likely response is suggested by some of the letters following publication of an excerpt in the *New York Times* magazine. One hostile letter writer observed that Friedan "would destroy feminism in order to save it and beat the Moral Majority by joining it." Another wrote: "Women who are the victims of rape, violence, and unpaid domestic labor will take little consolation from idealistic notions of co-parenting and corporate flexitime."

The Second Stage arrives at a time when women are visibly uncertain about their roles and abilities. They have made best sellers of two books, *The Cinderella Complex*, which holds that women display a deep inner desire to be taken care of that impedes career-mobility and independence and *How to Make Love to a Man*, whose title more or less speaks for itself.

But with the likely defeat of the ERA—or even with its unlikely victory— the women's movement will lose its unifying goal, notes *Boston Globe* columnist Ellen Goodman, who predicts the movement will decentralize and take on smaller targets. "People are going to have to be extremely inventive in bad times." Goodman believes that Friedan may be "onto something" in suggesting issues that are closer to home.

Says Friedan: "It was not easy for me to write *The Second Stage* because I know it shakes up some feminists . . . and that it is not going to be agreed to by all official feminist leaders. At a time when the gains that we have won, which I take very seriously indeed, are endangered, at a time when we are facing such reaction from outside, how can we raise questions that are going to be unsettling and upsetting to some people in the women's movement and create argument and discussion? But we can't keep brushing these questions under the rug because they are keeping us from the large support, the gains of equality that we deserve."

But it is also a personal statement. Children, she says, "certainly have been one of the basic satisfactions of my life. A new cycle will begin, the first of my children will get married next month, and I look forward very eagerly to being a grandmother, strange as it may seem. I can't wait to see what their kids will be like, to see them as parents. If I had to choose between giving birth to books and babies, that would be terrible. They both have been a part of my life."

She is in Sag Harbor, L.I., as she says this, in a home brimming with furniture from her marriage, mementos from her travels, and gifts from her children. A tear slides down her face. "I think it's kind of lovely that I'm going to spend the next month simultaneously getting ready for the birth of my third book and the first of my three children's weddings."

The reality is that this marriage of her son, Jonathan, would take place Oct. 11, and the book tour would begin Oct. 12, and somehow the living room had to be painted and the furniture re-covered before then, not to mention arrangements for the affair itself, an orthodox Jewish wedding for the bride's parents. And those glasses and plates.

For the moment, an instant in a radiant late afternoon, it was a wonderful, peaceful image, the Founding Mother about to become a mother-in-law. The beginning, as she said, of a new cycle.

The old cycle began sixty years ago in Peoria, where Friedan was born Betty Naomi Goldstein, the first of Harry and Miriam Goldstein's three children. Her father was a well-to-do jeweler who had started out with a collar-button stand on a Peoria street corner.

Had Friedan not been Jewish, had Peoria not been anti-Semitic, there might have been no *The Feminine Mystique*, she says today. Economically the Goldstein kids were better off than most of their contemporaries. There was no question that they lived on the right side of the tracks. There were a housekeeper and a maid. But socially they were outcasts. The adults were barred from the country club. The children grew up with good elementary school friends, only to be blackballed from the high school sororities and fraternities that ran the social life. "Come adolescence, one hit anti-Semitism," Friedan says. "I had a very early sense of injustice that I think came as much as anything from the experience of growing up Jewish in Peoria."

Friedan also had been born with an unfortunate nose and a tendency toward overweight. Equally as bad, she was extremely bright, which wasn't high on the list of feminine attributes.

Even after Peoria, this matter of looks and intelligence would continue to plague her. Reporters were always asking just how smart she was—was her IQ really close to 200?

As for her appearance, Friedan perceived early on she was no Betty Grable. When she acted, she got parts like the madwoman in *Jane Eyre*, a role that demanded "insane, maniacal laughter." Her boyfriends were *real* friends. Years later, she remembers "walking up Main Street in the sunset, and the boy with whom I started a magazine in high school put his arm around me and said, 'If you were a boy, you would be my best friend.' " All very well, but not a date for the prom.

When she and Carl Friedan divorced after twenty-two years, he would marry a model whose picture he flashed at the slightest provocation. His new wife (they have since been divorced) was charming and loving and occasionally shined his shoes, he told *Washington Post* reporter Myra MacPherson. "She's not intellectual, thank God."

And when Friedan got into a flap with attractive Gloria Steinem, there were those who suggested it was as much jealousy as any substantive difference. Friedan herself was not unaware that what the public generally saw were "monstrous ugly pictures of me, mouth open, fist clenched. And I would writhe and wonder. Was that really what it was all about—a mere petty power struggle among the girls? Gloria is assuredly blonder, younger, prettier than I am— though I never thought of myself as quite as ugly as those pictures made me. But my battles with Gloria in the Women's Political Caucus involved my most basic sense of what the women's movement was all about."

Friedan's mother had been women's page editor of the Peoria paper when she married. As the times dictated, she gave up her job, but continued to be active in community activities. At the same time, Mrs. Goldstein was perpetually discontented. "Nothing my father did, nothing he bought her, nothing we did ever seemed to satisfy her." Friedan wrote: "I didn't want to be like my mother."

Friedan went east to Smith College, where for the first time it was OK to be smart. She edited the school newspaper and started a literary magazine, but aspired to be a psychologist, studying with Kurt Koffka, a noted Gestalt psychologist, and others. After being graduated summa cum laude, she took a research fellowship at the University of California in Berkeley. She passed up the chance for another fellowship to pursue a Ph.D. As she wrote, "We walked in the Berkeley Hills and a boy said: 'Nothing can come of this, between us. I'll never win a fellowship like yours.' " Enough said.

She ended up *sans* fellowship—*and boy*—in Greenwich Village, sharing an apartment with other Smith and Vassar girls. With the end of World War II her friends now began marrying, and she was bumped from her job with a labor news service by a returning veteran. Carl Friedan, a summer-stock producer soon to enter advertising, arrived providentially and moved into her hot-water flat (the cold water didn't work).

During this period she was active politically. "Not about women, for heaven's sake! If you were a radical in 1949, you were concerned about the Negroes, and the working class, and World War III, and the House UnAmerican Activities Committee and McCarthy and loyalty oaths, and Communist splits and schisms, Russia, China, and the U.N. But you certainly didn't think about being a woman, politically."

These were glory years for the American housewife. The men were home and in charge once more. No more exhausting wartime jobs. She had done her bit, and the country needed her now to replace its population stock and buy its goods. In return, the housewife was endowed with all that was female and good. Friedan took note of titles from the women's magazines: "Let's Stop Blaming Mom"; "Isn't a Woman's Place in the Home?"; "Women Aren't Men"; "What Women Can Learn From Mother Eve"; "Really a Man's World, Politics"; and—a killer—"Nearly Half the Women in 'Who's Who' Are Single."

For her part, Friedan continued at a newspaper job after the birth of her first child. But when pregnant with her second son, Jonathan, she was fired. She was both furious and relieved. ("I had begun to feel so guilty working, and I really wasn't getting anywhere in that job.") The Friedans had moved to an amiable apartment cluster in Queens and Betty plunged into domestic life. When the census taker found her in Rockland County, in a big old Victorian house, she resolutely wrote "housewife" as her occupation.

The year was 1957, the year of Sputnik. Friedan agreed to do a survey of her Smith College class, now fifteen years past graduation. She expected to find them living marvelously contented lives, even though she herself was having these nagging feelings akin to guilt. ("Eight schizophrenic years of trying to be a kind of woman I wasn't, of too many lonesome, boring, wasted hours, too many unnecessary arguments, too many days spent with, but not really seeing, my lovely exciting children, too much cocktail party chit-chat with the same people, because they were the only people there.")

What she found instead was widespread discontentment among her educated contemporaries, not unlike her own. That discovery was the genesis of *The Feminine Mystique*, published in 1963, which held "the happy housewife heroine" was secretly suffering from "The Problem That Has No Name." It sounded like a virulent form of bad breath, but it was really another name for depression.

Here begins the book that would become the manifesto for the women's movement: "The Problem lay buried, unspoken, for many years in the minds of American women. It was a strange stirring, a sense of dissatisfaction, a yearning that women suffered in the middle of the twentieth century in the United States. Each suburban wife struggled with it alone. As she made the beds, shopped for groceries, matched slipcover material, ate peanut butter sandwiches with her children, chauffeured Cub Scouts and Brownies, lay beside her husband at night—she was afraid to ask even of herself the silent question "Is this all?"

Friedan beamed straight into those boxy little houses in the Levittowns of America as she wrote, "A baked potato is not as big as the world, and vacuuming the living room floor—with or without makeup—is not work that takes enough thought or energy to challenge any woman's full capacity. Women are human beings, not stuffed dolls, not animals."

The Feminine Mystique was an instant best seller. And Friedan, well, she had gone out and dyed her hair blond the summer she finished the book. Blond or no, after *The Feminine Mystique*, she claims to have been treated like a leper in her suburban community. The kids were even thrown out of the dance class car pool. There was this, at least: no more invitations to boring dinner parties. She was in demand, however, on the lecture circuit. And more and more, she heard people saying something like "What we need is an NAACP for women." The opportunity would come in 1966.

While Friedan was raising the consciousness of the masses, a Washington feminist underground in 1964 had lobbied a prohibition against sex discrimination into the Civil Rights Act. Their focus then shifted to the Equal Employment Opportunity Commission, where they were attempting to have sex definitions removed from the help wanted ads.

This was the issue of the day. You have to understand what was at stake here. How could a woman apply for a "help wanted—male" ad? It was as *verboten* as using a men's room. But that's where the good jobs were. These early feminists were getting nowhere. Their lack of success produced an undercurrent of irritation as a national conference of Commissions on the Status of Women was convened on June 28, 1966, in Washington. Friedan attended as a writer and observer, but shortly became much more, hosting in her hotel room a dissatisfied group who felt women needed an activist organization.

Unearthed by a NOW historian on that organization's tenth anniversary are several versions of what happened that night, none of them particularly flattering to Friedan, who was displaying an unfortunate capacity for acting out when people didn't agree with her. It is not one of her more marvelous qualities, and is one of the reasons she acquired a reputation for being contentious and difficult to deal with.

Everyone—including Friedan in *It Changed My Life*—remembers there was friction, stemming from the eagerness of some to start a feminist organization. Dorothy Haener of the United Automobile Workers would recall "an all-out shouting match" and Friedan showing one woman to the door, declaring, "You know, this is my room and my liquor, and you're perfectly free to say anything you please, but you're not going to use my room and my liquor while you're doing it."

Another, Nancy Knaak, a University of Wisconsin dean, said she got into a spat with Friedan when she wondered if they had explored all the alternatives. "Who invited YOU?" Knaak remembers Friedan saying. When voices were raised in her defense, according to Knaak, Freidan "thereupon stomped to the bathroom, entered, slammed its door, and noisily snapped the lock." Knaak stood her ground, and after about 15 minutes, she says, Freidan reappeared. The meeting ended with a compromise. Those who thought there could be change without a separatist organization would try to have the conference pass a resolution calling for enforcement of Title VII—the sex discrimination section—of the Civil Rights Act.

This effort was ruled out of order, and a temporary NOW was formed on the spot. Then on Oct. 29, 1966, 300 persons met in Washington to elect officers and draw up a statement of purpose. Friedan was elected president, a job she held for four years.

Friedan had certain deficiencies as president. She never learned to chair a meeting, having little patience for Roberts' Rules of Order, and wasn't particularly interested in the mundane chores of organizing. But, says Ernesta Ballard, longtime Philadelphia feminist, she has a "wonderful, exciting quality of making you understand things you couldn't understand and wanting to do something about it."

During those early years, NOW took major positions favoring abortion and the ERA and numerous minor ones on things like whether to scale dues to income and how many NOW chapters you could have in one city. Fortunately, there were some fun activities, like burning aprons in front of the White House (no bra was ever publicly burned, insist feminist leaders) and invading "men only" bars under the stellar blaze of TV lights. (Friedan took particular delight in de-sexing the Oak Room at the Plaza Hotel, which she had been unceremoniously cast out from years earlier.)

Somehow, though, the movement didn't seem to be making tangible gains. People still thought it was kind of cute, all those uppity females. So Friedan in 1970 called for a Woman's Strike for Equality to demonstrate some real clout. It was a huge success and, in a way, her finest moment. It did not hurt beforehand that there was a well-publicized fundraiser in the fashionable Hamptons, where a lesbian writer jumped naked into the pool and Friedan herself was photographed unaware that her dress had independently broken a drawstring to reveal her bosom.

It was also her swan song. She did not run for reelection that year, in part because she needed to earn some money and also because NOW was changing. In a sense Friedan didn't leave NOW as much as NOW left her. More radical feminists were emerging. Lesbians in lavender armbands, out of their closets and into the streets. Ti-Grace Atkinson (Remember Ti-Grace?) saying, "My impression is that the prostitute is the only honest woman left in America." *Ti-Grace, who had dug her up?* None other than Friedan, who had misjudged her ladylike looks and upper-crust accent.

Friedan's feud with Gloria Steinem and Bella Abzug, whom she accused of "female chauvinism" also dates from this period.

In the late '70s, under the leadership of Pittsburgh homemaker Ellie Smeal, NOW and disparate elements of the women's movement united in the fight for the ERA. But Friedan, who says she is "very supportive" of Smeal, maintains it was too late by then to repair the damage wrought by earlier sexual politics. In *The Second Stage*, she argues that "It is all very well for wiser leaders of the women's movement today to insist, correctly, that the Equal Rights Amendment has nothing to do with either abortion or homosexuality—that, in fact, it has nothing to do with sexual behavior at all. The sexual politics that distorted the sense of priorities of the women's movement during the '70s made it easy for the so-called Moral Majority to lump ERA with homosexual rights and abortion into one explosive package of licentious, family-threatening sex."

In her private life, Friedan was caught up in the aftermath of divorce after more than two decades of marriage. It was not an amiable split, to put it mildly. Friends could almost hear the breakup coming. Smashed sugar bowls, wine glasses, and the like. But for a long time Friedan resisted the idea of divorce. "I was scared of the loneliness," she would write later. "It took me five years to get the courage to do it."

For his part, Carl Friedan had been little heard from all those years, although *The Feminine Mystique* was dedicated to him. But after his ex-wife began publicly to talk about how he had resented her success so much he threw her notes all over the house, mild-mannered Carl vented his own rage at the way Friedan had portrayed herself as a victim of *The Feminine Mystique*—a rage that came pouring out in an interview with Myra MacPherson.

"I supported *The Feminine Mystique*," he fumed. "She had time to write it because she lived in a mansion on the Hudson River, had a full-time maid, and was completely supported by me. . . . Betty never washed 100 dishes during twenty years of marriage. . . . She has a great need to be independent on the surface. What she is actually is a very dependent little girl. And she keeps fighting that."

The divorce left Friedan rootless. Her two oldest children were in college. For money she was teaching, speaking, and writing, among other things, a regular column for *McCall's*. Though less involved during the '70s in movement politics, Friedan's pace scarcely slowed.

She traveled widely, to Brazil, Mexico, Italy, England. Wherever she went, she was recognized and often drafted to speak to women. Once when she thought she was safe on a mountaintop with a friend, a troop of Girl Scouts appeared. "Haven't we met?" their leader asked, calling the girls over. "Oh, God, I think, not here," Friedan wrote. "I wish I had worn a blond wig."

The *New York Times* unwittingly caught the frantic quality of her life in a fashion feature on how famous women organize their closets. "Organize my closet?" replied Friedan. (Instant guilt!) "That's exactly what I have to do today. It's the next urgent thing. My closet is complete chaos because I live completely different lives. There's my Hamptons country life. My public lecture life. My evening life. My messing around life. My traveling life. I spend half my time looking for things. . . . Plus I have an up-and-down battle about weight. That's another wardrobe. . . . You know what's really irritating? Those plastic bags from dry cleaners. You can't see what's in them. I'm going to organize my closet by blouses, skirts, and dresses."

At sixty, still a woman of great energy, Friedan has had a life in the past few years filled with metaphors for independence and stability. Three years ago, she bought her house, a charming white, 200-year-old waterfront cottage in Sag Harbor, where she has been spending increasing amounts of time. "She needed autonomy," says longtime friend and magazine editor Natalie Gittelson. "The house was an important symbol."

"I find it very satisfying," Friedan says. "It's given some rootedness which I badly needed." She lives alone, she says, "technically." The house over the summer has seldom lacked for guests—either children or friends. "My friends are a very important part of my life."

She has also learned to drive after decades of not doing so. And she has bought a Cuisinart.

A *Cuisinart!* It sits boldly on the kitchen counter near the round wooden table where she entertains friends. "She makes wild, marvelous soups," says Gittelson. "She puts lots of extraordinarily disparate ingredients in a pot and something wonderful comes out."

Friedan contemplates the future with characteristic enthusiasm. "I am going to do so many things for myself in the next few years," Friedan says. "Not just everything writing, lecturing, movement . . . blah, blah, blah." (Her *blahs*.) "I want to have more time reading, fun things, frivolous things, and adventurous things. . . . I'm thinking of getting a little boat. . . . I'm thinking next year I might plant a garden, and I want to do some fun travel, like a river raft or climbing some mountain in Nepal."

And, of course, says Friedan, there's that "One unfinished thing I'd like: I'd like to live with somebody again and make it work . . . But there's this damn public persona that makes it, I don't know, so hard."

At the moment, the public persona is on the road, publicizing her book, as daughter Emily puts it, "her last maternal duty to the women's movement." As Emily Friedan perceives it, "*The Feminine Mystique* was a statement to her mother, forgiving her mother for being who she was because she was that way for social reasons. *The Second Stage* is a challenge to me, me and my brothers, sort of saying 'I did this for society, now it's up to you.'"

My Side: Betty Friedan

Paula Gribetz Gottlieb / 1982

From *Working Woman* magazine,
(February 1982), 130, 132.

Nineteen years ago, Betty Friedan, homemaker and mother, wrote *The Feminine Mystique* and raised the consciousness of women across America. She wrote about housewives feeling inadequate because they did not fit the role of cheerful homemaker. As she explained in her introduction to the tenth-anniversary edition of the book, "Each of us thought she was a freak . . . if she didn't experience that mysterious orgiastic fulfillment the commercials promised when waxing floors."

Friedan began her writing career in the 1960s by contributing articles to several women's magazines but soon realized that these publications perpetuated the image of the childlike housewife—passive and happy in her world of kitchen and bedroom. *The Feminine Mystique* grew out of Friedan's alumnae survey of Smith College classmates. Their surprising answers about the role of women prompted her to write an article, which was turned down by several magazines. *Redbook*'s rejection letter said "[This is an article which] only the most neurotic housewife could possibly identify." The book followed these discouraging experiences.

After *The Feminine Mystique*, Friedan gravitated toward women who wanted change. She worked to create the National Organization of Women, a group dedicated "to take the actions needed to bring women into the mainstream of American society, now, full equality for women, in fully equal partnership with men." In 1966, Friedan was elected NOW's first president.

In 1971 Friedan helped form the National Women's Political Caucus, which crossed party lines to work on electing women to political office. During the next ten years, Friedan lectured, wrote magazine articles, worked for the passage of the Equal Rights Amendment and spoke at several universities on sex roles. Her research at Columbia University's Center for Social Sciences in New York led her to write *The Second Stage.*

In *The Second Stage* (Summit Books), Friedan discusses the problems of the women's movement, the superwoman phenomenon, the changes in the workplace and the need for women to work with men. Some book reviewers accuse her of writing to an elite minority of women and deny her claim that women have achieved personhood on the job and are ready not only to relax the political agenda of feminism but to work together with men for human equality. They feel that the radical edge of the movement still is vitally important. But many women were relieved to hear a founder of the women's movement say that there was more to life than a career; that they, too, deserved the fullness that life has to offer. Here are some excerpts from a conversation with Friedan.

WORKING WOMAN: *What prompted you to write* The Second Stage?
BETTY FRIEDAN: I have a continuing commitment to the women's movement—after all, I helped start it—and I felt that without this second stage, *The Feminine Mystique* would be aborted. Women could be stuck halfway through, and there might be a real reaction against the women's movement in the next generation. During the past few years I've traveled around the country, talking and lecturing, and I began to worry when I met women—young and not so young, especially women in their thirties—with awful conflicts about having children. They told me they were not going to have children, but I could tell they weren't very happy about the decision. Childbearing seems to me such a strong value of life. That worried me. Then this superwoman stuff began to worry me, too.

So, on the one hand, I was working this out theoretically in my university lectures and, on the other hand, I was observing younger women who had a whole new set of problems. I wrote a few articles about it, and I also raised some of these questions in my teaching and lecturing. I began to have an increasing uneasiness that something was going wrong. And I saw that the official feminist agenda, the first-stage agenda, was just not where these women were—they had other needs and problems to deal with.

WW: *What is the "feminist mystique" and why is it so dangerous?*
BF: A mystique is an image that shortchanges the reality of an idea or denies part of its totality. The feminine mystique that I wrote about tried to define women solely in terms of marriage, motherhood, sexual relationship and service of home. It ignored the woman as a person and, therefore, it limited, truncated women's possibilities. Now there is a danger that feminism, too, is becoming a mystique. There's a tendency to throw the baby out with the bathwater and to deny that part of the personhood does indeed come from traditional sources of women's identity.

When I said there was a danger of a *feminist* mystique, I meant an agenda so concentrated on that which has been denied—the ability and need of a woman to move as a person in her own right—that it denies that there are other aspects to her life. We had to break through the feminine mystique, but this is not to deny that those other aspects are also part of the personhood of woman. What is needed now is an integration of the two.

Just as the feminine mystique was a pseudo-glorification of the housewife that really denigrated her, so in a certain sense the feminist mystique glorifies career. It is a pseudo-glorification that makes women a prisoner of that career—passive to that career and shortchanged by it.

WW: *In your new book you call for the woman's movement to embrace the idea of family. Why is this so important?*
BF: We have to embrace our own roots in the family, our responsibilities to the family and our needs for family. And I mean families in all their diversity and in the realities that they change over time. We must understand that this is as an important a side of our lives as our careers are.

The Moral Majority, the radical Right, people like Jesse Helms [Republican Senator, NC], use the concept of family demagogically, and they play to real needs of people. I think that people are concerned about families. I don't believe that young people today have a good enough choice on whether to start a family or not. The reality that parents have to work outside the home is not taken into account by society in terms of the family. So we don't have the necessary restructuring of hours and aids in child care.

It is for the welfare of families that you need things like child care. It's a lie to wave the flag of family and then to prevent action on new solutions that real families—especially children—now need.

But it is our own paralysis and our blind spots that have enabled the Moral Majority to become so powerful. They don't represent any majority of people in the United States, but they certainly have taken up the flag for family life and God, and those are real values for most Americans.

You can't counter real values by not recognizing them, because if you don't recognize the real needs then you're dealing in obsolete truncated terms yourself. After all, there hasn't been a really strong effort on the part of the women's movement, on the part of many feminists to embrace the necessities of families today.

We have created a vacuum that the Moral Majority walked into. You don't fight the banners of people who say they are for the right to life. I say we are for abortion, but that's like being for mastectomy. We are for the choice to have children, for affirming the generative roots of women in families. We want to make it a good choice, good for the children in families as well as for the life of the woman herself.

WW: *You seem very optimistic about the changes in the workplace that you see as inevitable. Why?*

BF: As the number of women in the work force approaches 50 percent and as the majority of women are now working, the reality of work life has to lead to restructuring work—restructuring jobs as well as restructuring homes. Half the people in the work force give birth to children, and the other half now are expected to share the burdens of child rearing. And it's about time.

Furthermore, everything we know about technological development and the development of work and what's likely to happen in the next stage indicates that flexitime will evolve naturally.

The first stage of the Industrial Revolution may have required that people on the assembly line perform robotlike jobs, but things are changing. I've had interesting discussions with people working for the telephone company who demanded a whole new approach to the quality of work life. They insisted that they be given more autonomy in controlling their own work, instead of punching a time clock. People are insisting on more control over their work lives, and these issues go beyond just women.

WW: *With a greater percentage of women in the work force, child-care structures will change. What is your vision of the future of parenting in the U.S.?*

BF: The reality is that parenting is going to have to be shared between the mother, the father and the government.

The image of the soulless federal day-care system, of handing your child over to the state, is horrifying to women because their roots are in family and the idea of motherhood is so crucial to their identity. But women are facing up to reality. They can't keep running a home and take care of the children as their mothers did if they're also going to work outside the home. So what we need is diverse options for ensuring good care of children, giving mother or father some option to take parental leaves and reduce their schedules, or something like Milton Friedman's concept of the negative income tax or the voucher system, which the conservatives are suggesting for other purposes. We should institute a child allowance, which other nations do. Every person who takes primary responsibility for the care of a child or a dependent adult would receive a certain allowance paid as income, like a tax rebate. If the mother and father jointly share the responsibility of the child, then it should be paid to both. When they both work, then the child allowance is used to help pay for child care. Child care can be offered for profit or not for profit, by unions, by community agencies, by the local community using empty school buildings, or use a federal block grant for it. The single solution that we used to talk about in the early days is not feasible anymore: 24-hour child care, free for the children of all income levels, paid for by federal taxes. It was a dream. What's really important is that there should be a diversity of child care in the community that parents can control.

WW: *Why do working women feel that they have to be superwomen?*
BF: I call that "female machismo," and it stems from their mothers and grand-mothers. When the man had to define himself solely as the one who could beat up the other man or who scored bigger in the rat race of success, he had to hide his own humanness by excessive machismo.

When the woman had to define her whole identity in terms of the house and the children, it had to be a perfectly run home and there had to be per-fectly controlled children. And the superwoman syndrome evolved from these exaggerated pressures, not from the actual double burden of working in the office and in the home. In the rat race, men were willing to conform to exces-sive demands because that was supposed to be their whole identity. But in addition to these career standards, women have excessive standards at home (which don't necessarily have anything to do with the real needs of a healthy child or a livable home), handed down from those kinds of communities where the mothers derived their only power, status and control from the home.

WW: *How will the increased number of women in the workplace affect men and the nature of work?*
BF: The battle of the first stage was for women to break into a man's world. But in the second stage we're going to see the value of women's world, only it's no longer going to be woman's world or man's world—they're both going to be shared.

There's nothing wrong with ambition for women or with aggression, with assertiveness, with success. Let us all enjoy whatever of it we can. One of the reasons for the tendency of men to fall into the machismo trap and to have a gray and linear identity was because they were defined solely in terms of rat-race success. If in that competitive world everything rests on success, then men are passive to that and underneath they are really cowering.

What is liberating for men is to find other aspects of their identity—this is the other half of the women's movement. They can find their feelings, their real identity in the family in terms of the emotional relationships and the nurturing that strengthens anybody, not just the competitive drive.

But then how ironic if the woman would shortchange those parts that have given her flexibility and sensitivity, even probably longer life, fewer ulcers, strokes, and heart attacks. How tragic if she would sacrifice those nurturing parts of her personhood and let herself be boxed in by that narrow definition of career and success that makes her passive and helpless to the demands of the corporation.

WW: *What would you advise a* Working Woman *reader?*
BF: I'd say to her, "Don't exchange one half-life for another." We had to react against something, break through one mystique, break through a barrier, and we haven't completely finished that job yet. But it is not a good bargain to put yourself totally at the mercy of one half of life. Everything we know teaches us that the self rests on the twin roots of work and love.

Abilities are also needs. You need to use your ability. Aside from the economic needs, there are psychological needs—for status, identity, participation in the world, some sense of meaning—and the abilities themselves must be used by women and men.

WW: *Could you sum up the message of* The Second Stage?

BF: We must begin to ask new questions and, even though we don't have any answers, the asking will free the women now feeling in an unquiet way that they may be shortchanging themselves. It will free women just to see that there are problems with both the standards they have been accepting at work and at home. And that they have every right to want the fullness of life in both places. But in order to put it all together, they must begin to question the standards and seek new solutions that go beyond the agenda of the first stage of the women's movement. And these new solutions are going to be every bit as important to men in the next stage.

Betty Friedan: Her Brave New World

Curt Suplee / 1983

From *Washington Post*, (19 October 1983),
B1, B15. © 1983, The Washington Post.
Reprinted with permission.

Still Betty after all these years. There have been twenty since she published *The Feminine Mystique*, seventeen since she founded the National Organization for Women; two decades of ceaseless toil, wheedle and harangue, bending the stubborn American psyche to a new shape. And yet, Betty Friedan is talking so fast that the back ends of her sentences overrun the front, the syllables slamming into each other like a pileup on the Beltway. The moment seems so auspicious, the future so exciting. Ronald Reagan, she says, has "declared war on women" by weakening the laws against sex discrimination, cutting back on programs that benefit women and confronting the celebrated "gender gap" with mere tokenism. And women, she said, will be firing back: "In 1984, perhaps for the first time in American history, women have—and will probably use—their vast political power. Six million more votes were cast by women in the '82 elections than by men. Those extra votes are enough to elect a president, and women are going to make the difference next time." And as for the gap, "there won't just be a token woman in the cabinet, a token woman on the Supreme Court. Thirty to forty percent of appointments—that's the kind of standard we're going to hold a candidate to."

But didn't Friedan forecast a powerful women's vote in the '76 election, too? She stops abruptly, drops her face into an upraised left hand and shuts her eyes—a ritual of concentration. Then the rasping, breathy voice starts again, eyes still closed. "But the gender gap was only beginning to be visible in '76," she says. By 1980, "there was a 20 percent voting difference between men and women—the majority of women did not vote for Reagan." And since then, she says, eyes opening, face rising, arms flying out, women are showing "a greater outrage in their political behavior."

She's rolling now. The women's movement will become "the cornerstone of a new coalition that puts the priorities of life and human welfare above profits and advantages for a special few." It will include "that part of the business community still committed to free enterprise and the right to make money but who don't want to self-destruct the planet." And labor, since "labor itself will only continue to be a power if it organizes the service industries—which are so largely, uh, manned by women." A deep, gurgling chuckle.

A female vice-presidential candidate, she says, is a real possibility. "It was symbolic ten years ago for a woman to throw in her hat like Sissy Farentholdt. But it's all very serious and very real now"—in part because so many mainstream women's groups are sympathetic. "The American Association of University Women, the Junior League, the YMCA, even the Girl Scouts—all these organizations that are part of the establishment—they're all feminists! It's not just a radical outside minority." Finally, the vision looms triumphant. "By 1988, there will be a serious woman's candidacy for the presidency," and in twenty years "we will have the Equal Rights Amendment behind us, some form of child care, remedies for the Social Security inequities, and may well have a woman president."

These are among the issues she will address in her speech today when the Women's Research and Education Institute honors her with a twentieth-anniversary luncheon at the Capital Hilton. It is an unaccustomedly public role for the sybil emeritus of the women's movement, the Peoria-born psychologist who at sixty-two is long out of the workaday bureaucracy. "I retain my commitment," she says, but "in recent years I have played my role primarily as a thinker. I have the vision and the ability to put into words the dreams. But I never was good at maneuvering." Nor does she have to be, here in this Georgetown town house where a PR firm is busily shuffling her schedule of interviews and appearances.

Not that she undervalues her contribution. "*The Feminine Mystique*," she says bluntly, "was the beginning of it all. It made people conscious of what millions of women were feeling," and "people still stop me on the street and tell me

where they were when they read it." Then "I myself took the lead in starting
the movement in 1966 with the creation of NOW. In those days, it scared
women more than men."

In the early '70s, she organized the National Women's Political Causus with
Gloria Steinem and Bella Abzug, and—ever concerned with practical plans—
went on to organize the First Women's Bank and Trust. "You can spend just so
long on consciousness-raising," she said at the time, "and then it's like looking
at your navel." But by the mid-'70s, she suddenly found her influence waning.
"I didn't go along with the sexual politics" championed by *Ms.* editor Steinem,
Friedan says now, downplaying the bitterness of their rivalry. "It was a genuine
ideological difference."

Critics complained that Friedan was taking too much personal credit for
the movement and exploiting it to her personal advantage. For her part, Friedan warned in 1972 that feminism was in danger of devolving into mere man-
hating, that radical "female chauvinist boors"—abetted by "the lavender menace" of lesbian factions—were risking a national backlash. She accused
Steinem of "ripping off the movement for private profit" from the magazine;
and, in opposition to rising anti-male sentiments, declared in 1973 that American women were "now strong enough to see men not as breadwinners, not as
sex objects, not as enemies, but as human beings, brothers." It was not the
prevailing view, and Friedan ended up playing Danton to Steinem's Robes-
pierre.

Friedan wrote in *It Changed My Life,* her 1976 memoir, that "I was no match
for her—not only because of the matter of looks—which somehow paralyzed
me—but because I don't know how to manipulate or deal with manipulation
. . . I'm just an ugly little girl who can't deal with the realities of political
power or the accommodations it demands." But by the late '70s, the national
mood had mellowed; and in 1981 Friedan again became a major voice with
the publication of *The Second Stage,* her analysis of the future of feminism. "Over
the years," she says now, "basically, I have been right. Where I am now, I feel
very confident, even comfortable, with where the movement is—the large-
ness, diffuseness and diversity of it."

Indeed, she is positively bullish. "The ERA will happen, in my opinion, in
this decade." She expects that the requisite legislation will clear both houses
of Congress before the election, since "I don't think even Republicans have
the courage to vote against it" and "the old hysteria about bathrooms and so

forth" has faded. And she anticipates the new federal agenda will include "maternity leave, child care, flex time" as soon as "we get rid of the current administration."

She is equally ebullient in the face of apparent retrograde tendencies in the culture. If the covers of *Cosmo* and *McCall's* still hawk a welter of cosmetic tips and boudoir exhortations, at least the fiction has changed. "The heroines are different," says Friedan, a twenty-five-year veteran of writing for women's magazines. If moviegoers still slaver as John Travolta abuses his girlfriend in *Staying Alive*, at least today's films offer real parts for women. In the '50s, she says, the only role for a woman was "a wife or mother waving goodbye. It isn't much of a part." And on TV "there are women policemen, detectives, taxi drivers. There are still a few mothers waving goodbye, but the personhood of woman is with us now." And "I'm very interested in the popularity of movies like *Ordinary People, The Great Santini*, and *Tootsie*," which suggest a new critical attitude toward traditional masculine roles.

If sales of romance novels—with their atavistic depiction of women as mate-made masochists in the clutch of Mr. Wrong—have never been higher, Friedan says simply, "So? It's probably some remnant of the old dream. As life demands that women take on more and more complex responsibilities," and their freedom to choose increases, romances may "play to some yearning to escape from freedom. But an hour of nostalgia is not the reality." She sees a steady maturation in fiction written by women: from the novels of the late '60s and early '70s "wallowing in the victim state—the dreary martyred mother" into the rage of "The Women's Room" and beyond. "Now," she says, "we're getting some fine figures." Who? She can't quite think of any. But never mind: Her own "going-to-sleep reading" runs to mysteries and science fiction, especially "the wonderful new breed of women detectives" and s-f writers such as Ursula K. Le Guin.

And if some men are becoming uncomfortable with the lately modish "sensitive" persona of the '70s (as personified, say, in Alan Alda) and returning to a more conventional masculine image, "well, I don't know that I'll buy the idea that any man who has freed himself from macho has to be a wimp." That, she says, is the kind of "either/or stuff" she inveighed against in *The Second Stage* when warning women against adopting a "superwoman" self-image or a counter-feminine style of "bark and growl, with no softness, no sweetness." To do so is merely "reacting so totally against the feminine mystique that it's not free. It's defined by its opposite." Ditto for male "reactive wimpishness. The man that emerges from the ashes of macho will not be a passive wimp—he'll be free."

But the real "cutting edge" of change, she predicts, will take place as social structures begin to accommodate post-feminist reality. Among them:

- Americans must overcome "the family mystique"—that "image of the family locked into the past," with its single-family dream home and obsessive "together-ness"—without losing sight of the family's enduring value. That will mean brain changes, she says, both for "those who hysterically equate the family with one single form," as well as "certain kinds of radical feminists who are locked into rebellion against the family."
- Flexible work hours will be increasingly necessary for two-paycheck households, as will "new forms and ways of financing housing" and new modes of housing itself: "Not the conventional idea of a house or apartment, which still in a way is based on the feminine mystique—a suburban dream house arranged for poppa the breadwinner and momma the housekeeper, segregated away from the city where the work was done and political decisions made." Nowadays "the greatest increase in our population is people living alone like me." For them, as for working couples wrestling with new self-definitions and "those in states of singlehood," some quasi-communal housing is needed that "respects the individual need for privacy, but also the need for family-type supports—a commonality of sorts." It would include "shared services" like laundry facilities, gardens, kitchens and dining rooms for "flexible options of sharing," rather like "Swedish service housing."
- Child-care services must increase. "Talk about child care in this country somehow implies that it's either/or again. I think that children require the nurture of their own families," and "it's a vital experience for parents." But in 1983, "couples "don't necessarily have the grandmother down the street—and if they do, she's probably working." With city and state funding and additional tax credits, Friedan says, communities "could take advantage of neglected school and church buildings" for centers "near where people work."

And much more—a dozen thoughts skidding through the gravel of her voice, smashing into sentence fragments as the momentum builds. Still at full throttle, after a quarter of a century. "It doesn't stay still," Friedan says. "There is continually a new challenge if you keep going and growing."

The Emancipation of Betty Friedan

Marilyn French / 1983

From *Esquire* magazine, (December 1983), 510, 512, 514–18. Reprinted by permission of *Esquire*.

Betty Friedan sees her life almost as a miracle. She is as surprised at what she wrought as an explorer who set out to map an island and discovers she has found a continent. Trained as an intellectual, she became a political activist; deeply committed to the warmth, nurturing, and affection of family life, she became the leader of a movement perceived as antagonistic to those qualities; a woman of modest personal goals, she helped to initiate the "second wave" of a movement immodestly dedicated to changing the world. One cannot discuss her without discussing that movement.

Friedan's mother, like so many of our mothers, was unhappy with her life. She had been forced to give up her job on a newspaper when she married, a loss she lamented throughout her later life and which shadowed her pleasure in her family and home. She urged her daughter toward a career in journalism, but young Betty was fascinated by psychology at Smith and Berkeley and did work so outstanding that she was offered a graduate fellowship in that field—an extraordinary event for a woman in the Forties. She was dating a young physicist who resented her opportunity and threatened to break with her. She gave up the fellowship in a paroxysm of guilt and confusion, wanting to pursue her studies, but wanting most of all the love, the home, the children that were supposed to be everywoman's destiny. Like so many women, she wanted above all to avoid her mother's misery, her mother's life, and attempted to do this by renouncing her mother's values. *She* would not spend her life sorrowing over a lost career: she would embrace the man, the home, the children, and live in a bath of felicity. The physicist broke with her anyway.

She went into journalism after all, reporting for the labor press. She found the right man and married him. She was not forced to give up *her* job until she became pregnant with her second child: one maternity leave was deemed sufficient, apparently, and even the newspaper guild refused to support her protest, despite a contract stipulating the right to pregnancy leave. So far had things progressed in a generation.

Friedan continued to write, free-lancing mainly for women's magazines. She was fascinated by women who managed to attain excellence in a discipline—especially the arts—and to raise children at the same time. This was her own dream: a whole life, integration of all talents. She immersed herself in the magazines that were her market, studying them. Over time, she perceived a pattern. Her editors would cut references to her subjects' careers: they claimed a woman painting a crib was interesting to their readers, but a woman painting a picture was not. She had difficulty placing a piece on the natural childbirth of a famous actress: it was too "gory," editors complained. The reality of women's lives—physical, intellectual, emotional—was censored; what appeared was a fantasy, a picture-book image of happy female domesticity that pleased advertisers and presumably tranquilized female readers. Friedan began to analyze the fantasy; she interviewed housewives about the reality of their lives; she thought about the reasons for the promotion of such a false image. She gave the image a name: the Feminine Mystique.

In 1963 she published a book containing her findings, in which she described her personal dilemma and gave accounts of those who shared it. It was an immediate best seller, selling three million copies, and read by millions more. Friedan received thousands of letters from women grateful to her primarily for alleviating their sense of isolation. They had believed they alone felt as they did; they had thought, and many had been told, they were "sick," neurotic because they felt discontent, even desperate, about the vapidity of their lives. Everywhere, people talked about *The Feminine Mystique*; the phrase entered the language.

The women Friedan reached were mainly like herself—middle class with some education. Most were white, women of the American mainstream, mar-

ried, mothers; some had prosperous husbands. Inspired and validated by finding their own truth presented as truth, many of them changed their lives,
returning to school, entering the work force. But professional and single
women, whites and women of color, were also aroused by her book, locating
in the feminine mystique the barrier to their advancement; it was their image
in men's minds that led men to prevent women from achieving greater effectiveness and scope in their jobs. If Friedan's reputation rested only on this
book and the response to it, she would be noteworthy. But she went further:
she changed her own life.

Several factors converged at this time. The black civil rights movement had
stimulated important legislation, notably the Equal Pay Act of 1963 and the
Civil Rights Act of 1964. Discrimination in employment on grounds of race
was to be declared illegal. When it was proposed that *sex* be added to those
grounds, the House of Representatives dissolved in laughter. Martha Griffiths,
then in the House, was humiliated and outraged and threatened that if Congress did not keep "that joke" in the Act, she would force a voice vote on the
floor, exposing those who were against women. Margaret Chase Smith leveled
the same threat in the Senate. The word *sex* remained in the Act, but no one
expected it to change anything.

In 1961 President Kennedy had established a national Commission on the
Status of Women, which fully documented the second-class status of American women. Its findings, however, resulted only in the establishment of an
advisory council and fifty state commissions: more talk, no action, temporiz-
ing. The administration's poverty program had no women in decision-making
positions, offered no job training or educational programs to women, had no
plans for day-care centers, although the present "feminization of poverty" was
already perceptible—women and their children constituted 80 percent of the
clientele of urban welfare programs. Even the Equal Employment Opportunities Commission (EEOC), the agency supposed to administer Title VII (for-
bidding discrimination in employment) of the Civil Rights Act, had no women
in decision-making posts except for the presidential appointee, Aileen Hernandez. Indeed, it was discovered that the EEOC was planning to issue a
guideline to Title VII that essentially sanctioned continued discrimination
against women in employment.

The women who worked in government were outraged but could not act
openly; espousal of women's rights was grounds for dismissal, for women or

men. Women in media were in a similar position, as were academic and professional women. These women wrote or talked to Betty Friedan. Promoting her book took Friedan across the country and to Europe, and everywhere she spoke to huge audiences of women and listened to their protests. They urged her to "start an NAACP for women"; they insisted that Title VII would never be enforced for women unless they marched on Washington like the blacks. Women in labor unions described how the unions sided with management when women brought complaints, how women were silenced and intimidated at union meetings.

She was fired by the outrage she encountered wherever she went. She herself was astounded at the depth and scope of the problem she had named, at its pervasiveness in American society. Her book had thrust her into a central position, which she accepted with dedication and energy. She went on lecturing; she traveled continually, lived out of a suitcase, spent her nights in drab motel rooms. Ironically, this woman who cherishes the warmth and intimacy of family life had to sacrifice it to a struggle in which she had, accidentally it seemed, become pivotal. She missed her children; her marriage was foundering; but she worked on with the euphoria of those who suddenly see a passage to freedom. Under pressure from women in all aspects of life, she finally decided to found a political organization devoted to gaining women's rights, and in 1966, with a small group of women of different races, she founded NOW, the National Organization for Women, the first new feminist organization in nearly fifty years. For in 1920, after passage of the Nineteenth Amendment granting women the vote, the "first wave" of organized feminism in America essentially collapsed. The women were exhausted; the fight for suffrage had taken seventy years and had drained more than two generations of women. Some stalwarts continued to fight, among them Alice Paul, who in 1923 succeeded in having the Equal Rights Act introduced in Congress. But for the most part, women trusted the vote to provide them with a voice. It did not and could not, in a nation in which both major political parties are controlled by the same forces, forces intent on maintaining a society stratified by economic inequality largely determined by sex and race.

Thus, NOW's Statement of Purpose had to declare, once again, that women are human—an assertion, Friedan says still, that turns the entire culture upside down. Her statement proclaims NOW to be dedicated to equality for women and to political action as a means of achieving it. It declares that black and low-paid women are particular victims of our society; that women are excluded from postgraduate educational institutions and professional associations; that tokenism is unacceptable. It affirms the continuing importance to women of childbearing and child rearing, but rejects the middle-class division of labor, which places the economic burden of the family entirely on men. It locates the arena of its action within the boundaries of American law and outside alignment with any political party.

NOW grew swiftly and was extremely effective, largely because it was a mainstream organization. There has been feminist protest at least since the fifteenth-century writer Christine de Pisan, the first of a series of European intellectuals to protest laws and attitudes based on the idea that women are subhuman, property, and exist for men's sake. Women of all classes thronged to early Christian and, later, early Protestant sects, which offered them at least moral or spiritual equality with men—the opportunity to die with men before the lions or at the stake. Poor women who could no longer feed their families rose up courageously before and during the French Revolution and, in fact, helped to precipitate it. Women composed a heroic segment of early socialist movements, drawn by a vision of equality and social justice.

But it has been exceedingly difficult to unify women. Although they constitute a separate caste, as Simone de Beauvoir has pointed out (caste is conferred at birth and is unchangeable; class is conferred at birth, but can be changed), they are also members of different classes, the classes of their families, to which they feel they owe primary loyalty. Although females are at the bottom of every class and although women in general value felicity more than power, their common cause is obscured by the clashing of classes, races, religious and ethnic categories, and subcultures. Yet without some unity among women as a caste, nothing changes for women, whoever rules the roost.

Friedan's creation of a mainstream women's movement was therefore an extraordinary achievement. It was not performed in a single stroke: after establishing NOW, she and other leaders had to struggle daily to enable NOW to survive and grow, to be heard over the ridicule of the external world, including the media, and to pierce the silence of women's fear. In those years, Friedan was catapulted into international prominence; she became the symbol of the women's movement. She worked tirelessly, literally day and night: she lobbied, she organized, she raised funds. She drew women from across the country into a ferment of activity. If she was often a guest at the White House, she also visited women in labor unions and worked closely with women of color and tried to enlist them in the organization. Her energy seemed limitless: faith and joy buoyed her.

The first battle fought by NOW was to pressure, successfully, the commissioners of the EEOC and the President to rescind the guidelines tolerating sexual discrimination. The immediate consequence of this was the employers, who had recently been forbidden from dividing job advertisements into categories of "colored" and "white," were also prevented from advertising "Help Wanted—Female" or "Help Wanted—Male." Once this had been done, NOW initiated a series of lawsuits against companies that refused to hire women in jobs traditionally reserved for men—as telephone line workers, railroad workers, and others. It fought against "protective" legislation decreeing that women could not lift more than thirty-five pounds. It took up the case of stewardesses who claimed discrimination because they were forced to leave their jobs if they married or when they reached thirty-five. The airlines mounted a tough fight against the EEOC and NOW. So elaborate and expensive was their defense that Friedan came to recognize the economic motive of institutions in maintaining sexist discrimination. By letting women go at thirty-five or before, the airlines saved the costs of pensions and promotions. By keeping women in low economic status, many companies maintained a reliable low-paid marginal labor force who could be hired when needed and fired if an industry had to contract for a time. By hiring young unmarried women, or older women whose children had grown, industry gained the benefit of energy and experience without having to provide raises and advancement.

Maintaining a noncentralized structure offering considerable autonomy to community chapters, NOW in its early years focused action through the establishment of task forces on the treatment of women in the media and textbooks, employment, sports, and marriage and divorce laws. Women came to NOW for help in fighting sex discrimination in their jobs, in establishing standards for day-care centers, in banning segregated living arrangements on college campuses, and more. NOW used political pressure—picketing, marching, lobbying, and media events as well as legal action to fight, one by one, the seemingly unending barriers to women's full citizenship. In 1967, under Friedan's guidance, NOW voted to work for the passage of the Equal Rights Amendment, which had languished in committee since 1923, and for access to legal abortion. These positions led some women to resign from the organization. But once a woman has arrived at a feminist perspective on her life and society, there is no retreat from that realization, and these women formed their own organizations, like the Women's Equity Action League (WEAL), that worked with NOW on issues of shared concern.

In 1969 Friedan joined with Larry Lader and others who supported legal abortion to found what was to become NARAL, the National Abortion Rights Action League. At its inception, the men involved saw it as principally designed to protect doctors who performed abortions; they did not consider abortion a feminist issue and were appalled at the linkage of the two. Friedan rooted access to legal abortion firmly in the basic human right to control one's own body and reproduction. On this ground, abortion became a feminist issue. After the Supreme Court decision of 1973 affirming this right, abortion-related deaths of women dropped by 600 percent.

NOW had many major achievements in those early years. It conveyed to the nation at large the fact that discrimination against women exists; it transformed ridicule of the women's movement by the media and other institutions into serious attention; it was instrumental in the building of a corpus of judgments and laws requiring equity in education and in hiring and promotion. It helped to get the ERA passed by the Congress. It also performed two more amorphous but extremely significant functions.

First, it generated many spin-off groups; some, like WEAL, dissociated themselves from NOW because they could not support a particular position (abortion, in this case), yet continued to work on other projects with NOW. Some, like NARAL, were formed because a single issue had grown too complex and demanding to be handled by the parent organization. This was the case also with the NOW Legal Defense and Education Fund, started in 1970 by Friedan and Kay Clarenbach. Although women lawyers invariably worked for and with NOW *pro bono*, the many lawsuits NOW was involved with were still expensive. The Fund was designed to raise and distribute money for such actions. And in 1971 Friedan, with Bella Abzug, Gloria Steinem, Liz Carpenter, Clarenbach, and others, founded NWPC, the National Women's Political Caucus, designed to support candidates for all levels of office and in the judiciary who support the elimination of racism, sexism, institutional violence, and poverty. Each of these organizations has been extremely effective, and remains so.

Second, NOW functioned as a centrist organization, around and against which other groups could align themselves. More-radical women argued that to work for the assimilation of women into a society that was inherently unjust and unworthy was an unworthy act; more-conservative women, fearful of further weakening men's sense of responsibility for their children and the women who raise them, renounced any claim on "rights" that might, they felt, contribute to that process. In the late Sixties various groups tried to take over NOW. Younger women, radicalized by the Vietnam War and by their treatment by men within the antiwar movement, founded formal and informal feminist groups; many also joined NOW. These women represented a wide spectrum of opinion and were intellectually sophisticated. Some were socialists of various "sects"; some believed lesbianism to be the only fully feminist position, and they demanded that NOW affirm this. Since feminists were invariably attacked as "dykes," they should counter this attack by proclaiming, "We are all lesbians," much as King Christian X of Denmark vowed to put on the yellow armband with the Star of David if the Nazis decreed all Danish Jews must wear them.

Friedan's response to these new elements was both personal and political. She was shocked by the idea of a public declaration of lesbianism. She writes, "I am not that far from everywoman" (insofar as everywoman exists), and reminds the reader that she was born in Peoria, Illinois, a symbolic Middletown. But she also felt, with many other NOW leaders, that to take such a position would be a tactical error: she felt lesbianism as a political stance to be antimale, and her own position, from the beginning, had been to gain rights for women without alienating men, but rather seeing them as fellow victims of a divisive, repressive, dehumanized society. A mainstream person, she envisioned social change within capitalism, not through violent revolution or even evolution to a socialist system she considered authoritarian and still unequal.

For several years, these conflicts seethed within NOW, occupying the energies of many women and leaving deep wounds behind—especially the struggle between members of the Young Socialist Alliance (YSA), a branch of the Socialist Workers' Party, and the centrists. But the arguments broadened the thinking and awareness of the entire group and deepened its understanding of the nature of the barriers to the equality of women. In time, NOW reasserted its original mainstream character; dissenters formed other spin-off groups or dropped out of organized feminism (not out of feminism itself) altogether.

The conflict exhausted Friedan, who struggled throughout to prevent NOW from fragmenting into sects. In 1970, divorced and in need of money, she stepped down as president of NOW. Aileen Hernandez, one of the original founders, took over. Friedan's last major act in NOW (although she is still an important member) was to organize the Women's Strike for Equality in 1970. Its centerpiece was to be a march down Fifth Avenue in New York, but Mayor Lindsay had denied the women a permit. Nevertheless, they assembled, nearly fifty thousand women who had for the day abandoned their jobs or their homes to march for equality. When mounted police tried to stop them, Friedan told the women to join hands across the street: "And so we marched, in great swinging long lines, from sidewalk to sidewalk, and the police on their horses got out of the way. And people leaned out of office windows and waved. . . ." The march, the strike, created tremendous awareness nationwide of the women's movement and added to its moral force: it was a huge success.

Friedan returned to writing, teaching, and lecturing; she has been visiting professor at a number of universities in the past fourteen years. In 1976 she published *It Changed My Life*, an account of the early years of NOW. In 1977 she helped to heal the internal split over lesbianism by supporting the proposal for sexual preference at the National Women's Conference in Houston: the hall exploded with cheers and applause.

In 1981 she published *The Second Stage*, an exhortation to women and men to see feminism not as a movement antagonistic to traditional female roles and values, but as a humanizing force in society at large. At present, she is at work on a book on aging, to be called *The Fountain of Age*, searching for ways to see and experience age as a positive part of life. Acute to discrimination, she has discovered that most research on age has been conducted on men, who provide the standard for discussion of the subject, although women in general live longer than men and more of them face extreme old age alone. But both men and women are, Friedan believes, denied personhood after sixty.

If Friedan no longer stands as the spokeswoman for "the" feminist movement, that is partly because there is no single movement, but many, all sharing the same ultimate goal and a few basic principles, yet differing about means and methods. Many feminists diagnose the malaise of the entire Western industrial world as being rooted in sexism. If they are right, the creation of a more humane and just society, which is the goal of feminism, requires change more fundamental than feminists have previously recognized.

Betty Friedan has remained true to her principles, personal and political. She has been and remains a bridge between conservative and radical elements in feminism, and an ardent advocate of harmony and humane values. Her affirmation of the family in *The Second Stage* is a passionate plea for general awareness of the inclusive nature of feminism: its vision of human wholeness; its repudiation of laws and customs that deny men expression of their emotions, sensitivity, and nurturing qualities and deny women expression of assertive intellect, action, and a voice in society. Friedan will stand in history as an initiator of the "second wave" of feminism and as one who has never wavered in fidelity to its larger vision.

A Feminist in the Late '80s

Bettyann Kevles / 1987

From the *Los Angeles Time Magazine*,
(17 May 1987), 8. Reprinted by permission
of Bettyann Kevles.

The phone hasn't stopped ringing since 9 a.m. and Betty Friedan has risen three times from her bath to answer it. It's past 11 and she's still not ready to leave her Sea Colony apartment in Santa Monica for a noon lecture at USC. "Who is it?" she calls from the bedroom.

"USA Today," I answer.

Twenty-four years ago, Friedan wrote a book called *The Feminine Mystique*. A classic of feminist literature, it expressed the latent discontent many American women felt with their position in society and helped trigger the women's movement worldwide. Three years later, in 1966, she helped found the National Organization for Women and was its first president. She still has an uncanny ability for articulating the needs of women of all ages.

Her historical role in advancing women's rights has been likened to Thomas Paine's in the eighteenth century, when his pamphlet "Common Sense" energized Yankee discontent on the eve of the American Revolution. It is not uncommon to hear her compared to earlier feminist leaders Susan B. Anthony and Elizabeth Cady Stanton.

Friedan's concern these days is for the future of the movement that she helped launch. "The suffragettes disbanded after winning the vote in 1919," she points out—and two generations later, American women were back in the kitchen, living within the confines of a new mystique: An ideology that

74

insisted that a woman belonged at home, enjoying the greater world only vicariously, through the accomplishments of her husband and children. The advances of the last two decades have been substantial, but feminists today have more to do than maintain a holding pattern. To remain viable, Friedan believes, the women's movement must have a forward momentum. Its next goal should be a reshaping of both society and the workplace, which she believes are geared toward a "male model." In this new world—no longer just a man's world—women would not be forced to choose between family and career.

"There are powerful forces in America today, right-wingers and evangelists who threaten to re-impose earlier roles on women," she tells a packed auditorium of mothers and daughters at the Westlake School for Girls in Bel-Air one day. These daughters are the people she wants to reach now, members of the "I'm not a feminist, but I'm going to be an astronaut" generation who listen incredulously to Friedan's descriptions of life with girdles and curfews. She is not asking for their gratitude. She is cautioning vigilance.

On this April morning, while she prepares for the day, I find myself running interference with the phone. Friedan emerges draped in a light blue terry-cloth caftan and grabs the receiver on the counter between the kitchen and the living room. "They want to know," I explain, "if you have an opinion about the new short skirts."

Her demeanor changes like quicksilver. The comfortable matron is transformed, her toga no longer an after-swim cover-up but a cloak of authority. Standing as tall as her 5 feet, 2 inches allow, Friedan becomes a spokeswoman for the movement. "I am opposed to short narrow skirts," she pronounces. "They are undignified and denigrating to anyone over twenty. I shall continue wearing my skirts long and flowing and unhobbling and pretty."

It is hard to imagine Betty Friedan's mental map of Los Angeles. Having allotted just half an hour to get to USC from Santa Monica, she urges me to drive faster. She hates to be late and, in fact, seldom is. She has no patience with SigAlerts, freeway construction or lane changes. When things don't go her way her temper flares without warning, only to be followed by apologies.

She claims to drive on Long Island, where she summers, but she won't tackle the freeways in Los Angeles and for a few days I'm replacing her regular driver. ("Do you have a car?" she asked in a deep, raspy voice when I first befriended her in Massachusetts in 1981. "I need a lift. I don't drive in Cambridge.") She likes to compare herself to author and non-driver Ray Bradbury. "It's perfectly easy to be a pedestrian in this city," she says, "as long as you have friends who will pick up and deliver."

She is usually driven to work in a red truck by a young woman she met at a local NOW meeting. It seems she is short-tempered with her, too, but the young feminist ignores the outbursts. "She is so busy. She does so much, and she doesn't even have a secretary," the woman says. Friedan juggles teaching, lecturing, writing and entertaining, aided only by an answering machine.

Friedan first came to live in California last year, as a fellow at USC's Andrus Gerontology Center. Her return this spring with a joint appointment at the school of journalism and the women's study center has brought her into the mainstream of university life. She's received a variety of invitations to participate in local women's groups. Some, like NOW, are open to anyone. Others, like the Trusteeship for Women, are by invitation only. The trusteeship, a semi-professional, semi-social group of accomplished women—including Marilyn Bergman, an Academy Award-winning songwriter, and Maureen Kindel, president of the Los Angeles Board of Public Works—has impressed Friedan by its ability to implement policy.

She marvels at the contrast between the Los Angeles that New Yorkers warned her about and the reality. "It was supposed to be plastic, and intellectually a wasteland." Her base at the university may skew her perspective, but she hasn't found Los Angeles so bleak. Angelenos would make her feel obsolete and socially ostracized, she was told; instead she has been squired to street theater and invited to Sunday evening screenings at Norman Lear's. She was also warned about "the cult of youth." But instead of a youth culture she has been reveling in cross-generational friendships, enjoying evenings with men and women in their thirties and forties, sixties and seventies.

"You know I left Peoria (where she grew up) for New York because New York was cheerier. Los Angeles is cheerier than New York. L.A. is to New York as New York is to Peoria." She likes that equation and smiles at the thought. The smile transforms her, subtracting years.

But the crucial difference, Friedan finds, is one of attitude. Friedan is still active in East Coast women's networks, and she has a "warm, affectionate relationship with New York NOW"—but she is finding life in California more upbeat. "Women here aren't cynical, or burnt out," she says. "There's a political energy. And they aren't locked into single-issue thinking."

When Betty Friedan first came to USC, she came to write—not about women but about aging. At the gerontology center, she was working on a book about "the age mystique." (She turned sixty-six on Feb. 4, and her eighty-nine-year-old mother lives at Leisure World in Laguna Hills.) At the Grace Ford Salvatori Journalism Building, where she returned this year as a visiting distinguished professor in journalism and as a leader in the program for the Study of Women and Men in Society, ten file boxes of notes for her book sit untended near her desk. She hasn't found much time to go through them. Women's issues keep diverting her attention. "Since I've been out here all these things have been happening and I have to respond to them," she says.

The role of women is her focus at the journalism school. On one recent afternoon, Friedan's students in her "Women in Media" class are waiting as she arrives with a group of guest speakers. Seated at a table in front of her class, she rests her chin on her hand as she waits for everyone to settle down. Then she stands, her fingers toying with the silver rope around her neck. As she addresses the class, her eyes dart among her students. The words tumble out swiftly.

"Don't think you ingratiate yourself with me with feminist rhetoric. It won't work if it's just rhetoric," she warns her students—all of them women—as she returns a set of papers. "You need concrete examples to make a point or it won't sell." This also sums up her approach to her work at the university. She is impatient with ideology and hairsplitting and demands practical solutions.

Today she introduces Wallis Annenberg, co-publisher and editor of *TV Guide*; Irma Kalish, president of Women in Film; Fay Kanin, the first woman president of the Academy of Motion Picture Arts and Sciences; Carolyn See, novelist and book reviewer, and producer Norman Lear. Kanin urges the students to "persist, be a pest," not be so thin-skinned or easily discouraged. All right, maybe "pest" is an unfortunate term, Kanin corrects herself, but whatever you call it, women need to be more aggressive.

But that isn't always enough. One of the panelists mentions the "glass ceiling"—the invisible lid on female advancement into executive positions—and the others nod. (Later, at a television studio where Friedan is taping an interview, a woman executive makes the same complaint—that women can rise only so far, and no farther. Strangers do not hesitate to tell her their woes. She always listens. She describes it as one of the responsibilities she has accepted.)

Friedan later turns the discussion to the week's reading assignment, *In a Different Voice*, by Carol Gilligan. The book argues that women think differently from men, that women are more sympathetic and compassionate. Friedan suggests that violence and brutality thrive on the screen today because of male dominance of the media, and that a female voice is needed to decry poverty, disease and the nuclear threat.

Never anti-male, Friedan envisions a future in which everyone will lead more fulfilling lives. As she sees it, "We are stuck at a midway point where we have won some new opportunities, and we are living with them from necessity as well as opportunity, but everything is still based on the male model." She pounds her fist in her hand to make her point. Why should women, the people who have the babies, have to follow a career timetable geared to men? "What is needed is a basic remodeling of American society into one in which women and men can have equal access to both family and career."

That is part of her message in *The Second Stage*, which was first published in 1982 and reissued last year with a new afterword. The second stage she describes is a feminism that takes the woman's movement past demands for equal opportunity in what has been a man's world, at the same time as it demands changes in that world. She is asking for a more flexible, compassionate society that takes into consideration familial as well as work-related responsibilities.

Without doubt she has moved in a different direction from other feminists. She opposes sexual politics—which pits men and women against each other—and single-issue politics—which, by focusing solely on pornography or abortion, for example, leaves other critical problems unaddressed. She is especially sympathetic with mainstream working women who, she sees, need new public policies that will allow them to *choose* to have a family, with the knowledge that they will be able to retain their jobs if they opt for children and that there will be adequate day-care available.

Last spring, she accepted an invitation from the women's center to take part in a series of lunches with prominent women in the community, which has since evolved into a monthly Think Tank headed by Friedan. "I didn't object to being used because there is a great need for new ideas, new thinking on feminist subjects," she says. At the first Think Tank, last spring, the issue of parental leave was raised. As a result of that discussion, Friedan's name heads the list of a coalition that opposed some traditional allies and filed an *amicus curiae* brief in the landmark California Federal Savings & Loan Assn. case, in which the U.S. Supreme Court upheld the constitutionality of a California law that guarantees a woman the same job, or its equivalent, after unpaid maternity leave. Along with groups like the International Ladies Garment Workers Union, Planned Parenthood and the California Federation of Teachers, Friedan insisted on the right of women to be workers and to bear children.

The issue split the national woman's movement. National NOW and the American Civil Liberties Union supported Cal Fed. They feared that different treatment for women harked back to nineteenth- and early twentieth-century protective legislation that discouraged employers from hiring women altogether. In the court's majority opinion upholding the constitutionality of the California law, Justice Thurgood Marshall enunciated the right of women as workers to have both families and job security.

At an April Think Tank meeting, the Baby M case is the topic of the day. The discussion attracts more than forty women to the lounge of the Hillel Building on Hoover Street. Besides USC faculty members and Rabbi Laura Geller, who is host, there are law professors from other universities, a city commissioner, union representatives, advocates for children's agencies, and representatives of Hollywood organizations such as Women in Film.

The discussion focuses on the issue of surrogacy, and emotions run high. Actress Susan Anspach announces that she is collecting signatures for a petition supporting Mary Beth Whitehead, the New Jersey woman who agreed to be artificially inseminated and bear Baby M for a childless couple. Friedan has herself signed a petition backing Whitehead, but she is sensitive to the complexities of the issue. The couple also have substantial emotional investments, she reminds the group; the interests of the natural mother, while paramount in her mind, are not unalloyed. She is harsh about one participant in the case: the agency that arranged the deal and may make more money off of it than Whitehead herself. To everyone's applause, she calls for prohibitions against "procreative poverty."

On pornography, another issue that has splintered the woman's movement, Friedan also retains her own vision. She brandishes a flier from a New York conference featuring Gloria Steinem, Susan Brownmiller and Shere Hite. They support legislation limiting publication of obscene material. Friedan opposes all censorship and believes that "the real obscenity is the feminization of poverty."

It is in everyone's interest, she believes, to see that families are well tended. Women are different from men because women have babies; but the differences of sensibility that may stem from unique biological functions are differences of degree, not of kind. She is appalled by the rhetoric of the feminist opposition. "They talk about male civil rights," she repeats, her voice breaking with outrage. "How can there be male and female civil rights?"

When film maker Dale Bell bought the old Friedan home along the Hudson River in rural New York, *The Feminine Mystique* was two years old and already a classic. The house was a nineteenth-century fantasy with three floors, turrets and a porch. Bell recalls that a little girl showed him around and stopped on the third floor to explain: "And this is where my mother wrote *The Feminine Mystique.*"

When he moved in, the living room walls were bright purple. He repainted them along with the rest of the house. In the study, though, the bookcases were labeled with words like "health," "education," "divorce"—topics in the book. He painted around them, historical landmarks to be saved.

The house has passed into other hands, but Bell has never lost touch with Friedan. He says, "There was a ghost in that house that connects our lives."

Ted and Pat Apstein, her oldest friends in Los Angeles, are connected to Friedan by another house in that same rural New York county—a stone barn where Friedan and her husband, Carl, lived before the Hudson River house. The Apsteins bought the barn from the Friedans thirty years ago. A decade later, they moved to Los Angeles; now, they find Betty Friedan remarkably unchanged since the days their babies toddled together. "More confident, but otherwise the same," says Ted Apstein.

It was Pat Apstein who found Friedan the Sea Colony sublet and then loaned her a sofa and table.

"I gave myself half a day to finish the apartment," Friedan says. "I wanted a nice, interesting coffee table, and a quilt for the bed." The prices on Main Street in Santa Monica where she had gone to shop were higher than she had in mind, but she was in a buying mood, so she stopped to try on a sweater. Her face is familiar to people all over America and so she wasn't surprised when a woman came over and thanked her for what she has done. In response,

Friedan asked her how the sweater looked. "Not right for you," the stranger advised. "What exactly are you looking for?"

"A coffee table," Friedan said.

The woman happened to have just sold her first script and was celebrating by redecorating. She happened to have a marble-top coffee table and took Friedan to see it. She was also selling a bentwood rocker, an antique mirror and a quilt.

So Friedan sits on the borrowed sofa, her books in front of her on the marble-top coffee table. There are photographs of her family, but she guards their privacy. When Carolyn See one day reflected, "My mother would rather have had a prostitute for a daughter than a writer," Friedan added: "So would my children rather have had one for a mother."

Divorced in 1969 and never remarried, she hasn't stopped enjoying the company of men—maybe more now than as a young woman. In *It Changed My Life*, a 1976 collection of her writings on the women's movements, she muses about a dinner with a new man, about how much fun it was relating to men in ways she hadn't been able to before she was married or during her marriage. Perhaps she had been too insecure, "or maybe I was too anxious to get married to really relax and enjoy the relationships with men before."

Writer Maurice Zolotow, who met Friedan around 1950 at a meeting of the Society of Magazine Writers, explains that "all of her friends are family." There are old friends passing through like Bob Hirschfield and Muriel Robinson from New York, who drop in one day at the Sea Colony apartment—she introduces them as part of "my commune family." After the divorce she rented a house in Sag Harbor, Long Island, with four other newly single people. They shared cooking and cleaning and provided surrogate families to one another. Hirschfield and Robinson met at the commune and married a year later.

"Betty was first among equals," Bob Hirschfield recalls. "She had the biggest bedroom and made most of the decisions." And took her turns with routine chores. He remembers the night she picked the greens for the community salad from the garden. "We didn't notice what we were eating until we swallowed. She had picked a whole salad of mustard."

Zolotow recalls that Friedan in the early '50s was "very energetic, warm, sexy and well-dressed." She was, and is, very feminine, a quality he does not find inconsistent with feminism, but which still surprises people when they meet her.

"Feminists can also dream of long-enduring love and marriage," Friedan says, sinking into the sofa beneath a Picasso hanging of knights and unicorns that she unrolls wherever she happens to be living. "I have nothing but admiration, and envy, for people who achieve that in life."

A question about First Lady Nancy Reagan brings back her public pose. "The reality of the role of the President's wife is we do look to her somehow as a role model for American women. I think she should have identified more with women's rights. In the first year she was only interested in $10,000 ball gowns. Now she comes into focus as a strong, tigerish wife."

But she does admire their devotion to each other, and calls Nancy-bashing a red herring. "The issue is Ronald Reagan's competence. There is nothing wrong with a strong First Lady. In fact," Friedan says, "maybe the President's wife should have a job title and job description and pay.

"As for Nancy's devotion to her husband, there seems to be a genuine bond and love between them. That is what is admirable. Everyone loves romance and the idea of enduring romantic love."

Rabbi Laura Geller introduces Friedan to a Hillel audience in the Taper Auditorium. The rabbi, 37, is a contemporary of Friedan's children and is both her student and mentor.

A decade ago, Geller tells the students, when she was newly ordained as one of only nine women rabbis in the United States, she discovered that the Reform rabbis were holding their convention in Arizona, which hadn't ratified the Equal Rights Amendment. She called Betty Friedan for advice: Should she boycott or attend the meeting?

Friedan advised her to attend and volunteered to come herself, which she did, addressing the women rabbis in an informal session. Geller tells the audience: "It is pretty clear I would not be a rabbi if there had not been a Betty Friedan" who paved the way for all professional women of her generation.

Now the older woman is sitting at the younger woman's feet as part of a monthly Torah study group. Friedan was not particularly religious until, a few years ago, she came to sense "a mystical connection between feminism and Judaism."

"Growing up as a Jew in Peoria, I knew what it was to be an outsider," she says. She sees this as having helped form her sensitivity to the underdog's view of things.

"I would not be the first in the history of the Jews to play the role of a visionary or prophet," she says, "a female Moses leading women out of the wilderness. . . . I wouldn't be the first in our history to take a sense of injustice and apply it to the larger, human category."

When anti-ERA forces pressured the Illinois Legislature before a crucial vote, they called the ERA a "Zionist-communist plot" and showed photos of mutilated Israeli girls in tanks. On other occasions, at International Women's Congresses in Mexico City and Nairobi, Friedan faced organized anti-Semitism.

In March, at a Torah reading at the Brandeis-Bardin Institute, she was asked to comment on the scriptural lines for the day. These were about Moses breaking the tablets on his descent from Mount Sinai when he saw the Israelites dancing around a golden calf. The words seemed especially apt to her: "This is about feminism, the way some feminists have stopped evolving. Humans always have a tendency to make graven images. That is what threatens the women's movement. It is dangerous to make a graven image of feminism. That prevents life from evolving, growing, changing. The answers of the '70s will not satisfy the questions of the '80s."

She acknowledges the "patriarchal ethic embedded in the Judeo-Christian tradition" but believes that strong women are also part of that tradition. In Judaism, Friedan has found spiritual support for her continuing quest for human liberation.

"Becoming proud of my identity as a woman, I learned to be proud of this other part of my identity, my Jewishness. That taste for authenticity that I got with defining myself as a woman gave me a taste for authenticity that brought me to Judaism."

After the landmark 1970 protest march on Fifth Avenue in New York, an event that drew more than 50,000 women and signified the coming of age of the woman's movement as a national phenomenon, she addressed an enormous crowd in back of the New York Public Library. In that moment of exultation she recalled that in "the religion of my ancestors men used to pray each day thanking God for not being women. And women prayed simply to submit themselves to the Lord's will. I said, not anymore. I believe women all over the world will be able to say, I thank you Lord for making me a woman."

Betty Friedan Is Still Telling It Like It Is

Marian Christy / 1990

From *The Boston Globe*, (14 January 1990), A14.
Reprinted with permission of *The Boston Globe*.

Betty Friedan will be sixty-nine on Feb. 4. She does not disguise her gray hair or her tell-it-like-it-is attitude. In this conversation in her fortieth floor West Side apartment, Friedan even suggests that seniority has its advantages. "I am at a stage where I am what I am," she says forcefully. "I am enjoying the strengths of my older self."

Friedan's 1963 best seller, *The Feminine Mystique*, presaged the women's liberation movement. She is working on a new book, *The Fountain of Age*, about the good side of aging. It is already being described as "elderly liberation."

An outspoken believer in continuous self-realization, Friedan, a 1942 graduate of Smith College, was interviewed days before embarking on a four-month assignment as visiting distinguished professor at the University of Southern California.

Friedan, a grandmother, was divorced in 1969 from Carl Friedan, an advertising executive, with whom she had three children. She was a "bored housewife" before she wrote *The Feminine Mystique*, the book that changed her life and the lives of millions of women forever. In 1966, Friedan founded NOW, the National Organization for Women, which focused on job discrimination, and was its first president.

"To be able to feel good about being a woman is something wonderful. I've accomplished that for other women. It's finally happened to me, too! Think about it: Freud was not wrong about what he observed about penis envy. It

84

was symbolic that men had a better deal in life. Men were freer to have ventures and adventures. Now women have been defined as people. Women are freer today. Women don't want to be like men. There's more and more of a sense in taking delight in being what they are. Still, there's a lot of unfinished business. It shouldn't be impossible for women to have it all.

"Actually, thinking about it now, I don't like the phrase 'having it all.' Nobody applies that phrase to men. The two aspects of life are love and work. That goes for men and that goes for women.

"I'm fascinated by marriage. What makes it work? Why does it have such a hold on us? I have the sense that, when it works, it's marvelous. When it doesn't, it's misery-making and constricting. I feel a sense of failure about my marriage. I was married for twenty years. I look back now and realize that there were happy times. My marriage had some rich, rewarding textures. To this day, my children make pilgrimages to all the houses we lived in. I can't go into these homes without bursting into tears.

"Yes! Yes! I wanted my marriage to work. Ending the marriage was the most difficult thing I ever did. I even went through a period when I denied the plan of ending the marriage. Even now, there's still a feeling of loss, of sorrow.

"Not many of my friends are married to the fathers of their children. I envy people whose marriages have evolved rather than dissolved. I also envy my friends who have made good, strong ties in their second marriages. There's no point in denying one's need for love, for closeness, for mutual support. However you find it—in marriage or outside of marriage—it's vital. Intimacy is one of the most important things in life. The moments I feel most alive are in moments of private intimacy and, of course, in large, passionate moments— like in the middle of my revolutions!

"Marriage partners do not necessarily become competitive when the wife makes more money than the husband. That used to be a fear when man's ego was defined completely by his bread-winning powers and women married for status and support. Now, there's less economic measuring in a marriage. But both partners have to feel good about themselves and have reasonable measures of satisfaction and rewards. Only when there is enormous economic discrepancy can you run into trouble. Or if one partner has a fundamental lack of confidence and becomes discontented, there can be trouble. As we move nearer to equality, women are capable of achieving some status and support for themselves. That takes some of the pressure off men and they can break out of their machismo aspect.

"I'm a good friend. I have a great capacity for friendship. Maybe it's because I'm not married. Friendship is a basic sustenance of my life. The deepening bonds with old friends, male and female, is very important to me. The more pain and joy you share with someone is what forges a friendship and bonds it.

"I've experienced great support from women and have given great support to women. But there have been instances when I have been pained by trashing, by knifing and by manipulation at the hands of other women. I felt an enormous sense of betrayal. In the guise of the women's movement, one sees terrible pettiness.

"I also accept the reality of ambition. I am ambitious. I've always felt that ambition is fine, necessary and should be acknowledged. If, somehow or other, ambition begins to corrupt your leadership, there's trouble ahead. I've seen that kind of ambition in the women's movement and in the political arena.

"I admire people who have somehow managed to achieve personal power in the spirit of service. To succeed, you have to be ambitious and shrewd. But you also have to have integrity and not let personal ambition corrupt larger purposes. I'm not interested in power battles and manipulations that happen when power becomes more important than purpose. Instead of trying to outfox, I generally retreat.

"On the other hand, I have no problem with finding the courage to confront real enemies. I take on the battle. I am pained by knifings based on rivalries and jealousies. That has happened to me sometimes. That happens to anyone who achieves a large kind of persona. Oh, I'm hot-tempered and very impatient sometimes. I can have a lot of arguments, even with people I love. I feel strongly about things. We're in changing times. Everything is shifting. Arguments on the level of 'change' can be zesty and good. I also know my fame has earned me both support and envy. Some desire to strike me down. I've been tested. I've used my life to good purpose.

"I can get defensive. I can get on my high horse. But I understand myself. I allow myself to feel my pain and my joy. How can you be alive and not feel? I don't need masks. I know what I know. I feel what I feel. As I get older, I am becoming more and more my real self.

"Look! I don't hide my gray hair. I like it. It has softened my face. After I wrote *The Feminine Mystique,* I came across the ad: 'If you have one life to live, live it as a blonde.' It was a frivolous idea and I decided to defend my right to be frivolous. I went to a beauty salon and told them to make me a blonde. They couldn't. So I became a redhead. When I went out into the sunshine, my hair turned green. Now I don't have the inclination to take the gray out of my hair at all. Why bother with all that now?"

Playboy Interview: Betty Friedan

David Sheff / 1992

From *Playboy*, (September 1992), 51–54, 56,
58, 60, 62, 149. Reprinted by permission of
Playboy magazine.

Wherever Betty Friedan goes, she gets the kind of attention normally
reserved for movie stars. But the people who approach her are not autograph
seekers. They represent a remarkable array of women of every race, age and
background. They usually apologize for bothering her and explain that they
just want to tell her one thing: "You changed my life."

Few people have affected as many lives—male or female—as Friedan, the
mother of the modern-day women's movement. In 1963 she finished *The Feminine Mystique*, a book that "pulled the trigger on history," as Alvin Toffler put
it. Amitai Etzioni, professor of sociology at George Washington University,
called it "one of those rare books we are endowed with only once in several
decades, a volume that launched a major social movement."

The book, which sold millions of copies, gave a name to the alienation and
frustration felt by a generation of women who were supposed to feel fulfilled
doing what women before them had done: taking care of their homes and
families. Friedan struck a nerve and received an overwhelming response,
including hate mail from people who believed that a woman's place was in the
home. Many women saw Friedan as a savior who showed that they were not
alone in their despair. It spurred them to demand more. As a result, life as we
knew it—relationships, sex, families, politics, the workplace—began to
change.

The Feminine Mystique made Friedan the champion of the fledgling women's movement that grew up around her and her book. In 1966 she co-founded the National Organization for Women, was its first president through 1971 and wrote its mission statement. She led the group's fights for equal opportunities for women, equal pay for equal work, better child care, better health care and more.

But the movement that came on so strong in the Sixties and Seventies seemed to fall out of favor during the Eighties. Headlines announced that feminism was "the great experiment that failed." Women seemed less attracted to NOW's agenda, and many of the movement's goals—passage of the Equal Rights Amendment, for example—faltered as a result of anemic support. Representative Pat Schroeder in *Time* admitted, "[Younger women] think of feminists as women who burn bras and don't shave their legs. They think of us as the Amazons of the Sixties."

Recently, however, the women's movement has moved back into the fray, emerging as one of the powerful political and cultural forces of this election year. Fueled by George Bush's move to outlaw abortion and aided by recent headlines—from Anita Hill and Justice Clarence Thomas to Mike Tyson and William Kennedy Smith—the movement has a renewed vitality and relevance.

Skeptics need only look back to April, when more people marched in a pro-choice rally in Washington, D.C., than had ever marched for any other issue in American history.

Noticeably absent at the rally was the women's movement founder, Betty Friedan, who had not been invited.

The slight was a clue that the current leaders of the women's movement are struggling among themselves and, moreover, struggling for a new identity. Friedan represents the movement's history, but she also speaks for a moderate branch of feminism. She has been attacked for this, most directly in a recent book about the movement, Susan Faludi's *Backlash*. In a chapter entitled, "Betty Friedan: Revisionism as a Marketing Tool," Faludi charges that Friedan betrayed the women's movement. According to Faludi, Friedan believed that the women's movement was failing because "its leaders had ignored the maternal call." In fact, Faludi charged that Friedan was "stomping on the movement she did so much to create and lead."

Such criticism is nothing new to Friedan. She's been facing accusations and denunciations from all sides since *The Feminine Mystique* was published almost thirty years ago.

Back then, Friedan was a wife, mother and homemaker, thrilled with modern appliances and recipes she clipped from *McCall's*. She had grown up in Peoria, Illinois, and moved to New York when she was eighteen. She attended college at Smith and prepared for a life as a psychologist or journalist. After graduation she worked as a magazine writer until she was pregnant with the second of her three children. She then followed the traditional path of most women at that time, giving up her career and adopting the type of life personified by TV moms. She began to understand a quiet frustration felt by huge numbers of women, a despair she named "the feminine mystique."

The movement launched by the book consumed her life. At first she was considered a radical, but as time passed, her views mellowed. She began to worry that feminism was forcing some women to exclude family life as a politically correct option. Fearing that women who were discouraged from marrying and having children would abandon the movement, Friedan wrote her second book, *The Second Stage.*

In that book, another best seller, Friedan blamed radical elements of the feminist movement for problems that arose in American families as women attempted to be superwomen, juggling husbands, children, homes and jobs. Many women celebrated that Friedan had once again articulated their plight, though other women, particularly some strident feminists, denounced her. She had, they said, sold out.

Friedan weathered those attacks just as she weathers the current ones, and she remains an outspoken and important leader despite her differences with such notables as Faludi and Gloria Steinem. At seventy-one, Friedan holds academic posts at New York University and the University of Southern California, and continues to write and to speak across the country.

Given the recent resurgence of women's issues, Friedan seemed the perfect subject for the 30th anniversary of the "Playboy Interview." Contributing Editor David Sheff, who recently talked about death and dying with Derek Humphry for *Playboy's* August 1992 interview, flew to Los Angeles to face off with Friedan. Here's his report:

"It took nearly two years of courting Friedan to get her to make time for this interview. We met on several occasions, each time in Los Angeles, where she teaches courses at USC in feminist thought and supervises a think tank on women's issues. To each furnished apartment she rented in L.A. she brought the same personal items to create a home away from her primary home in New York: family photos, prints, towels emblazoned with scarlet parrots and loads of books (from Carl Jung to *Backlash*).

"We met at one of the apartments. She gave my hand a quick shake and then moved to the bar, expertly concocting the strongest, spiciest bloody mary I have ever had.

"At a nearby café we talked about political candidates and the men's movement. She was good humored and easy to talk with until she transformed, inexplicably, and became cantankerous. She is, by nature, candid and argumentative, and her years as a controversial figure have made her fearless. It's a potent combination.

"I met with her twice more before she allowed the tape-recorded sessions to begin. We had several lunches, and I attended the USC course she taught and took notes during a think-tank session on women's issues at which Friedan presided. She spoke briefly and then said that the forum would start after everyone introduced themselves. As the women in the room said their names and what they did for a living, it became clear that this was a group of some of the most powerful women in Los Angeles—business leaders, judges, teachers, politicians and activists. When my turn came, I announced my name and indicated that I was a representative of *Playboy* magazine.

"There was a collective, audible gasp, some nervous laughs and many looks of horror. The tension was slightly defused when Friedan announced, 'Well, it's not like I'm *posing!*'

PLAYBOY: *A lot of women didn't like having someone from* Playboy *in their midst. Do you feel as if you're consorting with the enemy?*
FRIEDAN: First, I don't believe in talking only to the already converted. It is important to talk to men. Anyway, the magazine has changed since the days of the Playboy Bunny at the Clubs. I probably wouldn't have been speaking with you in those days.

PLAYBOY: *But the Bunny was basically a waitress at the Playboy Clubs. What was so objectionable about her?*
FRIEDAN: The Playboy Bunny dehumanized the image of female sexuality. It was part of the feminine mystique.

PLAYBOY: *We always viewed it with fondness, as a fun image of sexuality.*

FRIEDAN: But the image came at us from everywhere—from *Playboy*, from the ads and programs on television. It was the image of a woman solely in terms of her sexual relation to a man, in this case as a man's sex object and server of his physical needs. In other cases it was as a man's wife, a mother and house-wife. That is why it was objectionable. The Bunny may have been cute and fluffy, but it denied the personhood of women. That was the feminine mys-tique, when women were second-class people, less than human, more akin to children or bunnies. It denied the whole previous century, when women had fought for rights, including the right to vote.

PLAYBOY: The Playboy Philosophy *simply tried to present sexuality as a part of life to be celebrated, not denied.*
FRIEDAN: But what came with that was a denial of the rest of a woman. When women are supposed to serve men, sexually and otherwise, they have no other identity. There is no place for career women or for women who have lives that are not about pleasing men. Since the culture views women that way, women necessarily view themselves that way. The Playboy Bunny image of women's sexuality was an extreme Rorschach for a culture that completely denied the personhood of women.

PLAYBOY: The Playboy Philosophy *had more to do with the sexual liberation of men and women than with anything else. It was a reaction to puritanism.*
FRIEDAN: But sexual liberation is a misnomer if it denies the personhood of women. The first wave of so-called sexual liberation in America, where women were passive sex objects, was not real liberation. For real sexual liberation to be enjoyed by men and women, neither can be reduced to a passive role. When a woman is a sex object, it limits a man's enjoyment, too. Maybe some people still haven't caught on, but the best sex requires a deeper, more pro-found knowledge of oneself and the other person. In the Bible, sexual love was *to know.* It suggests something deeper. That is why the women's movement had to happen for sexual liberation to be real.

PLAYBOY: *Do you object to the celebration of sexuality in our pictorials?*
FRIEDAN: A celebration of women's bodies is all right with me so long as there is no denial of the personhood of women. I suppose sometimes women are sex objects—and men are too, by the way. It's the definition of women just as sex objects that bothers me. Women can celebrate themselves as sex objects,

they can celebrate their own sexuality and can enjoy the sexuality of men as far as I'm concerned. Let's have men centerfolds.

PLAYBOY: Cosmopolitan *tried it.*
FRIEDAN: Burt Reynolds? It's a good joke, but I think the truth is that women are less interested in dehumanized sexuality. Sexuality for women tends to be more about personal bonding. Sexuality divorced from that is not pleasing. Men, too, seem to be more aware that dehumanized sex is not satisfying as a total relationship. But *Playboy's* centerfold is fine. It's holding on to your own anachronism and it is not pornographic, though many of my sisters would disagree. It's harmless. I was amused to see that a recent graduate of Smith, my colleague, posed for a pictorial and defended herself by saying that she could celebrate her sexuality if she wanted to. I agree, even though *Playboy* strikes me as an odd mixture of sex—sometimes juvenile—and forward intellectual thought. Alex Haley, who conducted interviews for your magazine, was my good friend. Christie Hefner is my friend and has been marvelously supportive of many causes—not only of free speech but the rights of women. *Playboy* articles and interviews are always quite brilliant and yet they are next to all this attention to women as sex objects.

PLAYBOY: *Back up. Did you say juvenile?*
FRIEDAN: I don't think there is anything wrong with celebrating women's bodies, but if that's all you're interested in, you're missing an awful lot. That's all I mean. I definitely don't think feminism needs to be equated with puritanism and the denial of sexuality. At the same time, I don't approve of anything that reduces women to sex objects, and I really disapprove of anything that degrades women or depicts them as the object of violence. The fact is, there are things far worse than the centerfolds.

PLAYBOY: *Last year there was a demonstration in Berkeley by a group of women who were offended that a man was reading* Playboy *in a restaurant. Would you have attended?*
FRIEDAN: It seems like a waste of time. I am for the liberation of human sexuality, not the repression of it. Most of all, I am for freedom of speech.

PLAYBOY: *Beyond* Playboy, *how do you see the connection between the women's movement and sexual liberation?*
FRIEDAN: As women moved against sex discrimination in employment, education and public accommodations, as there were marches and class-action suits

that focused on employment, it affected the rest of women's lives. As women began to use their own names, to have their own careers, to move into fields that had exclusively been men's before, they earned self-respect. Without self-respect, what kind of sexuality can anyone have? As women gained self-respect, their sexuality was vastly enriched. There was more and better sex all around. When women were enjoying sex more, men were, too.

There were fascinating statistics that began to emerge by the end of the Seventies. There really was a lot more sex, and both men and women were enjoying it more. I've traced each decade of the women's movement according to the early Kinsey studies about sexuality. There was greater sexual enjoyment as the women's movement progressed.

PLAYBOY: *Do you credit that to increased self-respect?*
FRIEDAN: When women are not people, when they are full of impotent rage directed against themselves, sex is not going to be lots of fun—for their partners or for them. The erotic experiences of many women were twisted by their self-images. And, of course, men played along with it, mostly because they didn't know differently. Masochism and self-denigration were considered normal sexuality for women. Before that, frigidity.

Jack Kennedy talked about political passion. Women experienced political passion for the first time because of the women's movement. They had the ability as human beings to shape their own lives and futures. Experiencing political passion was a prerequisite to experiencing physical passion. Women had been the objects of passion, but they weren't expected to experience it themselves.

PLAYBOY: *Some have claimed that the women's movement bred discord and increased the tensions between men and women, and that there was actually less sex, not more.*
FRIEDAN: There was less unfulfilling sex, maybe. And you're right: There was a time when it seemed that the women's movement was about women in a battle against men. But that's not what the movement was about. It used to be called the war between the sexes. That had a lot to do with the rage felt by women who had been put down for their entire lives. When the rage finally came out, no wonder it was excessive. The rage was taken out on individual men who were also products of obsolete, polarized, unequal sex roles.

PLAYBOY: *Is the war between the sexes over?*

FRIEDAN: It needs to be. As women began to find their strength, they directed their rage in fruitful ways to change their lives. They moved away from passive, impotent rage. I think women could then love men for what they are. I think that men were relieved when things changed, too.

PLAYBOY: *Not all of them. Some men rue the day you wrote* The Feminine Mystique.
FRIEDAN: But many more were relieved because the liberation of women meant the liberation of men. It was an enormous burden to be a man. There was a masculine mystique, too.

PLAYBOY: *What was it?*
FRIEDAN: Men had to be supermen: stoic, responsible meal tickets. Dominance is a burden. Most men who are honest will admit that. When things began to change, men were released from the enormous pressure.

PLAYBOY: *What's behind the current men's movement?*
FRIEDAN: I think it's partly a reaction against feminism, partly envy of feminism and partly a real need of men to evolve and break through the burden of the masculine mystique, the burden of machismo. It is a burden that comes when the definition of masculinity is dominance in a society where dominance is not a survival technique anymore. It requires men to suppress their feelings and their sensitivities to life.

PLAYBOY: *And yet you disapprove of the men's movement?*
FRIEDAN: First of all, there didn't need to be a men's movement the way there needed to be a women's movement.

PLAYBOY: *Some men obviously disagree.*
FRIEDAN: Well, there is no men's movement—except all of history, of course.

PLAYBOY: *But the men who flock to men's groups clearly have needs.*
FRIEDAN: Listen, the women's movement was about the personhood of women, not the impersonation of some idea of what women are supposed to be.

PLAYBOY: *And you think that is what the men's movement is about?*
FRIEDAN: Robert Bly's retreats are trying to teach men to be male impersonators. They are trying to embrace some mystique that is more obsolete than ever. The idea of putting men back in loincloths and giving them drums to beat and encouraging them to yell like cavemen is regressive, not progressive.

The good part is that they can also cry and have feelings. But a lot of it seems phony.

PLAYBOY: *You said that the men's movement is partly a reaction against feminism. How?*
FRIEDAN: The explicit or implicit message is that the feminist movement has made wimps of guys.

PLAYBOY: *Some men do equate feminism with emasculation.*
FRIEDAN: They don't understand feminism, then. The practical result of feminism is freeing both women and men from the burdens of their roles.

PLAYBOY: *Warren Farrell says the women's movement "is not a movement for equality but a movement for women's maximization of opportunities."*
FRIEDAN: And as an excuse, they tell men to go out there and reassert their masculinity. It's aggressive toward women. But the feminist movement has not made wimps of men. I think many pressures affect men that make a definition of masculinity based on violence—sorry, that was a Freudian slip—based on dominance almost impossible. If men and women don't face these things together, nothing will change. Men and women need to find ways to be intimate and to support one another and join together against the real enemy.

PLAYBOY: *You seem to be waving a white flag. But many women seem angrier then ever toward men.*
FRIEDAN: I've never bought the "down with men" idea—the male patriarch, the male chauvinist pig. There's a little truth in it, but it ignores the larger truth. The first stage of the women's movement was getting access to the world that had been, until then, completely dominated by men—the world of employment and government. We had to take control of our destiny. It was not a sex war against men but a question of breaking through polarized, unequal sex roles. But so much has changed. The people who criticize the women's movement discount it, but women have made enormous strides.

PLAYBOY: *Yet there seems to be more hostility between the sexes now than there has been for a long time.*
FRIEDAN: And we have to be very careful not to fall into the trap of fighting among ouselves. The real danger now is that the whole society is being attacked. The rage and frustration that is increasing as a result of the economic crisis is being manipulated into a scapegoat phenomenon.

PLAYBOY: *Scapegoating whom?*

FRIEDAN: Men blame women. Women blame men. Look around. There is an increase in racism against blacks and Latinos. The blacks and Koreans in L.A. The riots in Los Angeles were a result. I've been warning all year that the rage and frustration from the economic decline of this country was being manipulated into racism and polarization of one group against another. Well, it exploded in L.A. The denial of the American dream to the outright poor and homeless, as well as to the middle class and blue-collar workers—whose jobs and security are being squashed—built the rage. The trigger was the Rodney King verdict. To my dismay, Bush, Quayle and the others try to blame it on the decline of the family, on single parents and welfare mothers, while they continue the policies that make the top one percent get richer and everyone else more insecure. It is not going to end with the riots in Los Angeles until the real problems are addressed. In the meantime, they encourage racism, anti-Semitism, gay bashing and Japanese bashing. There is an increase in violence against women and against all minorities. There seems to be an increase in the number of crimes against anyone weaker in society—minorities, women and even children. It's causing a backlash against all the progress we've made.

PLAYBOY: *That's a buzzword of the women's movement now since Susan Faludi named it in her best seller. Explain the backlash.*

FRIEDAN: It's the reaction to all the progress we made. Women were being portrayed as strong and independent. But just as we were making progress in the culture and that progress was being reflected in the media, there was a backlash—you can see it on TV and in advertising. They are barometers of where the culture as a whole is going. Women's roles in movies are appalling.

PLAYBOY: *What are some offenders?*

FRIEDAN: *Pretty Women, The Silence of the Lambs*—two of the most successful movies of the past year or two.

PLAYBOY: *Is your objection to* Pretty Woman *that a prostitute was portrayed as the ideal woman?*

FRIEDAN: The movie's message was that, in effect, the way for a woman to get ahead is to find a rich man who will buy her pretty clothes. We were succeeding in doing away with the Cinderella story, that all a woman needed to be complete was a Prince Charming. Women were doing it on their own. This woman was "saved" from prostitution by a man.

Another big thing in TV and movies is portraying women only when they are in jeopardy. I thought it was absolutely outrageous that *Silence of the Lambs* won four Oscars.

PLAYBOY: *Yet Jody Foster and the director, Jonathan Demme, insist that it's a feminist movie.*
FRIEDAN: I'm not saying that the movie shouldn't have been shown. I'm not denying the movie was an artistic triumph, but it was about the evisceration, the skinning alive of women. That is what I find offensive. Not the *Playboy* centerfold.

PLAYBOY: *But* The Silence of the Lambs *had a female hero who fought back against violence toward women and triumphed.*
FRIEDAN: But even she was seen to be manipulated by this evil monster. Instead of showing women in jeopardy, the new trend is to show women in jeopardy who then survive the jeopardy.

PLAYBOY: *Isn't that an improvement?*
FRIEDAN: I tell you, women are tired of seeing themselves as passive sex objects in jeopardy, whether or not they end up prevailing. Yes, it was a well-done film, but aesthetic criticism can't be value-free. If I had been voting for the Academy Awards, I would not have voted for it.

PLAYBOY: *At least you must have been happy with* Thelma & Louise.
FRIEDAN: I loved it. It was a breakthrough movie. I was amused that some of my men friends were describing the movie as female fascism because of the violence. They said, "So you want women to be a violent as men?" Come on. Those women defended themselves—against rape!—and otherwise shot up an oil truck and made sure to shoot air holes in the truck of the police car so the offensive state trooper was able to breathe. You do not see air holes in the truck in *GoodFellas* or in *The Godfather.*

PLAYBOY: *Were you disturbed by the fatalistic ending—Geena Davis and Susan Sarandon doing a* Butch Cassidy and the Sundance Kid *into the Grand Canyon?*
FRIEDAN: Maybe that's another Rorschach. It is very hard to see how women who take back their lives can get away with it. They had to be punished. I wanted them to be able to go back and live a different kind of life. It was one example, though, of women who were strong, complex characters. There used to be more, but they are disappearing.

PLAYBOY: *On television, whom do you count among them?*
FRIEDAN: *Cagney & Lacey,* which is off the air. The only ones left are in *Designing Women, Murphy Brown* and *Roseanne.*

PLAYBOY: *Do you view the women in those shows as positive role models?*
FRIEDAN: They are strong women with personalities and lives of their own. They are not dependent on men.

PLAYBOY: *But they're also pretty wacky. For all her fiery independence, Murphy Brown is neurotic. She almost went over the edge when she became pregnant.*
FRIEDAN: It's true. They won't let her enjoy it, will they? But at least she's a strong, complex woman and she's getting great ratings.

PLAYBOY: *Dan Quayle doesn't like her. He singled her out as a symbol of what's wrong with American families.*
FRIEDAN: As a woman at a conference said the day Quayle made that stupid speech, he used a fictional woman to insult a lot of real women. Some single women are in that position against their wishes. Some have chosen it. The fact is, they are doing the best they can. For him to blame them for America's ills is to scapegoat women who have made alternative choices. It's typical to sound off about women, to blame the victims. America is in decline, however, because of people like Quayle and his boss, who have refused to address the fundamental problems of this country. Murphy Brown is affirming to women. And no matter what Dan Quayle says, America loves her.

PLAYBOY: *Where does Madonna fit in—backlash or in the forefront of the women's movement?*
FRIEDAN: I think women identify with Madonna as much for her guts, her strength, her politics and her business acumen as for her role as a sex object. Whoever said feminism shouldn't be sexy?

PLAYBOY: *What has caused the backlash?*
FRIEDAN: First of all, it is exacerbated more by the economic crisis than anything. All the progress women made—in spite of the best efforts of the culture and media—seemed unstoppable until the economic crisis came along. The economic crisis begins, and who is blamed? Men blame women. If they weren't working, there would be enough jobs.

The media have played their part by suggesting en masse that women should go home again. They have popularized the idea that Ronald Reagan espoused ten years ago when there was a small turn for the worse in the economy. He said, essentially, that there would be no unemployment if women went home again. *

PLAYBOY: *You're not suggesting that the economic crisis was perpetuated to put women back in their place, are you?*
FRIEDAN: No, but that is the result. The people responsible would rather have us blaming one another than blaming them. That's the point. And the people responsible are also the ones most threatened by the empowerment of women. Women have been the largest group in society that, until recently, was passive and easily manipulated. Women are not a ten percent minority, they are a fifty-three percent majority. When women discover their power and assert it to control their own lives, they're not easily manipulated anymore.

PLAYBOY: *But the economic crisis hurts everyone.*
FRIEDAN: Here's an example of the way the backlash works. What is the current hysteria over abortion really about? Why are we still fighting the issue? The right to abortion is basic and symbolic of all the rights that women have won. It is a symbol of autonomy and independence.

The authoritarian elements that were threatened by the success of the women's movement get us to focus on abortion instead of on them, to divert the rage from those who are really profiting. The rage that men or women have a right to feel when they have lost their economic security is diverted to abortion.

PLAYBOY: *But the abortion issue doesn't go away because some people believe abortion to be wrong. Or do you see it as some larger conspiracy?*
FRIEDAN: I don't believe in conspiratorial theories of history. I don't even think the feminine mystique was a conspiracy. There is just a convergence of many things. But that doesn't mean that the focus on abortion is anything other than a red herring. The autonomy and independence of women is genuinely threatening, not to all men but to those who want to exert authoritarian power. *Roe vs. Wade* was nineteen years ago. To force the women's movement, year after year after year, to mobilize to defend the right of women to control their own bodies—a right that we thought we had won nineteen years ago—is appalling. We have to fight it, we must, because the right of controlling our reproductive

processes is basic to the personhood of women. But defending that right takes away the passion that we also need to put behind other issues: child care, equal opportunity, affirmative action.

This nation is decades behind European nations in birth control. Why don't we have RU 486 here?

PLAYBOY: *Is it because men want to keep women barefoot and pregnant?*
FRIEDAN: The men who are running things do. Many people do not want things to change, so they divert us. We focus on abortion and sexual harassment and welfare mothers. The welfare mother has been made the Willie Horton of the 1992 election.

PLAYBOY: *The Republicans in particular have been citing welfare moms as an example of the system's failure.*
FRIEDAN: The welfare mother is not who people think she is. She is not black, she's white. She's not a teenager and she doesn't keep having babies and she doesn't stay on welfare her whole life. She actually has one and a half children and then she gets off welfare. But the stereotype, the Willie Horton welfare mother, is black, fourteen or fifteen years old and she keeps on having babies. They want us to think she is responsible for America's economic crisis, not the politicians and the people who are profiting. The fact is, you could give every existing welfare mother a hundred thousand dollars a year or take her off welfare altogether and it wouldn't solve the economic crisis. Still, otherwise intelligent men, instead of discussing the culture of greed and those excessive corporate salaries and bonuses, talk about the welfare mother.

The fact is, attacking abortion, the welfare mother, people of other races, gays, is a diversion of energy that should be going toward confronting basic political and economic problems of this society. Instead, it comes down to clashes between the races and violence against women.

PLAYBOY: *How, specifically, to violence against women?*
FRIEDAN: All the groups that have been moving toward equality are pitted against one another. Men and women are feeling the pressures of the recession. Remember, many, many women now carry the burden of supporting or helping to support the family. Still, men have been defined as having those roles, and the frustration of men today must be enormous—losing their jobs, barely getting by. The rage is funneled against the groups that have been

moving toward equality. Men take it out on women and the minorities who are supposedly taking their jobs because of affirmative action. Or they take it out on the Japanese for destroying the American economy.

PLAYBOY: *What should people do?*
FRIEDAN: They need to be alert to the danger of becoming polarized. Instead of fighting among ourselves, we must move with a new political urgency to save our democracy and the freedoms that are under attack. That is what is really going on. If we don't, we are playing into their hands and inviting fascism.

PLAYBOY: *Do you see fascism coming?*
FRIEDAN: Remember history. What preceded fascism in Nazi Germany? Economic chaos and the loss of a sense of national power. That caused people to scapegoat one another. Eventually, citizenship was taken away from the Jews. Then feminist organizations were outlawed and the rights of women—not only to abortion but also the right to work in professions or to hold political office—were taken away. Women were reduced to children, kitchen, church. Freedom of speech in Germany was suppressed altogether. Racism was taught in the schools in the name of science. And then there was war and the Holocaust.

There are many parallels. Art—called degenerate art if it was abstract or openly erotic or sexual—was suppressed by the Nazis. It all sounds pretty familiar, doesn't it? Look at what happened inside the National Endowment for the Arts. The art that Congress wants the NEA to suppress may not be to my taste and it may shock, but there are dangers to freedom of speech if we rely on sexual pluralism or anyone's sexual revulsion or shock.

PLAYBOY: *Some feminists support recently proposed legislation that will hold pornographers responsible if crimes are committed by people who were thought to be under the influence of pornography. Would you suppress pornography?*
FRIEDAN: The New York chapter of the National Organization for Women came out against that legislation and I'm very proud of them. Women cannot let the pornography issue be misused. Once you suppress freedom of speech for any reason, it will come back to haunt you. The *Webster* decision that forbids doctors from counseling about abortion is a suppression of freedom of speech. The same people would eventually have us banning books—*Our Bodies, Ourselves* is threatening to them. *The Feminine Mystique* was banned.

PLAYBOY: *How important were the Clarence Thomas hearings for the women's movement?*
FRIEDAN: It's the most significant thing that has happened in years. I think that Anita Hill is an absolute symbol of a paradigm shift in the women's movement, from being the victim to being empowered.

PLAYBOY: *Even if it didn't succeed in blocking Thomas' nomination?*
FRIEDAN: Even if it didn't. Thomas should have been blocked even without the sexual harassment issue because it was unconscionable that a Supreme Court nominee would not declare himself on the fundamental right of women to control their own reproductive processes. Regardless, consciousness-raising took place in the whole nation when women saw Anita Hill stand up and when we saw, day after day, the outrageousness of an all-male Senate Judiciary Committee and a nearly all-male Senate that just didn't get it. Women got it, and it's not going to go away.

PLAYBOY: *But Thomas was confirmed and the majority of Americans, the majority of women, according to polls, disbelieved Anita Hill.*
FRIEDAN: I'd like to see those polls in a little more depth. It's not surprising that women as well as men believed Thomas. We have had centuries of male authority that has influenced us all. Also, the hearings were conducted in a way that was set up against her. The Republican Senators savagely tried to destroy her character, and the Democratic Senators sat there like wimps and let them do it. A lot of women will not forget that. Wait until the elections. I have never seen women as angry. Women who vote! Furthermore, Anita Hill was not destroyed. She will go down in history as a heroine. As a result of Anita Hill's actions, women across the country are now emboldened to blow the whistle on sexual harassment.

PLAYBOY: *Has the issue been blown out of proportion, so that relationships in and out of the workplace are strained?*
FRIEDAN: I don't think so. The reason the issue became so big is that many women were being subjected to behavior that was inexcusable. If some people are nervous about it, then fine. It will mean they will be more conscientious.

PLAYBOY: *But many men and women bemoan the fact that even flirting is suspect. Do you really object to a little healthy flirting?*
FRIEDAN: We are talking about harassment, not flirting.

PLAYBOY: *Are you worried that the attention to sexual harassment is a diversion from economic and political issues?*
FRIEDAN: I think it is a great step forward that women don't have to dwell in the victim state, but that issue is, once again, men versus women. The sexual war is the focus, and we don't focus on jobs, repression or the inner cities.

Our larger agenda right now, it seems to me, is to join with men in demanding a new politics and culture to replace the culture of greed of the dozen years of Reagan and Bush.

PLAYBOY: *Does that mean you're supporting Clinton for President?*
FRIEDAN: I think it's essential to defeat Bush. I am not excited about any candidate that has come along, but Bush must be defeated. Still, whether any emerging leader is even sufficiently understanding of these issues—since they are all men—I don't know. Whether Clinton or the other Democrats are going to be as stupid as Dukakis was and give up what is probably their most potent source of support, I don't know.

PLAYBOY: *How did Michael Dukakis alienate women?*
FRIEDAN: As the 1988 presidential campaign began, there was a big gender gap. Women favored the Democrats. But Dukakis believed the conventional Democrats' wisdom, which was to clothe themselves as Republicans and refuse to be viewed as prisoners to any special-interest groups, including women. The women I worked with came up with commercials that would appeal to women. Cher would have done them. However, the Committee to Elect Dukakis wouldn't let us.

PLAYBOY: *Because he thought it was a liability to be associated with women?*
FRIEDAN: Exactly, and he was crazy. By the end of the campaign, there was no gender gap. And the people who ran the Dukakis campaign didn't even understand that they had thrown it away. I hope that Clinton doesn't do it again, because what used to be dismissed as women's issues are now the main issues of the campaign.

PLAYBOY: *What do you think about Ross Perot?*
FRIEDAN: America is yearning for a man on a white horse. The idea that he doesn't have to subject himself to the democratic process gives me a feeling of déjà vu. Other times it led to Mussolini and Hitler. Perot also seems to have some of this Bush–Quayle obsession with conventional family values. He

has said he won't have gays in his cabinet. He has said that we don't have enough money to address issues such as parental leave and child care. He appears to want to cut social programs, but cutting social programs is what got us to the riots in Los Angeles.

PLAYBOY: *Even as you talk about the new direction the women's movement must take, there is speculation that it has faltered. Has it?*
FRIEDAN: So many articles say the women's movement is dead. But because the right to abortion is threatened, more people marched on Washington last spring than ever marched for any issue. It is very much alive.

PLAYBOY: *Surveys have shown that women, especially younger women, don't identify with the movement. They may favor reproductive choice, but they don't relate to feminism.*
FRIEDAN: They may not relate to the word feminism, but the great majority of women, young and old, completely subscribe to the entire agenda of the women's movement, from equal pay to equal access to advanced jobs and professions to child care to choice regarding abortion.

PLAYBOY: *Then why won't they call themselves feminists?*
FRIEDAN: The trouble with the media, and even some of the women's organizations, is that they have too narrow a vision of the women's movement. They look at it the way it was fifteen years ago and don't recognize how far it has come. Young women say they're not feminists, but they don't have to be. They take for granted feminist rights. Yet women, when they see their rights are in danger, will march and act. Look at what happened in Washington. Women have power that is greater than anyone acknowledges. In Illinois, a relatively unknown black woman with very little money was able to defeat a Senator who was considered undefeatable, who had been in the Senate for twenty-two years. In Pennsylvania, a woman candidate beat the state's lieutenant governor and is now running against Arlen Specter. In California, two women won their party's nomination for the Senate. There are women who are going to be elected like that all over this country this fall. I don't think any of the presidential candidates understands that.

PLAYBOY: *But the majority of women don't consider themselves to be feminists. Representative Pat Schroeder suggested that it was because of the archaic image of feminists as bra burners, radical lesbians, men-haters and women who choose not to shave under their arms.*

FRIEDAN: There may be something to that. The media have done everything they can to discredit the movement. They glom on to the extremist voices in the movement with which many women want to dissociate. More so, the message in the Reagan–Bush era, served up by the media, was that feminism itself was a dirty word. The propaganda campaign was effective. It said that you would not get ahead in your career if you were considered a feminist. It said that you could not be a reasonable parent if you were a feminist. "Feminism," like "liberalism," was portrayed as being regressive and unpopular—as were civil rights, affirmative action, welfare and social programs. Some of the campaign against us has had to have an effect.

PLAYBOY: *Some people thought that successful women were no longer feminine—that they were taking on the character traits of fiercely competitive men. Do you agree?*
FRIEDAN: The depiction of career women as monsters, à la the woman in *Fatal Attraction*, is another cause of the backlash. No wonder women have questions about going for it.

PLAYBOY: *In politics, some of the most successful women—Margaret Thatcher and Jeane Kirkpatrick, to name two—seem as macho as any of their male counterparts.*
FRIEDAN: Well, I'm not sure that's true. When you are the first woman in any field, it's very hard not to follow the male model. There is no other model. It's only when women approach critical mass that you begin to see them show characteristics of leadership that really use the qualities associated with women.

PLAYBOY: *What qualities?*
FRIEDAN: Maybe it's because women are the people who give birth to children, but something has enabled them to be more sensitive to the cues of life. They nurture. The more they can use that in the public sphere, the better.

PLAYBOY: *George Gilder has charged that the women's movement is out of touch—it's elitist and most women don't want it. Is there any truth to that?*
FRIEDAN: I'm really losing patience with the attempts to polarize women. The power and the glory of the women's movement is that it crossed all those lines. It has affected every woman. When they say that the women's movement doesn't represent the average woman, they are intentionally dividing us.

PLAYBOY: *Do you admit that the women's movement itself, because of all the infighting, is partly responsible for alienating women?*

FRIEDAN: That's part of the tendency to blame the victim. The organizations on the cutting edge of the women's movement are still doing a valiant job of protecting the rights we thought we'd won in the first place. They still fight for rights, from affirmative action to equal employment opportunities to the right of choice in the matter of abortion.

PLAYBOY: *But there's still fighting within the women's movement, isn't there?*
FRIEDAN: Yes, and the first thing we have to do is redirect our focus. If women are alienated from the women's movement because it is antagonistic toward men, I understand that. One of the reasons I am doing this interview is that I think the movement has to become one of women and men. Maybe the women's movement has to be superseded by a larger political movement.

PLAYBOY: *What you're saying is heresy in some radical corners of the women's movement.*
FRIEDAN: It depends on what you call radical. I think that a radical vision of society has to go beyond women's rights—not to sacrifice them but to go beyond them.

PLAYBOY: *Have the extreme wings of the women's movement alienated many women?*
FRIEDAN: I'm tired of all the infighting and blaming. The media play it up, too. I agree, though, that the women's movement must be for all women.

PLAYBOY: *The president of NOW, Patricia Ireland, has admitted she had a lesbian relationship in addition to her marriage to a man. This has turned off some women. Are you concerned about that?*
FRIEDAN: I don't think a woman must be defined in terms of her sexuailty. At the same time, I never objected to sexual preference, and I think that it's a positive, life-affirming thing that women are able to find and define their sexuality in diverse ways.

PLAYBOY: *Still, many women simply can't relate.*
FRIEDAN: Yes, and focusing on any single issue that divides us prevents us from getting anywhere. I have been pitted against the lesbians in NOW, and the lesbians have been pitted against me. When we allow that, we are playing into the hands of those who would diffuse our focus and our power. My biggest concern is polarizing women against one another. My definition of feminism includes Patricia Ireland and Gloria Steinem and women staying at home. I am against polarization of women against women, whether it comes from Dan

Quayle or Susan Faludi or Camille Paglia. I'm also not for any rigid, narrow definition of feminism. A women's movement has to include divergent life-styles and it has to continually evolve to meet the needs of women. Women's rights are going to go down the drain if we alienate one another and fight one another.

PLAYBOY: *Might women drift away from feminism because it criticizes their choice to stay home with their children?*
FRIEDAN: I think that's correct. I worry about the factions in the women's move-ment that say there is only one way. Of course women who want families and careers are alienated from a movement that says you have to choose.

PLAYBOY: *You described your stand in* The Second Stage, *for which you were written off as a sellout by the more radical factions of the movement. Susan Faludi said you were as bad as the men who said that the women's movement was failing because "its leaders had ignored the maternal call."*
FRIEDAN: Women are the people who give birth to children, and that is a necessary value in society. For the great majority of women, no feminism that was opposed to family would work. I never believed that feminism was opposed to family. Feminism implied an evolution of the family. Feminism was not opposed to marriage and motherhood. It wanted women to be able to define themselves as people and not just as servants to the family. You want a feminism that includes women who have children and want children because that's the majority of women. I think Susan Faludi's book is important because there is a backlash. But she makes me part of it because of this stand.

PLAYBOY: *Have you discussed it with Faludi?*
FRIEDAN: Yes. And she's told me that she's taking that criticism of me out of the British edition. [*Editor's note:* Faludi denies she is making any changes regarding Friedan.]

PLAYBOY: *Faludi also says that your optimistic prediction—that "men will not fear the love and strength of women, nor need another's weakness to prove their own masculinity"—never came to pass. If she's right, then her view is understandable.*
FRIEDAN: It was changing. There was a sharing of the responsibilities between parents so that each person could fulfill himself or herself as a person.

PLAYBOY: *Yet the new, younger leaders of the women's movement don't seem to buy it.*

FRIEDAN: Faludi is right that the backlash has undermined much of the progress we made. But the answer is not to ignore that most women want families. The women's movement started with many women who already had children and didn't want to be defined solely in those terms. On the other hand, having children was of great value to our lives. It remains one of mine now that I see my children and grandchildren growing.

PLAYBOY: *But many women didn't see motherhood as a choice for a liberated woman.*
FRIEDAN: That's why I wrote *The Second Stage.* I saw my daughter's generation growing up with ambitions for careers, yet also wanting to marry and have children. They had real problems putting it all together. They saw it as a personal problem—that it was their fault—because they had an image of feminism that didn't include a family. We had to deal with that. Feminism had to focus on restructuring the society so it would support women who wanted to have careers and families. We had to work for parental leave and job sharing and other flexible work arrangements. It meant there were equal responsibilities for men in the home.

PLAYBOY: *What about the women who tried working and who realized it wasn't all that it was cracked up to be? They wanted to return home.*
FRIEDAN: That's a myth of backlash, too.

PLAYBOY: *A recent Roper poll says that fifty-three percent of women say they would rather stay home than work.*
FRIEDAN: What those polls show is that the great majority of women want a different work arrangement when their children are little. It does not show the majority of women would abjure opportunities for careers. The polls show that women do not necessarily want to spend their lives in the rat race the way men do. They want to have a new mix—children and work. They are leaving corporations and starting their own businesses, not to go home again but to work in situations that are more flexible. They're saying that women don't want to choose the mommy track versus the fast track. The best companies are discovering that the women they want on the fast track also can be given flexible work arrangments. It will allow them to keep women who are assets to the companies.

PLAYBOY: *Do you admit that some women want to stay home to raise a family?*
FRIEDAN: Some might, but those women want other things that the women's

movement brings them. Some women want to have their kids and then go back to school, and then go to work where they can add a whole new dimension to their lives. Other women want to do the opposite. The main thing is that women want choices.

PLAYBOY: *It's been said that children suffered because of the women's movement. Women gained the opportunity to work and kids were abandoned.*
FRIEDAN: That's enormously regressive thinking, though you certainly see that attitude portrayed in the media.

PLAYBOY: *But research indicates that kids are suffering. It might not be good for kids to have both parents working twelve hours a day.*
FRIEDAN: Both parents should not be working twelve hours a day. That's where job sharing comes in. Flexible hours and parental leaves, for both parents. President Bush vetoed a minimal parental-leave bill. That alone is reason enough to throw him out of office.

PLAYBOY: *Do you agree that kids, in the meantime, are the victims?*
FRIEDAN: The argument is that women should go home because kids are being abandoned by work-obsessed parents. First of all, the reason both parents work twelve hours a day is an economic issue, not a women's right issue. Both parents have to work. They need the money. Children suffer because of the economy. Both parents have to work and there is no support, no child care, no flexible hours. Children are being victimized, but not because women went back to work. Research indicates that when women went back to work, by necessity or choice, there was no bad effect on the children—depending, of course, on family circumstances and other factors.

PLAYBOY: *But some of the research is disturbing. A study showed that drug use is proportional to the amount of time kids spend without parental supervision. It says that latchkey kids are prime candidates for drug problems.*
FRIEDAN: You have to look at all the variables. Studies I can show you prove that it is positive for children when their mother, like their father, has a fulfilling career. The children will then have role models of strong women. It gives girls more confidence.

PLAYBOY: *But—*
FRIEDAN: [*Angrily*] Let me finish. The children tend to be more independent, and they do not suffer any more proneness to drugs or delinquency.

PLAYBOY: *Our studies seem to contradict each other.*

FRIEDAN: I'm sorry. It is part of the backlash that would have women who have chosen to lead fulfilling lives blamed for drug abuse. The message is the same: Stay home. The fact is, kids do better in families where the men and women balance work, time spent with each other and with the children. They do better in those circumstances than in traditional households. To imply that you can solve these problems—drugs, unemployment—by women going home is backlash.

PLAYBOY: *Do you agree with Susan Faludi that the idea of the biological clock is part of the backlash, too—another way to make women go home, or at least feel guilty about pursuing their careers?*

FRIEDAN: I don't. Again, women want the choice. Many of them want to be mothers. If they are on a career path that doesn't allow them any flexibility, so that they have to choose which track they're on, they get angry because they are in a no-win situation. I think Susan Faludi can be ardent about it because she is young and she hasn't had to make the decision for herself yet.

PLAYBOY: *Some would see that as a comment of the backlash: A feminist can insist on career over motherhood while she's young, but as soon as her biological clock starts ticking louder, she'll think differently.*

FRIEDAN: Feminism cannot dictate the decision to all women. Women have to be supported in all the different ways they decide to become fulfilled. That's what I've believed since the beginning.

PLAYBOY: *Was there a formative event that made you a feminist?*

FRIEDAN: There wasn't any one thing. There were many things. It was almost accidental. But mysteriously, miraculously, all the disparate parts of my life and the frustrations came together in *The Feminine Mystique*. It was a reaction to the life I was living.

PLAYBOY: *What was it like?*

FRIEDAN: I had been working as a reporter after college. My mother had been very unhappy. She was unfulfilled. To marry my father, she gave up a job at a newspaper and was never satisfied after that. It was as if she had given up, and I lived with that discontent, not understanding it. She dreamed of me having a better life. She never had been able to go to college and she dreamed of me going.

I did go and I pursued a career. I gave up my ambitions and then my job in order to become a suburban housewife. Soon, my life was PTA meetings and dinners and housecleaning and having coffee with my neighbors. Housewives were supposedly living this dream life, but, of course, there was something wrong.

PLAYBOY: *How did you come to understand it?*
FRIEDAN: I was aware that something was wrong. I described it as the problem that had no name. I began writing about it, about my experience and the experiences of the women I knew who were suffering. It took five years to write.

PLAYBOY: *Did the response surprise you?*
FRIEDAN: At first the response was terrible. No one would publish it. When I finally found a publisher, they printed only three thousand copies. But as soon as it was out, women read it. It spoke to them and it had an incredible effect. More and more were published. Women wrote me about their relief to realize that they were not alone in feeling this anguish. Not all women. Many were very threatened. But it changed a lot of lives.

PLAYBOY: *Including your own.*
FRIEDAN: Yes.

PLAYBOY: *What happened?*
FRIEDAN: I spoke about the book and heard from women everywhere. I continued writing and talking about the feminine mystique. Women began to fight back. It enabled me to go on and help to start the National Organization for Women, the National Women's Political Caucus and the National Abortion Rights Action League, the Women's Forum and many other things.

PLAYBOY: *And you've said that that activity was behind your divorce in the late sixties?*
FRIEDAN: It was a difficult time, and certainly the women's movement gave me the strength to do something about it. I have some regrets. I was married for twenty-two years and there were some happy times. In some ways I look at it as a failure that it ended. Ending it was difficult, but it was more difficult living with things the way they were. I understand it more in hindsight, of course, like everything else.

PLAYBOY: *How would you characterize your relationship with your peers in the women's movement? What kind of a relationship do you have with Gloria Steinem?*

FRIEDAN: I knew Gloria before she was involved in the women's movement. In fact, I remember trying to get her to join with us when we were going to go into the Plaza Hotel and insist on being served in the men's bar. She wouldn't have anything to do with it then.

PLAYBOY: *You've clashed with her on many issues.*
FRIEDAN: We tangled a lot. I was really opposed to the radical chic, anti-man politics she espoused: "A woman needs a man like a fish needs a bicycle." There were other things. I didn't like it when she went to the League of Women Voters to support the ERA and, in her speech, said that all wives are prostitutes. I thought it was politically unwise, and I fought it within NOW and within the women's movement generally. I fought attempts to push the women's movement out of the mainstream, and that put me in opposition to Gloria. But now, in my wise maturity, I see that all of it contributed. Gloria is a survivor and a fighter. She contributed a lot. She is a good role model for women who choose not to marry or have children. She showed that it is possible to have a good life. I don't think that most women want to go that path, but it's important to have a model for those who do. She also has made a real contribution to the women's movement with *Ms.*

PLAYBOY: *Steinem, in her recent book,* The Revolution from Within, *discusses what she calls "the real enemy within." She feels that women have to look internally to deal with issues about self-esteem. How do you feel about it?*
FRIEDAN: I have not read her book, though I have read the reviews. I'm glad that it's a best seller and that she's making lots of money on it and that she's not going to be a bag lady. Furthermore, the fact that it is a best seller is marvelous proof that the backlash isn't working that well. Women are reading Steinem and Faludi, and therefore they are still concerned. But I worry about *The Revolution from Within* if it feeds the idea that the problems women face are just personal and internal, that psychoanalysis or some version thereof could solve them. I don't think that's true. I would like for women to see now that they have a new set of problems and that they need political solutions for those problems.

PLAYBOY: *How does it feel to be on the outs with some factions of the women's movement? First, Susan Faludi says you're part of the backlash, and then you aren't asked to speak at the pro-choice march on Washington.*

FRIEDAN: I'm not going to lie. I'm very hurt when I feel trashed by the leaders of the organizations that I helped to start. But I'm not going to indulge in the media's delight at exacerbating the divisions between us. I do admit that I was really hurt that I wasn't asked to speak at the rally. I seemed as if I were the only leading American woman that wasn't, you know.

PLAYBOY: *Why were you excluded?*
FRIEDAN: Someone doing my oral history was told that it was because I always get quoted by the media and these other women wanted to be quoted. I think they should be, but it isn't necessary to trash your foremothers. I have a lot of courage and guts to fight the enemy, but I get really hurt. I hate to admit it. It's sort of a de-Stalinization of the women's movement—their attempt to write me out of history, though I don't think that will happen.

PLAYBOY: *Do you acknowledge that the younger, more radical voices may better address the needs of the current women's movement?*
FRIEDAN: I think Susan Faludi is very important. I tell people to buy her book. I assign it to my students even though she criticizes me. But everyone knows that movements that discount their history and don't learn from their mistakes repeat them. I hope these young people don't make that mistake.

PLAYBOY: *What do you think about Camille Paglia?*
FRIEDAN: How can you take her seriously? She is an exhibitionist, and she takes the most extreme elements of the women's movement and tries to make the whole movement antisexual, antilife, antijoy. And neither I nor most of the women I know are that way.

PLAYBOY: *How about Naomi Wolf, who, in* The Beauty Myth, *says that anything— from advertising on—that makes women self-conscious about their bodies is evil. Do you agree?*
FRIEDAN: It is an important book. I am outraged by the pressures that enable surgeons or manufacturers of silicone gel or anyone else to profit by inducing women to mutilate themselves. Silicone breast implants, plastic surgery, excessive dieting are anathema to me. I object to blue-jeans ads that seem to show these women who are still children as inviting rape or having just been raped.

PLAYBOY: *But you seem to draw lines Wolf doesn't draw: She would strongly criticize* Playboy's *Playmates.*

FRIEDAN: Remember, the fact that I have given you this interview does not mean that I endorse the centerfold. It's all right to look, but anything that does not show women as total beings cannot be endorsed. I am trusting that you communicate these issues to men caught up in the mystique. Look at women like women can look at men but never forget, for a moment, the complete, complex personhood of people.

PLAYBOY: *How do you see things changing in the future for you personally?*
FRIEDAN: No major changes. I am still working, no longer on the politics of the women's movement but on the larger vision. I'm also writing a new book, *The Fountain of Age.*

PLAYBOY: *What's the fountain of age?*
FRIEDAN: I see the mystique of aging as similar to the feminine mystique. Again, it denies the personhood of individuals who get older. It's about viewing age not as a decline from youth but as a unique stage of living. Because we spent that time fighting the feminine mystique, we gave ourselves a head start in the battle against the mystique of age. We stopped defining ourselves vis à vis men—as mothers, wives, sexual objects—and we discovered new joys in ourselves and in other women, and in men, too. Similarly, when we break through the mystique of age, there will be new joys in the rest of our lives, for men and women. That mystique is the next one to fight.

PLAYBOY: *Given the history of the women's movement, are you hopeful?*
FRIEDAN: The whole modern women's movement has taken place in only the past twenty-five years, and so much has changed. Women now make up forty percent of the students in the law schools, sixty percent in the journalism schools, forty percent of the M.B.A.s. But they are only now beginning to move in significant numbers into the middle and upper ranks of the professions. Women were earning fifty-nine cents for every dollar men earned and now it's seventy-something. It's getting better, but there is a long way to go. And do you want to know something? The countries where men's and women's earnings are more comparable are the countries that have policies of child care and parental leave. They are countries that accept the fact that women will continue to be part of the work force and that women are the people who give birth to children. And they are countries doing better economically than we are.

PLAYBOY: *You've blamed the media for much of the backlash, but you just indicated that sixty percent of journalism students are women. If so many women are becoming journalists, won't things change?*

FRIEDAN: For a course I'm teaching, "Women, Men and Media," we monitored the front pages of the newspapers to see the percentage of time women were mentioned, photographed or quoted. The number was fifteen percent. Women are fifty-three percent of the population. That meant that forty-seven percent of the population occupied eighty-five percent of the space on the front pages. The same was true in broadcast news. Women were sought for comment on broadcast news fifteen percent of the time. Even in the study we did last February, during a time when all kinds of stories of great importance to women were breaking—the Mike Tyson rape case, silicone gel breast implants, Anita Hill—the experts sought quotes from men. Well, the media are still controlled by men. The editors and news directors are men. That's a symbolic annihilation. Is it a conspiracy against women? No. But it surely is a blind spot coming from the all-male definition.

PLAYBOY: *What will it take before there'll be a woman in the White House?*
FRIEDAN: Maybe four more years.

PLAYBOY: *Any nominees?*
FRIEDAN: Ann Richards. Not only was she elected governor of Texas—Texas!—but what she's done as governor is a very interesting story and a bellwether. And Texas is the most macho of states. See, we've come awfully far. That's why I don't understand the media's jumping on this talk about the death of the women's movement. If you think about it, there are millions now where there were a few of us at first, millions of women who have the training, the professional opportunity, millions who have changed their lives, taken control of their lives. Why do you try to dismiss it? You just try to find all sorts of ways to whittle it down and dismiss it, when the reality is right in front of your eyes. It's threatened now and we have our work cut out for us again. Maybe it's wishful thinking on the part of the people who keep talking about the death of the women's movement. Well, they have another thing coming. We're not going anywhere.

Portrait of a Feminist as an Old Woman

Michele Kort / 1993

From *Los Angeles Times Magazine*, (10 October 1993), 11. Reprinted by permission of Michele Kort.

"I'm an incorrigible bohemian—paper napkins and all that," Betty Friedan announces, apropos of no particular question. She clears her grandchildren's toys off the couch in the living room of her cozy, cluttered, clapboard house, which sits on the edge of Sag Harbor, Long Island.

"I started coming here in 1970, and it was more bohemian then," she continues. "There were a few rich people, but they didn't bother us. But now there are so many rich people!" It's a pleasantly cool afternoon in Sag Harbor, the picturesque former whaling village in the Hamptons, where Friedan and about 2,500 other heat-escaping New Yorkers spend the summer.

"And I'm losing my tolerance for stand-up cocktail parties of any sort; I want to *sit down*," she adds with a certain vehemence. When Friedan speaks in her hoarse, almost preacherly tone, the italics and exclamation points are almost visible. "But on the other hand, I've got so many friends out here, and we're all stuck. It would take too much *energy* to find a new place and make new friends."

This is a woman who knows exactly what she thinks about everything. By knowing herself, and taking her own ideas seriously, Friedan has often identified her personal experience as a sign of the times. Her feeling of entrapment and malaise thirty years ago articulated itself into the revolutionary book *The Feminine Mystique*; political frustration twenty-seven years ago led her to found

117

the National Organization for Women, and the dread and denial over her own aging encouraged her to write her new tome, *The Fountain of Age*. Friedan has made a career of recognizing and politicizing her private concerns and then weaving them into the national discourse.

"Betty's a very self-aware human being," is how her old friend Natalie Gittelson, author and former New York Times Magazine editor, pegs her. "She's always interesting—particularly on the subject of Betty."

But she is not always pleasant. Though she claims she's mellowing at age seventy-two, she still frequently expresses herself in the vernacular of a revolutionary—anger, outrage, protest and an aggressive stubbornness. She doesn't care if everyone likes her, as long as they listen to her.

Today, though, Friedan is in an almost giddy good mood. She's about to launch *The Fountain of Age* after ten years of research and writing. It's got "big book" written all over it, and not just because it weighs in at 600-plus pages. Just as *The Feminine Mystique* added a new expression to the lexicon—and launched, she'll tell you with no undue modesty, the second wave of American feminism—this book reveals another mystique, one that denies the continuing "generativity," the strengths and creativity, of those on the other side of sixty-five.

"In the middle of writing it, I felt very bogged down, and I romanticized in my memory that *The Feminine Mystique* had *sung* out of me," Friedan recalls of the book's long gestation. "And then, about two years ago, I saw that it was adding up. I realized that it's there, and it might even be important"—her voice drops; for a moment she sounds almost humble—"in somewhat the same way as *The Feminine Mystique* was. Although that's always a bad thing, you know. If you think you're competing with something like *The Feminine Mystique*, which had such an impact, you'd kill yourself. But to my surprise, it's turned out that way, I think. A man I know who's just about to turn sixty read the book and said, 'It's changed my whole thinking about everything!' And if men are saying that. . . ." This is obviously music to her ears. She giggles with pleasure.

In the book, Friedan surveys the research, collects anecdotes and uses her own adventures—like going on an Outward Bound expedition when she was in her early sixties—to demonstrate her thesis that aging is more opportunity than problem. It is a book weighted down with information but illuminated by touching, often confessional, moments. Menopause, she says, is simply a transition, not necessarily a hormonal nightmare. Mental health doesn't automatically decline after the 40s. Keep changing, she tells her fellow aging explorers, keep finding purposes and projects, maintain your automomy. Break the rules.

The *Wall Street Journal* has called the book "wise and challenging" and Friedan "a brilliant conceptualizer," but the *Washington Post* wondered if "older Americans of color might not have added some important perspectives." The *Los Angeles Times* surmised that "readers not turned off by her occasional nervous preening will find much to enlighten and provoke as they join her in the contemplation of possibilities." But on this day, no reviews have come out yet, and Friedan's basking in the pre-book-tour glow. If the book catches on, she could be hailed once again as the catalyst of a movement, this time as a modern-day Ponce de Leon who helped usher in an era of upbeat geriatrics.

And she could once again become a leader. It's a position Friedan courts and, some say, demands. And it's a position she's been too often denied in recent years. She long ago earned her place in history as the grande dame of the modern women's movement, or as she herself put it at a Clinton-Gore rally last fall, "the mother of you all." But as her own feminist philosophy—concerned more with assuring equal roles for women than with questioning the patriarchal underpinnings of society—eventually was criticized as rigid and conservative, her celebrity was eclipsed by younger, more radical and more glamorous spokeswomen such as Gloria Steinem, Catharine A. MacKinnon, Alice Walker, and Susan Faludi. In the past two decades, Friedan has remained a household name and is a usual suspect when a quote is needed about an Anita Hill or a parental leave act, but she is no longer a ranking member of the feminist vanguard. Now Friedan has a new, eager group of the disenfranchised to champion, and it seems a welcome relief after the sort of ostracism she has felt. "Betty knows how to move on," says Gittelson. "She did what she did, and you could say that she passed the torch or the torch was wrested from her, but whatever happened she didn't fall down in her tracks. She moved on."

Right now, Friedan is moving with a slight limp. It is the only overt sign of a health crisis she endured this year; in fact, for a brief time, she thought her latest book would be published posthumously.

In April in Los Angeles, where she's spent the past seven winters teaching a course at USC's business school and running a think tank on women's issues, she had what she thought was a breath-shortening flare-up of her asthma. It turned out to be heart failure, caused by an infection on her heart-valve wall. In early May, she had the valve replaced with an animal's, but, as she loves to tell the story, "My Jewish heart rejected the pig valve." So she needed a human one—she even called old friend Donna Shalala, now secretary of Health and Human Services, to see if she could help track one down. On May 17, she got her human valve and had her second open-heart surgery in two weeks.

That should have been an excuse to take a long rest, but Friedan had a book to sell. Just two weeks later, Natalie Gittelson remembers hearing Friedan ask her daughter, Emily, a pediatrician, if she and her husband, a cardiologist, would accompany Friedan to Miami for an American Booksellers Assn. meeting; Emily agreed. Gittelson asked Emily, "Do you really think she'll be able to make it?"

"No way!" said the daughter. "I'm just humoring her."

Nonetheless, there was Friedan wheeling onto the stage—she used a chair because of a disc infection in her back, she insists, not because of the heart surgery—and delivering a rousing talk about vital aging to a captivated crowd. She told them, "I want as many people as possible to read this book, so there's no way I'm going to spend ten years writing it and then not get out of the hospital and come talk to you." By being there, she proved a thesis of her book—that age shouldn't limit even the most extraordinary acts.

Today, Friedan looks tan and healthy, having spent the summer "lying fallow" and not slave to a book deadline for the first time in years. Sprawled on the couch in Sag Harbor in a scoop-necked black sweater and pants, she runs her hand through her silver hair. "I'm just back to myself," she says, "and the one good thing that came out of it is that I weigh under 130 for the first time in forty years!" She's even been out dancing, one of her favorite pastimes. The surgical scar on her chest looks like a battle wound, and her vivid features—the substantial, down-curving nose and the droopy, basset-hound eyes—have softened. Friedan may have seemed prematurely old in her forties, especially while mediagenic Steinem stayed preternaturally young, but real age sits well on her.

Not that she went gently into her elder years. In the preface of the book she writes, "When my friends threw a surprise party on my sixtieth birthday, I could have killed them all. Their toasts seemed hostile, insisting as they did that I publicly acknowledge reaching sixty, pushing me out of life, as it seemed, out of the race."

She says she was depressed for weeks; the last place Betty Friedan wanted to be was out of the race. To combat that depression, she decided to confront the issue head-on; she took a fellowship at Harvard and immersed herself in gerontological research. She was soon struck by the discrepancy between the decrepit, often pathological image of aging presented by many of the "experts" and the old people whom she began interviewing. She noticed, for example, that for many women, menopause was not a tragedy.

"I ran into these women who were putting their lives together in a different way beyond motherhood," she says. "I saw how vital they were; they didn't even remember menopause. That was one of my first clues to *The Fountain of Age.*"

Soon she had a book in the works, and her depression turned into activist anger. In that, she's not unlike other female social critics, who, as they grow old, suddenly find the subject of age to be a fascinating frontier. In the past few years, Germaine Greer and Gail Sheehy have tackled menopause and points beyond, while Helen Gurley Brown, who ironically published *Sex and the Single Girl* the year before *The Feminine Mystique* came out, took on sex and the older woman in *The Late Show: A Semiwild but Practical Survival Plan for Women Over 50.*

Friedan's bottom line on aging is similar to her bottom line on feminism— liberation means having choices. And to make these choices possible, society must overcome its aversion and fear of aging. Which Friedan herself had to do before she could write her book.

"I had to write through my own extreme denial and dread," she explains. "But then at one point, I'm interviewing a woman in Palm Springs who was clearly my age and in a very short tennis skirt and had red hair. She said, 'Isn't it nice; I hear you're writing a book about these poor old people.' And I said, 'I'm not writing a book about them. I'm writing a book about us.'"

Among young feminists, Friedan is a shadowy figure; many consider her ancient history, almost in the same category as Susan B. Anthony or Elizabeth Cady Stanton. "When I speak to feminists my age, Betty Friedan's name rarely comes up," says Barbara Findlen, twenty-nine, who is managing editor of *Ms.* magazine and working on an anthology of writings of young feminists. "When it does, the overriding sentiment that I hear is that her work has become irrelevant. The impact of *The Feminine Mystique* is unquestionable," she adds,

"but at the same time, when you read it and her other writings now, you see
how limited and divisive her vision is."

But when *The Feminine Mystique* became a bestseller, suburban housewife Friedan was hailed as a liberator, and she suddenly became the leader and spokeswoman of a brand new movement. And for a while she seemed the perfect
choice. She was a natural polemicist and publicist, someone who could choose
the right issue to pursue and pick the perfect moment to bring it to the public
arena. In 1965, Friedan and other activists started to get increasingly angry
that the sex-discrimination section of Title VII of the Civil Rights Act of 1964
wasn't being taken seriously. A tearful Equal Employment Opportunity Commission lawyer took Friedan aside and pleaded with her to "start an NAACP
for women."

At a meeting of state commissioners on the status of women, Friedan
helped form the National Organization for Women. Officially born Oct. 29,
1966, with twenty-eight charter members, NOW's statement of purpose—"to
bring women into full participation in the mainstream of American society
now"—was written by its first elected president, Betty Friedan.

President of NOW for four years, she was also instrumental in the founding
of a number of other important feminist organizations—the National Assn.
for Repeal of Abortion Laws, now known as National Abortion Rights Action
League, the NOW Legal Defense and Education Fund and the National Wom-
en's Political Caucus. She took courageous early stands on abortion rights and
the ERA, among other key pieces of the NOW agenda. But as the years went
by, she found her celebrity increasingly eclipsed by younger, and hipper,
women. Friedan essentially led the "mothers" division of the movement, while
Gloria Steinem directed the daughters brigade. The mothers were trying to
escape the misogynistic world of the 1950s; the daughters were trying to avoid
ever getting into such a repressive rut.

"It was the difference between a glamorous, sexy feminism and a dowdy,
matronly feminism," says writer and former *Mother Jones* editor Deirdre English,
who points out that the male media acted misogynistically in setting up that
dichotomy. "But if Betty Friedan has been the only representative of feminism
out there," she says, "we (baby-boomers) probably wouldn't have become feminists."

For Friedan's peers—mostly white, middle-class, middle-aged, heterosexual
women like herself—*The Feminine Mystique* was a conversion experience. It

pointed out how everyone from Madison Avenue hucksters to Sigmund Freud and Margaret Mead had conspired to keep women in that gilded cage of no-other-option housewifery—and that it was time to break free.

But more radical feminists often preferred Simone de Beauvoir's 1949 *The Second Sex* or Kate Millett's 1970 *Sexual Politics* as their primary text. *The Feminine Mystique* did not speak to issues of class in the same way that some radical feminists tried to," says Catharine R. Stimpson, a longtime women's studies professor and current director of the MacArthur Foundation. "It did not speak to issues of race, and it did not speak to sexuality."

Indeed, the notion of "sexual politics"—encompassing everything from pornography to date rape to lesbianism—Friedan decried as "diversionary," which led to huge rifts. Friedan would dig in her heels on the issue and freeze out all argument. Her brusque, know-it-all, combative style antagonized women in the movement—and anyone else who may have caught her in a crotchety moment.

She was "one of the most difficult women in the world to work with," says Dolores Alexander, formerly executive director of NOW and currently an anti-pornography activist in New York. Friedan herself admits, without much contrition, to a *"terrible* temper," and her friends don't deny her eruptive personality. "She's always fascinating to me, but even Betty would never call herself a pussycat," says Gittelson. "She's strong-willed, she likes things her way. She's capable of great fury, sometimes over small issues."

While her friends accept her nature as part of the intriguing and often charming package—and have learned to talk back—she wore out many people in the women's movement and was increasingly cut out of the feminist community. "Friedan's a good thinker, and she's always had fantastic timing, but people won't follow her to the end like they will other women in the movement," says Judith Meuli, who, with fellow longtime NOW activist Toni Carabillo, has written a history of the modern women's movement called *The Feminist Chronicles: 1953 to 1993.*

The Second Stage, Friedan's third book, published in 1981, was the final straw for many of her critics. Ostensibly devoted to discussing the future of the women's movement, it was considered revisionist by many feminists. Friedan seemed to blame feminists for the inability of the movement to make further strides in areas of concern to mothers and families. In her 1991 bestseller *Backlash,* Susan Faludi accused Friedan of "yanking out the stitches in her own handiwork" by suggesting, among other things, that women reject confrontational politics—which Friedan had pioneered—in favor of a gentler "Beta" style and rediscover volunteerism. "(Her) solution puts the burden on women; the need for men to change barely figures in Friedan's new plan," wrote Faludi.

"It gave the false impression that NOW had not addressed issues of child care and homemakers, when in fact we had," says Carabillo of the book. "It was as if she alone recognized this need. It was not constructive criticism."

"Betty's influence after *The Second Stage* was minimal," adds Meuli.

Friedan has no apologies for the book or the controversy it generated.

"I think I was right. I'm not blaming anything on feminists at all!" she says, her voice rising. "What I had to say in *The Second Stage* was not the party line, which has become 'down with men' and ignores that the real empowerment of women is economic empowerment that comes from jobs and more self-respect. I also deplore and find ideologically and politically wrong a feminism based on sexual warfare, sexual politics. Warfare between women and men. I think that denies the complexity of the interdependence of women and men."

Some would argue that this polarization of feminism along anachronistic battle lines, with so-called "man haters" on one side, echoes the rhetoric of anti-feminists. But Friedan doesn't flinch. "I do blame the feminists—not feminists, because I'm a feminist—" she quickly backpedals, "but the so-called feminist organizations for not having given the priority they should to child care and parental leave, flexible work structures," she continues. "I'm not for supressing pornography; I'm for suppressing *guns!* Some pornography insults women . . . but *none of it is as dangerous as the guns that kill women and men!*

"It's wrong to make me an enemy or betrayer of feminism," she concludes, responding to the criticism that she has often called "mother bashing." "I'm trying—or I was trying—to take feminism to the next stage."

If open heart surgery couldn't keep Friedan from a book tour, criticism, even from her "daughters and granddaughters," never kept her away from the podium, the stage, the TV cameras. She wrote her books and magazine articles; she secured visiting professorships at universities in fields ranging from women's studies to business management. She turns up everywhere, delivering rousing speeches for groups as diverse as the Orange County Women's Club and the Mature Marketing Summit on topics from social psychology to flexible work structures to gun control.

In 1987, she came to USC, initially for her gerontology research, and because winters in Santa Monica are better for her asthma. She organizes, at both USC and NYU, an annual conference on women, men and the media, an area she has long understood. "She's really contributed to a number of different schools at USC," says USC business professor and author Warren Bennis. This year, her Betty Friedan Think Tank tackled such issues as sexual abuse, the L.A. riots and national health care. She currently teaches a course in the business school called "Changing Paradigms of Management," which gives her a chance to promote one of her pet theories that business is shifting "from a macho style to a maestro style," as Bennis puts it.

"She's a great moderator, and she seemed to be up on all the issues," says Lisa Miller, who coordinated the think tank last spring. But when asked what it was like to work with Friedan, Miller pauses, laughs and says politely, "Challenging."

Friedan divides her time among her Sag Harbor home, a river-view Manhattan apartment and a Santa Monica condo. She hasn't remarried since her 1969 divorce, but she's had her share of male companionship. She also nurtures a legion of friends from academia, the arts, media and business. For 10 years, Friedan shared a house—a commune, she liked to call it—with some of these longtime friends who, like her, had been divorced. Although she now lives alone, the close contacts have remained.

Journalist Richard Reeves and his wife, erstwhile L.A. political candidate Cathy O'Neill, are Sag Harbor buddies. When Friedan celebrated her sixty-fifth birthday, lyricist friends Adolph Comden and Betty Green wrote tuneful tributes. Former *Washington Post* Editor Ben Bradlee might turn up at a Friedan soiree; so might well-known sociologist William Goode. Friedan mentions she had dinner the other night with an old friend who's a famous sex therapist, her tycoon husband and Barbara Walters.

About twice a year, Friedan's own far-flung clan—three children, their spouses and eight grandchildren—rendezvous with her in Sag Harbor. She obviously revels in her family and sparkles around her grandchildren. She's the eldest of three children herself and remains close to her brother, Harry, a retired businessman, but not to her sister. "We're like oil and water," admits Friedan. Nonetheless, she wrote admiringly in *The Fountain of Age* of Amy's decision to switch careers from art to writing in her sixties.

The contacts, the high-powered friends, the peripatetic lifestyle are all a long way from Peoria, where she was born Betty Naomi Goldstein on Feb. 4,

1921. A Jew, she learned early what it meant to belong to the non-dominant culture. And if she needed a household example of the "fountain of age," she had one in her maternal grandfather, who lived to be nearly 100. But it was Betty's mother, with whom she had an admiring but stormy relationship, who taught her by example to be a feminist. It was the example of a woman who did not achieve her full potential.

"I sometimes think what really motivated me was a gut awareness of my mother's frustration," says Friedan. "I wanted women to be able to feel better about being women than my mother was able to. She had been women's-page editor of the Peoria newspaper, but when she married my father and started having kids, she had to stop working. She leaned too much on the children and her husband, and nothing we did was ever enough."

Her mother may have also helped inspire *The Fountain of Age*. Miriam, who died a few years ago at age 90, having survived three husbands, lived an active retired life at Leisure World in Laguna Hills, until her doctor advised her at age eighty-seven to step down from directing bridge games. "Too much stress," Friedan says. Her mother went rapidly downhill after that, and when her children finally had to put her in a nursing home, she died six weeks later. Friedan doesn't believe it was just old age. "Better to have the stress and take the risk," she says, and it's a theme throughout her book.

With her mother's prodding, Friedan went into journalism, eventually moving to New York City to work for a news service and then for labor newspapers. She rented a kitchenless basement apartment on West 86th Street and met Carl Friedan. Seven months later, they were married.

Carl went into advertising, and the couple eventually moved to suburban Rockland County. They had three children, Daniel, forty-four, a physicist; Jonathan, forty, an engineer; and Emily, thirty-six. Pregnant with Jonathan, Friedan was fired from her job, and it was almost a relief. She no longer had to fight her mother's fate; she could embrace it, listing her occupation as "housewife." In 1957, she began designing what should have been routine questionnaires for her fifteen-year Smith College reunion; thinking she might write a magazine article, she expanded them to examine more deeply the experiences and feelings of her fellow alumnae. The response from these well-educated, ostensibly happy housewives had an "Is that all there is?" ring, and Friedan began considering that there was, as she'd dub it in *The Feminine Mystique*, a "problem that had no name." Yet.

She started the book in the New York Public Library and finished it on her dining room table while the kids were at school. "It was like secret drinking in the morning," she says. Friedan admits there may have been a little "benign neglect" of the youngsters while she labored away for five years, and the still-mystiqued ladies of Rockland County ostracized her for things like hiring a taxi when she was too busy to take her turn carpooling. But "I enjoyed being a mother," she says, glancing fondly toward the kitchen where Emily, here with her family on their semi-annual visit, is preparing gazpacho. "And the proof of the pudding is that all three children are doing well in love and well in work. And they are wonderful parents themselves. That's the most you can ask for."

The Feminine Mystique sold more than 60,000 hardcover copies, and more than 2,320,000 paperbacks are in print. As her career took off, her marriage ran aground. After the divorce, ending more than twenty tumultuous years, Carl Friedan blasted his ex in an interview, claiming she "never washed 100 dishes during twenty years of marriage" and that his new wife made chicken soup and shined his shoes. Friedan laughed and replied, "All I can say is, to each her own. I'm so mechanically inept, I can barely shine my own shoes."

During her recent illness, however, she felt a renewed appreciation for the bonds of friends and family. In fact, Carl flew out to see her when she was hospitalized. "I had a feeling of such support," she says. "You wouldn't believe."

This celebration of support and family ties is one of the main themes of *The Fountain of Age*. Hardly angry, hardly obsessive, it may prove Friedan's contention that she is finally mellowing. The fact that she included, in a positive way, the ties among aging gays and lesbians seems further proof, and will certainly amaze those who have never forgotten her strident and anti-lesbian stance when she was president of NOW.

Ivy Bottini, a former president of the New York chapter of NOW, remembers the shock she felt when she gave Friedan a lavender armband to wear during a 1969 march for women's rights on New York's Fifth Avenue. "It was to show solidarity with our lesbian sisters and their oppression," says Bottini, now a Los Angeles realtor and lesbian who was once a Long Island housewife. Many people took the armbands, including Gloria Steinem. But Friedan looked at hers, threw it down and ground her heel into it.

"My point was, 'How can you have a women's movement and leave a huge amount of women out?' " says Bottini. "But Friedan just never got that. She

doesn't understand that lesbianism is the bottom line of the women's movement. If you can't get past the fear of being thought of as a lesbian, whether
you are or not, then you never are really free. She's still talking about equal
rights. Sexual politics is civil rights."

Dolores Alexander thinks Friedan came up with the term "lavender menace," and Bottini believes Friedan was one of the people who engineered a
"purge" of lesbians from the NOW leadership, urging inactive members to
attend an election meeting and vote out Bottini from the presidency, which
they did. A 1973 Friedan essay in the *New York Times Magazine* smacked of
downright paranoia; Friedan even claimed a woman was sent to seduce her
and then blackmail her into silence while unnamed lesbians took over NOW.

Bottini, who despite their differences found Friedan to have a likable, fun
side, laughs when she remembers her encounter with Friedan three years later,
at another march down Fifth Avenue. Pushing through the crowd, Bottini,
who was visiting from L.A., found herself face-to-face with her former neme-
sis. "Are you back?" Friedan asked. "No," Bottini said. "Good!" Friedan replied.

Although Friedan does not apologize for her actions, she does admit that
she has grown more open-minded. "When I first came to New York, the whole
question of homosexuality made me uneasy," Friedan acknowledges today. "I
mean, I'm very *square!* Very Middle America. I had many friends who were
lesbians, but I didn't know it. And when I did know it, I didn't particularly
want to know it.

"I never wanted to suppress anyone's sexual preferences or wanted people
to be persecuted for them," she adds, "but what I objected to was equating
feminism with lesbianism. After all, I wrote a whole book objecting to the
definition of women only in sexual relation to men. I would not exchange that
for a definition of women only in sexual relation to women."

Some have neither forgotten nor forgiven Friedan's early stance. But in
1977, at the National Women's Conference in Houston, she delivered a mea
culpa of sorts, and received a huge ovation, for seconding the resolution to
protect lesbian rights. "Finally she was sounding like the intelligent woman
she should have been sounding like all along," says Dolores Alexander.

Today, Friedan's voice is calmer, less judgmental. In *The Fountain of Age*,
some of the most moving testimony, about finding intimacy in old age among
a "family" of friends, came from gay and lesbian friends she interviewed. "I
found them easier to interview, in a weird sort of way. It was much harder to

ask a heterosexual couple," she practically whispers, as if Peoria were still listening, "about the reality of their sex life."

Still, when she writes about intimacy in her own life, she can be touching but coy. She never mentions in this book or others, for example, why she hasn't remarried.

"Oh God, I don't know," she says. "I *think* I would have liked to. I *say* I would have liked to. I've had such a hectic life through these years. Who knows, maybe I will before the end. I think it's better not to live alone, I'll tell you that, although I'm not lonely. But it would be nice to always have someone to go to the movies with. To say nothing of sharing the day-to-day intimacies.

"Intimacy is a very . . ." she pauses for a long beat ". . . fascinating thing. I have a deep sense of the importance of intimacy, I have a deep need for it. And I have a great sense of how I and others push it away. After all, the fear of intimacy is probably the fear of really revealing yourself.

"It always has been easier for me to see what's happening out there and figure it out than it is to live through it and finally do it myself," she says pensively. "And maybe one of the things that happens in my book,"—she brings the discussion back to the promotional realm—"is that you become more and more comfortable with yourself. You don't have to hide anymore. And that opens up possibilities.

"I'm still in the middle of it, you understand. I don't pretend I have all the answers for myself personally. But I think I know more clearly what the questions are."

Betty Friedan: *The Fountain of Age*

Brian Lamb / 1993

This interview was broadcast on C-SPAN
"Booknotes," 28 November 1993. Reprinted by
permission of C-SPAN.

BRIAN LAMB: *Betty Friedan, where'd you get the name for your book,* The Fountain of Age?
BETTY FRIEDAN: That it's not the "Fountain of Youth." Everybody in America is obsessed with the Fountain of Youth, the old Ponce de Leon. And what I saw, once I was really going on this track that led me to the book, that what's wrong—a mystique of age more pernicious, pervasive than the feminine mystique—is somehow a definition of age only in terms of decline from youth and not as what it is, a period of human life that most people didn't even used to have, that should be seen as a new period of human life in its own terms, hence *The Fountain of Age.*

LAMB: *At what age did you go on Outward Bound?*
FRIEDAN: I think it was in my early 60s.

LAMB: *Why?*
FRIEDAN: Well, I told myself that I was doing it to do research for the book, because of the kind of people I was looking for—women and men that would continue to develop and evolve and that didn't fit that deterioration and decline. And I was already beginning to see that a strong element of that was adventurousness, a willingness to risk, an ability to risk in ways you couldn't do when you were younger. And I figured I'd find them on this, but really, secretly, it was something I'd always yearned to do myself, that wilderness

130

exploration kind of thing. And in my long married life and then in my hectic life since my divorce—all this women's movement and lecturing and this—I'd somehow never done this wilderness stuff, so I really wanted to do it myself. And then, of course, what it became was a metaphor of the whole search for the fountain of age.

LAMB: *Can you remember where it all started—I mean, the Outward Bound thing? Who went on it?*

FRIEDAN: Oh, well, that one, it was their first time when they experimented— Outward Bound was this rigorous wilderness survival thing that Peace Corps trainees used to go on. And they decided to do one for people 55 plus—over 55. It was called Going Beyond, and this was the first one like that. And we met somewhere at some airport in the South and the first thing we did, we went river rafting on the Chattahoochee River, sort of Tennessee, Georgia— wherever the movie *Deliverance* was done. And there was this wild river rafting and the rapids, and then there was 24 hours alone in the wilderness sites. It was traipsing through wild territory without a guide—with just a chart, compass and so on and so forth. And then it was this cliffs and rapelling. I finally said, "I don't have to prove myself this way." You know, that's why I say the whole thing was a metaphor. And it was quite marvelous.

LAMB: *And you didn't tell people your last name when you started this?*

FRIEDAN: No, I don't think we told people our ages, and I don't think we told people our last names nor our professions. It was just, maybe, what city we came from or something like that, but it was no real identifying thing. So I wasn't seen through my mask, as it were—my persona, the great feminist, here. And we became great friends. There was a retired insurance executive from North Carolina, Earl Arthurson. He was a big, burly man, Dartmouth class of '38, it turned out, and he was the oldest of our group.

And he was then in his 70s, but he was clearly the leader. I mean, there were men there 55, and he sort of somehow had to really hang back sometimes and let some of these others take the lead. I'm not a jock so he'd help me over the fences or cliffs or God knows what. And I had a terrible time getting my backpack adjusted right and he was always very helpful. Of course, the feminist stance is to not accept such help but, please, I needed all the help I could get.

LAMB: *And what'd you learn about yourself?*

FRIEDAN: Well, I was able to do it, and the adventurousness of it was terrific. It was great fun for me to just be on my own without having to wear my public mask. And I loved it. Then toward the end, when there was some rappelling thing which I really didn't master enough to feel in control of it, and I was going to swing out around this cliff and I was scared to death—and I think rightly, because I didn't feel rightly in control. I hadn't done it enough to feel in control of it. For the river rafting, they gave us some learning period and I did it. I could do it all right. But this I didn't feel in control of and I just finally said, "Get me out of here." And so then one of the other women, when she came down she said, "You've given me the courage to do it." I said, "I've given you the courage to do it?" Here I was, I thought, a coward that said, "No, I'm not doing this." I finally said, "Take me out of here," and they had to lift me up off the cliff. And she said, "No, if you had the guts to do that and say, 'This is not for me,' then I could do it."

LAMB: *What was the reaction when people found out who you were? And had anybody figured it out?*
FRIEDAN: The women knew, but they kept my cover. But these guys were amazed.

LAMB: *None of the men knew who you were?*
FRIEDAN: No. This was 10 years ago—they knew who I was once it was said, but how could they recognize me? I was in all these sweat pants and this gear, and I really didn't look like I look on television, not that I look so great. Anyways, so one of them—Earl—we became great friends. My protector, see. He always claims—I don't know if he's telling the truth, but I think he really didn't know who I was—"I wasn't taken by your fame. I was taken by your gusty spirit." But every year he comes to New York and takes me dancing at the Rainbow Room. He's a wonderful dancer. Then he's one of the people that really is the fountain of age.

Here he'd been all these years this big-shot in North Carolina, Charlotte, a big insurance agency, and a pillar of the community and all that. And he had nursed his wife through 10 years, I think, of lung cancer. After she died, he took a lot of cruises, traveling. He was lonesome, but he's such a good dancer, and so he would, in his courtly style, dance with all the ladies that outnumber the men on these cruises. So he got offered a job as a cruise host, and he spends most of his time now on these fantastic cruises all over the place, where he's a host. He got me to go on one. Cruises are not for me, but I went for three days, just to see him in action. And he's having the time of his life. It's not your usual occupation for Dartmouth class of '38, or whatever he was, and the big-shot insurance magnate, but he's having this marvelous, adventurous last third of his life doing this.

LAMB: *What year did you write* The Feminine Mystique?
FRIEDAN: '63—30 years ago, it was published. I wrote it for the five years earlier than that.

LAMB: *Over those 30 years, what's happened to that book? Can you still buy it in book-stores?*
FRIEDAN: Oh, sure. I mean, it's assigned in colleges and in classes. I guess it's considered—it's on these lists of the 10 books through all time that have shaped history or whatever. And it's assigned in college courses in American history or sociology or whatnot, so young people are reading it. I'm amazed they still find it so applicable because we have changed so much since that book and breaking through the feminine mystique. But what intrigues me is that women of all ages still stop me, if they run into me in the airport or the street: "It changed my life." And they tell me where they were when they read it: "I was in the hospital having my third child," whatever—"I was doing this, I was doing that." It really did have this effect of putting into words what they'd been groping and yearning for, and it enabled them to take steps to change their life. And the interesting thing now is that with my book, *The Fountain of Age*, men—I mean, men and some women, too, of course—are having the same sort of emotional reaction that women had to *The Feminine Mystique*, of saying, "It's made me think altogether differently about the rest of my life."

LAMB: *How many copies did you sell, do you know, up till now, of* Mystique?
FRIEDAN: Oh, God. I don't know by now. Like millions of copies in about 20 countries. I have no idea how many, but years ago they were saying three million so it must be a lot more than that now.

LAMB: *What were you doing when you wrote that book?*
FRIEDAN: Well, I was, technically, a housewife in Rockland County, suburban New York, with three kids. I had been freelancing for women's magazines after I'd been fired from a newspaper job for being pregnant with my second child.

And what I later called the "feminine mystique" was filling me full of guilt for working. Even though my husband had been in the theater and was then starting in advertising, we needed my paycheck, but I'd been feeling so guilty. Now I'm fired. You couldn't look for a job with your belly out to here, pregnant, then—you know, not in those years—well, not now, too. So I was technically a housewife, but I couldn't quite get rid of the itch to do something so I was free-lancing for magazines, mainly the women's magazines, like secret drinking in the morning, because none of the other mothers in that suburb were working then. It was the end of the feminine mystique period.

And after about five years of writing according to this limited image that was supposed to be the image of the American woman then—solely in terms of her husband, children, home, nothing else—I got restive about it. And then there was the happenstance of doing the 15th reunion questionnaire of my Smith alumni. Since they were saying too much education is making women frustrated in their role as women—I had valued my education—I thought I was going to disprove that with this questionnaire of Smith '42. And instead it raised more questions than it answered. And then, when the magazines that I wrote for, one after the other, either turned it down or rewrote it to say the opposite and I took it back, I knew I'd have to write the book *The Feminine Mystique.* But I didn't have any sense then—I mean, every chapter I'd finish, I thought, "Gee, I must be crazy," because it so went against everything that was accepted as both the conventional and sophisticated truth about women. But the idea that it would have the impact it did—you know, they say it really started the consciousness part of the women's movement that led to the modern women's movement. In my gut I guess I knew it was very important, but I didn't have the confidence I later acquired. It's such a mystery to me that I was able to write that book.

The experiences and the skills, my training as a psychologist, a journalist, the life I lived enabled me to write *The Feminine Mystique;* but now with *The Fountain of Age* I had also the training that came from breaking through the feminine mystique and helping to give the vision of the women's movement. So I tackled this new problem, which is beyond feminism. It's a different problem, but I guess I was able to tackle that as I began to recognize that I was dealing with another mystique. I wasn't interested in age. Not me. No. I mean, I had the same dreary view of age as anybody in America, the same absolute denial. It didn't apply to me. But once I began on this little path—large path—

that led me to break through an even more pernicious, pervasive mystique, the mystique of age only as decline from youth, I guess all the 30 years from writing *The Feminine Mystique* to the women's movement gave me a way to more—well, I can't say more quickly, because it took me 10 years to write this book, but at least to be able to break through this other thing.

LAMB: *Connections—you point out Joe Duffey, who was head of the National Endowment for the Humanities, had some money for this project back in the late '70s.*
FRIEDAN: Well, when I decided I wanted to do this, I knew I had to immerse myself in research—in other words, a field that was new to me—to find out what research had been done on aging, because I saw that somehow there was no image of age except this nursing home-senility-Alzheimer's decline and deterioration from youth. But what I was seeing first in women and then even in men, too, is people moving into their 60s, 70s and 80s with vitality and even growth and development. And there was something wrong here, that women somehow had an edge on men in this, although the men were dying younger. So I didn't get enough of a publisher advance to do what I knew would have to be some years doing the research, so I went to see Joe Duffey, who was then the head of the National Endowment for the Humanities.

Now he's head of the U.S. Information Service in this new Cabinet. And I said to him, "Look, I'm not a Ph.D.—I've got no Ph.D. in sociology or geron-tology. I'm not an academic, but I want to do this book," and I called it "Changing Sex Roles in the Aging Process." That was my title then. "I want to do this and I need some help to get the research done and to make my way through everything that's been done so far, in addition to my own interviews." So he said, "Well, did you have a Ph.D. when you wrote *The Feminine Mystique?*" and I said, "No." And he said, "Well, your track record is good enough for me." And that was really pretty marvelous of Joe, I thought. And then the peer review—you know peer review? Well, the academics vetoed it, so he got pretty annoyed at that, but he gave me a chairman's grant and then Columbia University, the Center for Social Sciences, Jonathan Cole, who was himself a very quantitative sociologist, but recognized the value of the kind of qualita-tive sociology that I guess you could say I do. He took me to McGeorge Bundy at the Ford Foundation and they gave me the rest of the money that I needed. And that was all a great help because it took me a lot longer than I thought it was going to.

LAMB: *Where do you live now?*

FRIEDAN: I have an apartment in New York, and I feel more rooted. I have a little old house in Sag Harbor, an old whaling town on the Sound. And that's where my kids bring my grandkids, and that's where I did most of the writing. And then four months of the year I teach in Los Angeles at the University of Southern California. And in the fall I'm a visiting professor at New York University, so four months of the year I live in a different place each time, in Santa Monica or L.A.

LAMB: *You mention in the book several times that you feel better after going through the book process than you did before—about aging.*

FRIEDAN: Well, I wrote myself into a completely new place. It was very liberating. It's mysterious in a way, but I was absolutely in denial. I mean, I age— please. What was it they say to me, "What's this I hear, Betty, that you're writing a book about age?" And eyes would glaze over, and I'd say, "Oh, no, no, no, no, no, no, no, no, not me. I mean, you've got it all wrong." Here I am, the flaming radical, the cutting edge, but age. Because I had the same dreary view of it, absolutely denial as anyone else. And I'd say, "No, no, I've got this far-out hypothesis about women and men and changing sex roles, not the aging process." And then, when I actually started working on the book, I took a fellowship at Harvard at the Institute of Politics at the Kennedy School where I taught *The Second Stage,* a book that I just finished. I taught that seminar, but otherwise I could use the resources of the university. I figured I'd immerse myself in whatever research had been done on aging. In that great university all I could find was medical school, Alzheimer's, nursing home, ethical issues—when do you pull the plug? I'd go to these conferences and the gerontological meetings I was beginning to attend, these paneled halls and the young Turks in their white coats with research money for aging, and they would talk about "them" with the same contemptuous compassion that reminded me of something. It reminded me of the way the male experts on women used to talk about the "woman problem," all those years ago. And I'd come out feeling so depressed. That didn't interest me at all, this Alzheimer's, nursing home.

And then I began to interview women and men—that I was finding much more easy than I thought I would—who were clearly very vital in these years beyond 60 and beyond 70, even beyond 80. I remember one I interviewed in

Cambridge beyond 90. And they were continuing to grow and develop. So that would exhilarate me. Then I began to feel depression, exhilaration, and a kind of weird panic. And I thought, "What is wrong with me? What was wrong with me?" I'd never had that much writing block before. And then I realized what was wrong with me. I just had my own 60th birthday. And I was furious when my friends threw me a surprise party on my 60th birthday. And I felt very hostile to them and they were very hostile to me to have done that, because I was as much in denial as anyone else.

And then one day I was interviewing in Palm Springs, and there was this woman—she was clearly older than I was. She had flaming red hair, but the white roots were visible. She had a very short miniskirt—tennis skirt with crepey legs underneath and she said, "Oh, how nice. I hear you're writing a book about those poor old people." And I said, "No. I'm not writing a book about them. I'm writing a book about us." And she said, "Oh, not me. I mean, I will never be old. Not me." And I began to do what I had to do to write this book, which was to break through my own denial. I had to be able to say "us" and in my own reality, which didn't fit any of these images. Then I found, in the research, all kinds of facts that defied this image of deterioration and decline that for most people now takes place only at the very end of life—just before death or well into their 80s. And even if you measure with the test standardized in youth, the decline is not what the image is—or it's just begun, a measurement of what evolves.

Youth is not the peak, you know. There are qualities of—we don't even have words for them in this society—wisdom, qualities that emerge in you if you're not still just looking at yourself, trying to pretend you're young long after you're not young really anymore. Even if you have five facelifts, you're not going to look young. You look like a mummy, without any character, without any experience. When I wrote *The Feminine Mystique*, I talked about problems that had no name. When I began to look into women—and it was easier for women, but also more and more new kind of men—who are moving into a different kind of age—they might be called pioneers of a new kind of age because there are no role models, no maps, no guidance—I see strengths that have no name.

LAMB: *Should people have to retire at 65?*

FRIEDAN: There are certain words that absolutely we must protest against.

Retire is one. Old is another. Old, static and it's got this whole connotation of decline, deterioration and state. Older is OK. People growing older, don't deny the person here. Retire—you retire from society. You go into a retirement community. You're supposed to be out of the larger community. We should not buy all this. Even forced retirement—losing your job because of your age—is supposed to be illegal, you know it's happening, that people are being forced out, eased out, downsized out, and not only in their 60s—in their 50s. And they can't very easily find another job, even if they dye their hair, try to phony their age.

I protest the idea that you must retire from society at age 60, 65, 70, whatever, when you've got all this ability and experience. You could retire or be forced out from a job or even be burned out and want to leave, but not retire from society. Move from one structure, one project—career lines that were really based on youth—to something else. But we are retiring all these people—this fastest-growing group of people in our whole society—from being productive members of the society, to be just a drain or a burden or be made invisible, walled out of sight in a continuing care community, as if their only identity now is as objects of terminal nursing care, when they don't even need that until just before their death or, you know, in a very advanced age.

You know, this is a new period of life to be lived, years that people didn't used to have. Life expectancy at the turn of the century was 45 for men, 46 for women. It's over 75 now. It's nearly 80 for women, over 72 for men. New years of life. Without road maps, without role models, we will be the pioneers of a new age. And behind us are the bulge of the baby boomers, getting into a trauma as they approach their 50th birthdays. A woman was interviewing me the other day and she said, "Oh, this book has come just in time for me." And I looked at her. She was a lovely looking young woman. She said, "Just had my 30th birthday." They, with all their numbers, created the youth culture, the songs of the '60s, the Beatles, all that, but they will take this revolution, which will be the revolution of the turn of the century, over the top.

LAMB: *Do you have a living will?*
FRIEDAN: Absolutely. And I'm going to see to it my kids have something that you can't really put in your living will: never, ever, ever put me in a nursing home.

LAMB: *Why?*

FRIEDAN: That image of deterioration and decline is so awful—it's no wonder that people deny age in this country. That is a reality in nursing homes. A high proportion of people in nursing homes are defined as senile. Some of it is real senility, but to my surprise, only 5 percent of people over 65 have any kind of senility, including Alzheimer's. But if they don't have it when they come in, through the absolute dehumanized, infantilized treatment of the nursing home—the sedation, if you will—they will acquire the signs of senility. What we need are not more nursing homes. What we need are more measures that are not necessarily medical, that will enable people to stay in their own communities and in their own homes—because you can't deny death. At the point where such a life is not possible and you really do have a terminal condition, then we have the hospice movement, which does not intervene with high-tech machinery to give people an extra week or day or month of painful life where you can't really function, but enables you to face death in the midst of your own family and friends as painlessly as possible. We don't deny death, but death should be in the midst of life.

LAMB: *You dedicate this book "To the memory of my mother, Miriam, and my father, Harry, who made a larger life possible for me." What did they do for you?*
FRIEDAN: I grew up in Peoria, Illinois. My father was a brilliant man, but he was an immigrant with no higher education, though he read philosophy every night after dinner. He sent his youngest brother to Harvard Law School and was inordinately proud of all my intellectual accomplishments. My mother grew up in Peoria and went to the local college, Bradley. Then she was the women's page editor of the newspaper there, but, of course, she had to quit that when she married my father and started having kids. She couldn't wait for me to get into junior high school and try out for the paper. I edited the college paper at Smith. That was one of the most fun things in my life. But she insisted that I get a good education, and my father said to me on his deathbed, "Don't come back here." You know, in other words, go beyond. Go beyond. My father died too young. He was in his early 60s and he had that premature kind of heart—the male role and the inability to even express the pain you may be feeling. He endured the anti-Semitism of a Middle West small town at that time and the pressures of the Depression and all that. My mother lived till she was 90. It was my mother's frustrations that I think gave me the psychological motivation for the women's movement. But my mother,

at the age of 70-odd, after burying her third husband, got herself licensed as a duplicate bridge manager.

She's always been a brilliant card player and she would toodle around. She lived in Leisure World in Laguna Hills, California. She would toodle around running the duplicate bridge tournaments into her 80s, with the prodigious feats of memory that required. And if I was coming out to California and I knew I'd be on TV, I'd say, "Oh, God, I've got to go see Mother." It terrifies me to drive in California because I can't stand the freeways, so it's not so easy to get from LA to Laguna Hills. So I'd call her up and I'd say, "Mother, I'm going to be in LA in two weeks. Can we meet?" "Darling," she would say, "I'm so busy. Why didn't you let me know longer in advance." I mean, she was no pathetic old lady being dependent.

LAMB: *You've mentioned Leisure World. What do you think of the Leisure World-type places?*
FRIEDAN: I spent a lot of time interviewing in those places and there were some people that seemed to make a good life for themselves there. They were mainly people that took responsibility for organizing the community. But even the physical appearance of the place, where it's walled off from the larger community, where the whole life can be structured around sort of busy, busy play, clubhouse activities, walled off from the whole continuum of life, generations—something about it was like this mystique of age, this denial of the personhood of age, translated into bricks and stucco. Even the luxurious age of ghettos, I don't think, are the wave of the future if we break through this pernicious definition of age just as decline. I was very interested to see, a couple weeks ago, a story on the front page of the *New York Times* that more and more people—older people—are coming back from Florida and those retirement communities in New York—dirty, busy, complex New York, with all its problems, but where there's so much life going on and where you can take the bus, take the subway, walk to things.

LAMB: *In your dedication, you also talk about Daniel and Jonathan and Emily and Raphael and Caleb. Is it Natalia?*
FRIEDAN: Yeah, Natalia.

LAMB: *David, Isabelle, Laura, Brigitta and Benjamin, "whose mother and grandmother I am."*
FRIEDAN: Proud of that, right.

LAMB: *How many of those are your children?*
FRIEDAN: Well, there's my three children, Daniel, Jonathan and Emily. And then my eight grandchildren—six blood grandchildren and two step-grand-daughters. They are actually from Iceland. My oldest son, who's a theoretical physicist, married the only woman physicist of Iceland, and she had two daughters from a previous marriage and now they have this wonderful little baby, my youngest grandchild, Benjamin.

LAMB: *Have you ever sat down with your kids and talked about aging?*
FRIEDAN: Not as such. I mean, they've all gotten copies of my living will and when I said to them, "You know, I'm going to leave you the house in Sag Harbor jointly," they said, "Oh, we've already had a meeting about it and we're going to"—how they were going to run it, and use it as a joint place to come with all their kids so they can come together. But the family ties of my children with each other and with their father and with me are very strong. And I like that. And in the dedication of my book, *The Fountain of Age*, as you see, the first part of it says that, on the wall of my kitchen in Sag Harbor, there's some Hebrew letters from a song—Hebrew songs from generation to genera-tion. I don't know, they had had some parties there and someone had tacked that song on the wall and I love the look of Hebrew letters, anyway.

But in that kitchen is where we all get together and I have this long, long dining table which will hold now the 14 of us when we're all in residence. And so from generation to generation. I mean the last chapter of my book, *The Fountain of Age*, is generativity, the freedom to risk, age as adventure and generativity, because I think, finally, in what evolves, there is a sense of the affirmation of your whole life as you've lived it and in the history, and then some great sense of the meaning of that life and that your life is a part of the continuum that will live after you, through your children, through your grand-children, but also through your human generativity that's not just biological.

For me it's been the women's movement and also the social and political causes to make the world better that somehow are a part of my morality, and even this last 10 years' task of breaking through the mystique of age, the fountain of age and what may come of that. My sense is, even from what's already happening, that there are implications here for revolutionary social change. I can't predict what form it will take any more than I could have predicted the women's movement after writing *The Feminine Mystique*. But I think it will happen and I'm open to what happens. I'll follow the leads where they come.

LAMB: *In the generativity chapter, you talk to a lot of people that the audience will recognize—Norman Lear, Jonas Salk, Hugh Hefner and others. I got some sense that maybe when people get older, they change the way they think about things.*

FRIEDAN: Well, it was interesting to me that, for instance—well, take Norman Lear: he's one of the men I admire most in this society now, who somehow very successfully and effectively used television in the most non-didactic but marvelous way—"All in the Family" to open larger social values to this society, to transcend the polarization and even racism—in the most open way and then doesn't stop. What did he call it? Act 3?

LAMB: *He did get to Act 3, yes.*

FRIEDAN: And then he very openly now professes a certain spiritual dimension, very openly is concerned with saving the environment and with People for the American Way protecting the liberties of America from censorship that has been plaguing the television industry. Or even Hugh Hefner—here is Hugh Hefner, with the whole *Playboy* thing and the Playboy bunnies and all that, and in his later years, he liberated himself from the rigid reaction against the sexual puritanism of his youth. And he'd handed over *Playboy* to his daughter, Christie, who's really quite a wonderful woman. And he's liberated, not to have to just try to shock, defy the rigidities of his youth. He can move beyond that. And this is what I see happening to people when they continue to grow and develop. In ways that all those years of psychoanalysis may or may not have done, you're liberated from the conflicts and the rigidities that hemmed you in before.

LAMB: *If you live as your mother lived, you've got another 20 years to go.*

FRIEDAN: I hope. I mean, that would be nice. What you read from the last line of the book—it's really quite true. Somehow in the process of writing this book I've liberated myself. Somehow I have moved from this denial and dread of age to an affirmation of where I am now, which is a very unknown place. I feel that things are changing all around me and I am more myself. I am myself, with all my faults. I've had pains in my past and bad things can happen to me still. It's all a part of it, but I am there finally and I am very interested and open to changes that are happening. It's not true that you have to love the way you loved when you were 30 or not love at all.

It opens you to whatever happens in a way that's different from youth. In some ways it's the same, but it's different. It's different and it opens you to new dimensions in your intimacy and your friendship. I was invited to go on an expedition in the rain forest in the Amazon, which has always been a fantasy of mine, in January, and I'm going to go, if I can assure myself that there's going to be no mosquitoes, because I can't stand mosquitoes. It's like I'm open. I'm open. And it's exciting.

LAMB: *When you teach at USC—University of Southern California—what do you teach?*
FRIEDAN: Well, I lead a complex academic life. I run a project in the School of Journalism called Women, Men and Media, that's funded by the Freedom Forum and that monitors in an ongoing way the media—the mass media, images of women and men. *The Feminine Mystique,* after all, was a breaking through of the media image of women, and *The Fountain of Age* is in another way women and men. At the Leadership Institute of the School of Business, I run a think tank which had been up to now new dimensions of feminist thought. It included activists, policymakers and academics. This year's going to be on thinking for a new age and risking new ways of loving and living together and of working and of money and of medical care and health care and new social and political values.

I also teach a course and lectures in the Leadership Institute of the School of Business on management and diversity. There are threats to that now and there are enormous possibilities. With the experience of women, with the experience of people that are older than the conventional, with racial differences, we have begun to embrace and use diversity. The downside is that there has to be some new grasp of all this and of the importance of it and maybe even some alternate work structures to come out of it. I also teach in the professional writing program. I do half of a seminar and my part is writing from personal truth and social observation.

LAMB: *How about at New York University? What do you teach there?*
FRIEDAN: I teach the Women, Men and Media and the diversity and management.

LAMB: *In this last chapter, you mentioned the Dominican nun: "She recounted her own lifelong struggle to name herself. 'I am a lesbian nun. If I had a choice, I would be exactly who I am.' She told of the long years when she had no close friends at all." What was the point of that one?*

FRIEDAN: Well, it showed her evolution to an authenticity about herself, do you see? This is what the research and my own interviews show, that if you continue to grow and develop through the years—in the new years of life that are open to you—you become more and more authentically yourself. You shed the masks and that is enormously liberating. And finally, with all its pains, you affirm the life that you have lived and you put it all together. And I was very struck by that account of hers—I found it somewhere—that she had lived so much of her life denying an essential part of herself according to a mask and she finally got rid of the mask.

LAMB: *You wrote about Helen and Richard Dudman.*

FRIEDAN: Oh, yes. They were one of my first senses of the pioneering, adventurous possibilities of age. I got to know them when he was the head of the Washington bureau of the *St. Louis Post Dispatch*. She had been women's page editor of the *Washington Post* and then she had been working for public broadcasting. She should have been made manager of the station there in Washington when it opened up, but she was passed over for a man. She was real mad and they decided that he would take early retirement. They had a shack on an island—well, it was a cabin—in Maine. In the little town near their island a radio station was for sale, and so they borrowed the money and bought the radio station. She ran the station. He kept working in Washington till the station began to be in the black, and then they started a whole new life for them—then he took early retirement.

But in his favor, he said, "I'm not going to stay on in this town once you've had the power that being a leading journalist gives you—then you don't have that any longer and you hang on. Instead I want to make a new life for myself." I go to see them in Maine. This radio station is a great success. He helped her. I mean, she was running it. He helped a little in the news division, but he began to do his own thing with not only building boats, which he had intended to do. I don't think he's ever going to get that boat finished, but he's doing north-south editing and teaching journalism in the Third World countries from a center in Hanover. And she's about at the point where she's handing over the radio station to their daughters, who moved up there, too, with their kids, so she can go with Richard on some of these Third World adventures. They are really role models for the fountain of age.

LAMB: *You found Flora Lewis, who writes a column from time to time for the New York Times, but who used to be their foreign correspondent.*

FRIEDAN: I interviewed her about the last year I was working on the book. She had come to speak in LA, and she took the lecture so she could go see her mother, who was in a nursing home. Flora, after all those years as a foreign correspondent and a columnist, had made a new use of her experience, lecturing all over Europe. She's committed to the one-world international thing. She's a brilliant, brilliant woman and it really interests me when you ask people like the Dudmans or Flora Lewis, but let's not assume that everybody that I interviewed was something glamorous like a foreign correspondent.

I interviewed plenty of women on Social Security who also were making new lives for themselves. And if you try to get them to put into words the difference between what they feel about themselves now at 70—something compared to 50, it's really interesting how their judgments are not so rigid, black and white, how they've acquired a new ease. They see things whole. They've got a kind of a comfort and assurance and authority. They know who they are. They don't care so much what other people think. You can see it in their faces—I really recognize it. I recognize it when a woman reaches that point. Suddenly there's a new serenity and assurance and a radiance in her face.

I know one woman and she's a marvelous woman that I know in California, and she just looks so different. I don't know, she's maybe not quite as thin as she used to be. She's stopped dying her hair and she used to somehow not project the confidence that she has now and this sort of comfort with herself. I mean, strengths that have no name—I don't even know the word for it but there it is.

LAMB: *Several times you mention Marlene Sanders.*
FRIEDAN: Well, Marlene Sanders is one of my best friends and we've been through a lot together. She called me in the middle of the night when she was the first woman to be made vice president for news of a network. Even when network people were not supposed to be political, she was one of the large underground of women in the networks that supported the movement and did what they could do. Now we run the Women, Men and Media project together with Nancy Woodhull. Because she's close to me, I could observe all these interesting little things, like when she was widowed. Jerry, her husband, was a wonderful man. She finally sold the big apartment that they had and she's in a smaller, but very perfect for her, sunny, airy new space. I like to see

the way she copes. Marlene is a very clear-headed person—much more clear-headed than I am, I sometimes feel. And so she's made these changes in her life in a very good way and I like to see it.

LAMB: *Do you have another book you plan to write?*
FRIEDAN: At this moment, my dear, I am so relieved to get this done. You know that for seven years I shipped back and forth across the country 20 boxes of papers, of notes, of books, because each year I'd go for my Spring-Winter teaching at the University of Southern California. I was drowning in all that research, and the fact that I finally finished the book is such a liberation. And I don't know. I don't want to do another heavy book like that. I'm going to do short stuff. Maybe I'll do a column. Maybe I'll do a program like you. Maybe I'll do a detective story. Maybe I'll write science fiction or a novel, but no more heavy books.

Betty Friedan: Now She's Making Waves in *The Fountain of Age*

Alice V. Luddington / 1993

From *Geriatrics*, (December 1998), 52 (4).
Reprinted with permission from *Geriatrics*.
Copyright by Advanstar Communications, Inc.
Advanstar Communications, Inc., retains all
rights to this article.

Will her new bestseller launch a liberation movement for older Americans, as *The Feminine Mystique* did for women in the 1960s?

Feminist Betty Friedan, author of *The Feminine Mystique*, marked that book's thirtieth anniversary this fall with the publication of a new work, *The Fountain of Age*. In this exclusive interview with *Geriatrics*, Ms. Friedan, now age seventy-two, talks about a new movement toward vital aging that aims to liberate older Americans from the "age mystique."

Q: *You begin* The Fountain of Age *by describing your reluctance at age sixty to confront your own aging.*

A: It took me ten years to write this book. It was the hardest thing I ever did. The first few years, all the gerontological meetings I went to were unutterably depressing. All this dreary stuff—Alzheimer's and nursing homes and incontinence and memory deficit. But then I would go out and interview people who were vital after fifty, after sixty, after seventy, even after eighty. Men and women who clearly were continuing to grow and develop. And they exhilarated me. They were much easier to find than I thought they would be. They were all around and in all walks of life. And I wondered if changing the very way you think about yourself could have an effect on the aging process.

Q: *What really convinced you to write this book?*
A: I took a month and looked at every possible major magazine, looking for images of people who might be age sixty-five or older. Photographs, illustrations, ads. And I couldn't find any. So I went down to age fifty, and even then I couldn't. A few rich, powerful men in the news stories. No images whatsoever of older women. Even the ads trying to sell women anti-aging creams would have a young model's face, with maybe one line painted on it.

There were articles about the "problem" of age—these disgusting people that refuse to die, that are living on in such enormous numbers, the "greedy geezers" who are spending all the Social Security, and all of that. But there is never any image of anyone over fifty, over sixty, over seventy doing anything that anybody wants to do in this society. Loving or playing or winning, working or contributing. It is striking, this degree of denial. I remember when I was interviewing in Palm Springs, and a woman with flaming red hair who was clearly older than I said, "Oh, how nice, I hear you're writing a book about those poor old people." And I heard myself say, "No, I'm not writing a book about them. I'm writing a book about us." And she said, "Oh, no, not me! I'm never going to be old."

Q: *If not the "age mystique," then how do you now view aging?*
A: Age is a unique period of human life. Although it's enormously various from individual to individual, the period of vital health in age is increasing, as is longevity in general. Life expectancy today is over seventy-two for men and eighty for women, so one-third to one-half of life may be lived over the age of fifty.

I found very startling things buried in the research. I was amazed to discover that only 5 percent of Americans have Alzheimer's. I was amazed to discover that only 5 percent have senility. I was amazed to discover that men and women aging in the community did not show major deterioration until just before death or well into their eighties.

We have to get beyond the age mystique and begin to see age as a new period of human life. Do you have to love the way you loved when you were thirty or not love at all? Do you have to work the way you worked when you were thirty or not work at all? Do you have to meet your human needs the way you met them when you were thirty or be lonely, sick, and passive victims of age?

A person can continue to grow and develop if one doesn't buy that self-fulfilling prophecy of deterioration and decline. People continue to grow and develop, become more and more themselves after fifty, after sixty, after seventy. They become more whole.

Q: *In this process, what do you believe the role of the older person's physician should be?*
A: Physicians should look on age in terms of its reality, not the mystique that makes us want to avert our eyes from it. People over sixty, over seventy, over eighty, are people, with all the complexity of people. Certain developmental things can happen to them, but deterioration and decline are not inevitable.

When I took some classes in aging at Harvard, the young gerontologists in their white coats would talk about them. Do we burden them too much by asking them to take part in the decision of when we turn off the machine? And the way they talked about them reminded me of many years earlier when the male experts on women would have a conference on the woman problems—them. What do we do about them, these neurotic suburban housewives?

Doctors who treat age itself as disease may not get it. Doctors who maintain that paradigm of medicine only as diagnosis of disease and cure may not get it. People can live for many years with certain conditions. The "fountain of age" is some spring of vitality that I found in people who have recovered from strokes, who have had bypasses, who have serious arthritis. You function. The point of medical care for the last third of life is to maximize function, not necessarily to diagnose and cure.

Certain measures, even those non-medical ones that probably have to be prescribed by a doctor to get paid for by Medicare, can enable people to stay in their own homes, to live independently, to get out and about in the city, to keep on driving. These may be more important than pills, of which all too many are prescribed just to keep older people quiet or get rid of the symptoms.

Q: *What if Medicare doesn't pay physicians to spend that much time with older patients?*
A: Then we have to get after Medicare, don't we? It may be true of all people, but it is certainly true of older people, that expensive, high-tech tests to diag-

nose an isolated symptom are not as important as some sense of the person and how they function.

Q: *For women, one indicator of aging is menopause. How have attitudes changed?*
A: After I wrote *The Feminine Mystique* and would be invited to lecture, I would ask my host to get together for me women who had combined marriage, motherhood, and some profession beyond the home. There were not many such women in any town at that time; the great back-to-work, back-to-school movement had not yet begun. And the women tended to be older than I, because my generation was at home bringing up the baby boomers. But they looked wonderful, these women. They were vital. They looked much more alive than the suburban housewives that I interviewed, who were younger.

And in passing, I happened to mention the menopause. Well, menopause was not something we ever mentioned out loud at that time. It was considered the end of your life. It was terrible, unmentionable. But one after another, these women would say, "No, I didn't have menopause. No, I never had that." Well, of course they had ceased their menstrual cycle, they were no longer reproductive. But they thought they hadn't had menopause, because it was no big deal. They had not taken to their beds with depression. If they had hot flashes, it hadn't debilitated them. And somewhere in my fifties, when I was all involved selling the women's movement, I didn't have the menopause myself.

Q: *In your book, why do you take such a negative view of estrogen replacement therapy?*
A: What is happening today is a new medicalization of menopause. Hormones are big profit makers, and the degree to which these hormones are being pushed really alarms me. A whole generation of women is being told to take these drugs—whether or not there's any real indication—from the time they miss their last period, maybe for the rest of their lives. It's like giving caterpillars injections so that they will never get out of the cocoon and turn into butterflies.

I'm not saying that a woman with a serious problem of incipient osteoporosis might not be well advised by her doctor to take hormones. But not everybody, and not for the normal menopause.

I object to making women be guinea pigs. The returns of the research aren't in yet. It's only now that the Women's Health Initiative of the NIH is doing controlled random study. But the research is indubitable that hormone replacement therapy increases your risk of uterine and breast cancer.

Q: *You describe "the nursing home specter." Why are older people so terrified of nursing homes?*
A: Even at their very best, nursing homes remove a person from the society of the living. In some nursing homes, the personnel don't even call people by their own names. It is just assumed they are no longer people. Too often they are treated as helpless children, sedated or put in restraints to keep them from being a bother to personnel.

In Ellen Langer's research at Harvard, people on one floor of a nursing home were told, "Here's the furniture in your room. You'll have a plant, and the nurse will water it for you every day. We'll show you a movie every Wednesday night, and the nurse will come and get you." On another floor they were told, "It is up to you to rearrange your room the way you want. The nurse will give you a plant, and it is up to you to take care of it. We'll give you a list of the possible movies, and you can decide whether and when you want to go." Six weeks later, the ones who continued to make their own decisions and to water the plants themselves were significantly better in both their physical symptoms and mental health. They are better, and they moved better, and they were more social. Two or three years later, the ones that watered the plants and made their own decisions were still alive, and most of the others were dead. When people give up control over their lives and have no purpose to their days, it is a dehumanizing experience.

Q: *What about planned communities that offer increasing levels of care based on a person's functional level?*
A: I did a lot of interviewing in those manicured age ghettos, and I think they are the denial of age reified in wood and brick and stone. You wall older people off in adult play areas, out of sight of the rest of the community. And they are supposed to keep themselves busy with trivial pursuits. Instead, we need more services that are geared to helping people keep living in the community, either alone or with shared services. It is important to keep living where you can walk or take a bus to where real activities go on.

Q: *How does an older person—as you describe it—"die with life"?*
A: You have to face the fact that life will end in death. If you have a terminal

condition, you shouldn't waste your last days being hooked up to machines or in terrible pain from treatments that are not going to give you significantly more days of human function.

We are moving to a new morality in which choice is as important at the end of life as it is at the beginning of life. But choice at the end of life means more than just living wills and deciding when to turn off the machines. Older people are wrongly blamed for the enormously expensive portion of health care resources that are used in futile efforts to resuscitate them or keep them alive in the very end months of life, beyond the point of human function. Actually, people don't want to die this way.

The hospice movement is a very important development. People who are in the face of death can get help to stay in their own homes with their family and friends around them. The hospice enables you to face death as comfortably as possible, with as little pain as possible.

Q: *How has* The Fountain of Age *been received?*
A: Ten years ago, a book on age might not even have been published, much less become a best seller. The first printing, which was released in September, was 250,000 copies, and most of those were sold in the first month. This response is, I think, the surest signal that we are about to undergo a paradigm shift on the whole approach to aging—from aging in terms of "problem for society" to life as vital aging. This is comparable to what happened to women thirty years ago.

An Interview with Betty Friedan

Kathleen Erickson / 1994

From *The Region*, (September 1994), 16 (3).
Reprinted by permission of The Federal
Reserve Bank of Minneapolis.

Twentieth century history has been driven by great conceptualizers—from Freud's theories of the subconscious to Henry Ford's assembly line. For the women's movement, the great post-war conceptualizer has been Betty Friedan, author of *The Feminine Mystique, The Second Stage,* and most recently, *The Fountain of Age.* It was Friedan's *Feminine Mystique* that initiated a fundamental re-thinking of how women defined themselves, their responsibilities and their choices in the post-war world. It was Friedan who, in *The Second Stage,* challenged the direction of some within the women's movement who have veered toward an increasingly separatist view of women's issues.

And today it is Friedan who emphasizes economics, not sexual politics, as the basis for women's continued progress toward equality. *The Region* met with Ms. Friedan at her home in Sag Harbor, New York, to talk about women and economics.

REGION: *Your writing seems to suggest that achieving gender parity in income is the highest priority for achieving overall gender equality. Is that what you mean to say?*
FRIEDAN: Economic equity is an enormous empowerment of women. Having jobs that provide income means that women can be a more effective force, a more equal force, in the political process. Women with income take themselves more seriously and they are taken more seriously.

I don't mean to say that income is the only benefit women gain from working. Yes, you have to have money to live. But there is something beyond monetary rewards. It is essential to be a part of the ongoing work of society. I've interviewed men and women who've burned out on their jobs, or lost jobs, that have started on new career paths that aren't going to provide the same level of income or status, but that end up being more satisfying. The concept of being part of a community is very, very key to longevity and the quality of one's life. It's a very important theme in *The Fountain of Age*, where I'm looking particularly at issues affecting older men and women.

So it's the two together, income and being involved in a meaningful way in a community that I see as being important. But to address the specific issue of equity, there's no doubt that income is the bottom line.

REGION: *Is that a bottom line on which women have focused?*
FRIEDAN: A poll was done a couple of years ago by the Ms. Foundation and the Center for Policy Alternatives in Washington. The poll asked women— women who were selected across race and class lines—what are the most important issues facing women today? Overwhelmingly, the answers that came back, regardless of the women's race or class, were: getting jobs, keeping jobs, getting promoted in jobs, and how to put jobs together with family, relationships, other parts of women's lives. So yes, I'd say women have the economic bottom line in focus. Having said that, I'd have to acknowledge that within the women's movement, there are certainly those so-called radical feminists, who feel the key issue facing women today is oppression by men. And for these women, progress can be achieved only through a kind of "down with men, down with marriage, down with motherhood" approach.

I'm not politically correct on this point. I abhor political correctness generally, but most particularly in connection with feminism. Implicit within feminism is the need to be responsive to change, responsive to the fundamental conditions of life. To focus on male oppression is to deny the fundamentals. While I can understand the legitimate emotional freight, the anger, that attaches to men's and women's historical roles, I don't see this view as getting us anywhere—and more importantly, I see it as keeping us from dealing with the real conditions that women need to address. Indeed, I see common ground on which men and women must stand together if real progress is to be made.

Certainly a great deal had to change to allow women to begin to achieve the measure of financial and emotional independence women have today. But at this point in time, having raised consciousness regarding women's potential, having put reproductive freedom solidly in place along with legislation that makes discrimination and harassment of women in the workplace illegal, we need to move on.

REGION: *From a public policy perspective, what needs to be done to further the objective of economic parity?*
FRIEDAN: Let me emphasize what I just said: What we're talking about is not just economic parity for women, but more economic choices for men, as well. And I see our needs as being both in public policy and in redefining the corporate bottom line.

Take for instance the corporate downsizing that is so widespread today. It's something that's affecting both men and women. It affects men who've been conditioned to expect the status and security of employment; it affects women who've only just made it into lower and middle management jobs, the jobs most vulnerable to downsizing. There's a risk here that men will begin to see women as the enemy taking jobs, and that women will see men as taking away from them the rewards they've worked so hard to achieve.

In fact, public policy should be addressing the root causes of downsizing and look at all the options, including shorter work weeks. Corporations need to define work in new ways, need to provide more support for job sharing, flex hours, and other policies that would offer a broader range of participation in the work force.

REGION: *When you talk about a shorter work week, one of the first obstacles that comes to mind is remaining competitive in the global market.*
FRIEDAN: What we're talking about here is how we define our public policy objectives, including economic policy. If our public policy objective is to assure broad participation in the work force, to free up men and women to work and raise families and to continue to draw on the experience and abilities of older men and women, as well, then our economic policies need to support that objective.

How do you do that, if you're a public policy maker? Well, maybe world leaders attending international economic summits need to spend more time considering how economic policies can support social objectives. Our economic policies get set at a very high level. What gets considered is the value of the dollar, trade agreements, interest rates. I'm not an economist and I wouldn't for a moment deny the importance of these larger issues. But more effort has to be made to integrate these larger, purely economic policies with social concerns. I don't think anyone fully understands the impact economic policy has on social outcomes. We tend, at the public policy level, to set our macro objectives and then clean up the micro impact in the political process. Social objectives should in some sense drive our economic agenda.

REGION: *Are there economists who are attempting to do this?*
FRIEDAN: Laura D'Andrea Tyson in the Clinton administration—and Robert Reich, too, at Labor—seem very sensitive to these concerns. But we need more people working actively to come up with a new economic paradigm that supports both growth and a more humanistic orientation within the workplace. The costs of not doing this are enormous. There is a great deal of frustration, that borders on rage, that politicians need to be responsive to. We're going to pay one way or the other.

REGION: *It's clear you've been busy writing. What else have you been up to?*
FRIEDAN: One of my objectives over the past several years has been to address economic issues in the context of people's real lives. I started out with a think tank on the evolution of feminist thought under the Institute for the Study of Women and Men at the University of Southern California (USC). That effort ran into problems because I didn't see eye to eye with people in women's studies. The think tank found a new home in the Leadership Institute at the USC business school, where I've taught for the last seven or eight years and hold the position of distinguished visiting professor. I've also given lectures there on women's experience in management and on diversity in management—lectures that are now given to all MBA students.

It has been interesting to me that the business school has been much more open and receptive to these issues than was the more traditional academic setting. I think the reason for that is the business school recognizes that these issues are real—to both employers and employees. Business school's constituencies are looking for solutions to these problems and business schools are being responsive.

On occasion I convene a retreat for women interested in economic issues—we met at the Xerox conference center this past January to deal with new economic thinking that is essential to women. And I'm going to be a

Wilson Fellow in Washington this fall, which will be a wonderful opportunity to focus on women and economics.

REGION: *Earlier you mentioned the need to redefine the corporate bottom line . . .*
FRIEDAN: I mean something rather broader than the "bottom line" in a profit sense. We need to redefine how corporations are organized and managed. There's increasing consciousness that a "command and control" style of management which one associates with a male model isn't necessarily what works anymore, especially with small to medium sized companies. There's increasing evidence that a more flexible management style, where responsibility is distributed up and down the line, is what works best. And that kind of management style is one that will allow individual workers more flexibility—men and women. It's also a style I think women are inherently well-prepared to implement and to be effective at within the corporate setting.

REGION: *What's your reaction to anecdotal evidence that women are electing to climb down the corporate ladder—that after investing a lot in education and training that prepares them to be full participants in the corporate environment, they opt out?*
FRIEDAN: I think it's tremendously important that women continue to be full participants in the corporate environment, and that they continue to seek the same responsibilities, opportunities and rewards in that environment that in the past have only been available to men. Having said that, I also would have to say we haven't gained much if we define success narrowly, if we see women as making progress only if they make it to the top of a corporation.

If women see a better future for themselves, financially, in human terms, or in terms of doing something that's more fulfilling than what's available within a corporate structure, they should go for it. And there's evidence that's exactly what they're doing. I've seen statistics indicating that women are getting Small Business loans at a rate six times greater than men. That means women are out there on the cutting edge of the economy. As I've already said, it's not clear that the male model of success is working very well for men these days. Why should women tie themselves to a male model of success—much less an outdated model? One of the true measures of achievement for women is that we're starting to create our own definitions, not just using the old definitions. And incidentally, there's also anecdotal evidence that suggests men are questioning the traditional definition of success, that men are "opting out." Men have a lot to gain from not being tied into a 9 to 5, corporate life as their only option.

REGION: *What about women who want to define success solely in terms of their role in the family. Is that an acceptable model for today's woman within a feminist construct?*
FRIEDAN: Of course it is, as long as it meets the woman's needs as well as the family's needs. I do think women who make that choice are doing so with some degree of risk. Research has indicated that women's standard of living fell enormously following divorce reform. Our courts, in divorce cases, haven't always been consistent in recognizing a woman's contribution when she's cho-sen to make that contribution within the home. I do think this has been a transitional issue, it has largely affected an entire generation of women who did not have independent incomes—but for women who chose not to work at paying jobs, the issue becomes one of judicial equity. And of course, apart from divorce, there is always the question of what happens to a woman who is left a widow where there isn't an estate to meet her ongoing needs? There's emotional risk, as well. If you put all of your skills and energy into other people—your children, your husband—and your children grow up and your husband dies or leaves, you lose the context of community I talked about earlier.

REGION: *Much of what you're saying would suggest that you see income as being the root of most of our social ills. Do you think income is more significant than race or gender as a determinant of success?*
FRIEDAN: There is no denying that there has been and is still discrimination on the basis of gender and of race. Furthermore, in a time of economic stress, there's a danger of women and people of color becoming scapegoats. But I do believe that access to employment and earning is key; once that's in place, many of the social problems are relieved. There's no question that the black middle class has benefitted greatly by the civil rights movement. But there is a large black underclass that still does not have access to jobs. If there's no clear road to income and status except crime, we should expect social prob-lems. You can't solve this problem without addressing the economic issues, and the same is true with gender.

REGION: *Is welfare reform necessary?*
FRIEDAN: Don't make the welfare mother the scapegoat for our economic prob-

lems. There are a lot of mistaken stereotypes here. The typical welfare mother is not necessarily black, she doesn't keep having children on welfare, and she doesn't have all that many children. And eliminating welfare all together would have an insignificant impact on the economy. As far as the suggestion that's being widely discussed—two years on welfare and that's it—that isn't practical if there aren't jobs at the end of two years. There have to be good jobs and good child care.

REGION: *Is the women's movement still relevant today—politically and in creating the kind of change you're supporting?*
FRIEDAN: It is certainly still needed. We've come a long way, but we haven't begun to go far enough. Where I think the movement is vulnerable is in what I've already mentioned: Creating battle lines—between men and women, old and young, black and white—isn't going to meet anyone's needs. It is also true that there is now a whole generation of women who take what's been achieved for granted. They don't understand the need to keep working to protect what we have and to achieve more. They think what they have is an irrevocable entitlement, when in fact civil rights, historically, have been won and lost before. We could lose ground again.

I had a call from a woman in Rhode Island. She was a reporter who wanted to do a story on why the women's movement in Rhode Island had died. By "died" she meant that no one was going to meetings, marching, chaining themselves to fences anymore. I told her, that's not what's needed anymore. We need to integrate our objectives for jobs into economic policy discussions. We need to be actively engaged in corporate settings, fighting for the kind of changes that will make the work place responsive to the changing needs of women and men. Marches and "events" were a necessary part of the evolution of the women's movement, but what was needed 75 years ago isn't necessarily what's needed now.

One of the remarkable changes that has taken place in the woman's movement since *The Feminine Mystique* was published is that women using their rights has been normalized. Important rights were won—on paper—75 years ago, but the women who used those rights were by and large women who didn't marry and didn't have children. And they were viewed in a negative way by society as being spinsters. Before *The Feminine Mystique,* the great majority of the few women who were in *Who's Who* were unmarried.

Looking at my own experiences, as recently as 1958, when I was a graduate of Smith, the best women's college in America, I knew nothing of feminism, I knew very little of the battle for women's rights that took place in the last century and in the first half of this century. I thought of feminists—if I thought of them at all—as a group of neurotic spinsters suffering from penis envy. I was, after all, a psychology major, and I'd been very much influenced by Freud.

When I started to examine my own life, my mother's life—that's when I began to question the limits of women's lives and the way we were defined. And it was shocking to find how much that had been forgotten, how it had atrophied because it had not been carried into the mainstream. We need to keep those ideals active in the mainstream.

REGION: *Where do you go from here?*
FRIEDAN: I've spent twenty-five to thirty years focusing on women's issues and the last ten years on women and men and age. As I said before, I see no solutions in terms of power blocks. What is needed is a new vision of community, a higher vision of the good of a whole community that transcends polarization of groups. Groups have been effective in the past in achieving equality. Now we're in a position where the only way progress can continue is through a new definition of community. What is positive today—and I saw this clearly in the research I did for *The Fountain of Age*—is that the narrow focus of material status, the need to conform, are viewed today as irrelevant issues. People are looking for meaning in their daily lives. That means that there's a potential for people to come together to protect the ongoing stream of life in generations to come.

REGION: *That's a good way to end. Thank you, Ms. Friedan.*

A Conversation with Betty Friedan

Denise Watson / 1995

From *The Virginian-Pilot*, (4 May 1995), E1.
Reprinted by permission of *The Virginian-Pilot.*

Betty Friedan had a run in her stockings. Not just a run. A RUN. A marathon of gnarled, off-black nylon and lycra that gaped and grew, zigged and zagged until it disappeared into the depths of her black skirt. But she didn't care. Why should she? The mother of feminism has spent half her life teaching women to care about things that matter most, and a run in a stocking isn't one of them.

Friedan moved women beyond the world of hosiery and other social tethers in the early 1960s when she chronicled the disillusionment of many housewives in her book, *The Feminine Mystique.* In 1966, Friedan founded the National Organization for Women and helped organize the National Women's Political Caucus. In her most recent book, *The Fountain of Age*, seventy-four-year-old Friedan tackles aging, and challenges folks to look at those latter years with acceptance rather than dread.

A visiting distinguished professor of public policy this semester at George Mason University, Friedan took a few minutes to discuss aging, the future of feminism and Newt Gingrich as she relaxed in her office on the college campus.

"There is this war now. This war on the welfare mothers. It's like the canaries in the coal mines," said Friedan, visibly tired but her gravelly voice still fresh. "The rage of that angry white male is being manipulated into a polarizing thing. . . . It's turning the white men, blacks, immigrants, the women against each other."

Here are some questions we collected from readers. Following are excerpts from that conversation.

Do you have any advice for a sixteen-year-old starting off and looking into the feminist movement? There are many negative things said about feminism. What does she accept and disregard?

"For a sixteen-year-old, the feminist movement has a lot to offer. Because now she can take herself seriously as a person, as a full person, and she has to make decisions about her own life, whereas her mother was supposed to only think about catching a man. Little girls weren't even asked, 'What do you want to be when you grow up?' Girls received, 'You're a pretty little girl, you'll be a mommy just like your mommy.'"

"We've done that in the women's movement for equality, which is the major expression of feminism. We've done that to the point where this sixteen-year-old and her generation can take for granted opportunities their mothers never even thought of.

"And I know it's been fashionable in recent years to say, 'I'm not a feminist. But I think I'm going to go to law school and maybe I'll be a senator, or a judge, marry a nice guy if I want to, when I want to.' All kinds of choices are taken for granted now. But I think it would be good for her to study the history of feminism because the rights that are taken for granted now, the opportunities that are taken for granted now, are in danger with this Contract on America group. What a war on women and children! And what a backlash against women! And to be prepared for that, to be able to say rather proudly and strongly, 'I am a feminist.'

"Let her disregard some of the rhetoric that the media sometimes plays up beyond its proportion in the movement itself. Feminism does not mean down with men, down with marriage, down with motherhood, down with sexuality. Those are some of what I consider distorted voices that have come out of feminism.

"But the reality of the women's movement for equality is that it's made life better for men as well as women. The fact that women are able to work now and earn, she doesn't earn as much as a man, but she earns more than she would've thought she could ever earn twenty years ago. The man doesn't have to be the sole breadwinner. It's better for the whole family.

"But there is a war now. This war on the welfare mothers, it's like the canaries in the coal mines. The rage of that angry white male is being manipulated into a polarizing thing. Gingrich and the attack on affirmative action churn the white men, blacks, immigrants, the women against each other. That is a diversion from the real economic imbalances leading to the growing frustration of the middle class men and women. But it's also a diversion to see it in too narrow gender terms because men are not the enemy here. Only some men, that are using their power to manipulate this backlash against women, against people of color."

Looking back at all of your work, is there anything you would have done differently?

"If someone had written my book when I was twenty years old, who know? I might've gone into law school and ended up on the Supreme Court. Or I might've been an archaeologist and lead great digs, or who knows what? I might've married later, but I'm glad I had the children I had. I think I've made good use of my life even though I didn't have a conventional career, but I have helped make the possibilities of life better for the next generation. That's why the women's movement, I think, is a miracle and a wonderful thing. A life opening, life-affirming evolution of our democracy of the last twenty, thirty years. That and the black civil rights movement.

"But I think we have to move on now. What I see so needed now is a new vision. I think we've gone as far as we can go with separate movement— women's rights, gay rights, black rights. At this point, there has to be confronting of the dangers of the backlash, of the polarization of groups against each other, while the rich are getting richer, and the Gingrich people with their Contract on America are going to destroy sixty years of social progress.

"I've been reading the papers in Washington very carefully and, with the many comments I've read, I have never seen lobbyists for business, big business, so openly writing the laws. As they are, sitting down with the Newt Gingrich gang and actually dictating how the laws should be written to get rid of the regulations that have protected the American people."

How does a woman who feels defeated from hitting the glass ceiling heal and redeem herself? What actions should she take?

"Well, I know what a lot of women are doing. They're starting their own businesses. They're leaving the corporate world and, in a certain sense, the cutting edge of our economy today is entrepreneurial. And more Americans today work for companies owned or managed by women, than the Fortune 500. But on the other hand, I don't think you give up the battle to break the glass ceiling. I don't think we can lie back and let Newt Gingrich and his gang get rid of affirmative action. Because the facts are, 95 percent of the top executives in management in every business are white males."

Who were the most influential people in your life?

"Since I am a product of psychological training, my mother and my father."

One woman says she's read all of your books but now wonders if the rise in crime and drug use among kids can be linked to women working outside the home.

"The research shows that's absolutely not true. That in the last forty years, where for the first time American women worked from choice and not just from drastic family emergencies, like desertion or alcoholism from a husband, all kinds of research shows that children of families where woman worked, were psychologically in better mental health, had more self-confidence, than children of full-time housewives."

Is your current focus on aging, and getting people to see aging as a positive instead of a negative aspect of life, more rewarding than your work in women's issues?

"It's an evolution, that's all. That I was able to write *The Feminine Mystique*, that I was able to start the women's movement was wonderful. As my grandson would say, 'Awesome!' And I look back and I'm marveled that I was able to do that, that I had the nerve.

"It's hard to even realize now how taken for granted that feminine mystique was. I hit a chord in so many American women and each one thought she was alone in that suburb, that sexual ghetto where nothing stirred between the house of 9 to 5, over 3 feet tall, that if she wasn't having an orgasm waxing the kitchen floor, something was wrong with her. That no matter how much she wanted those kids, her husband and all that, the appliances, the station wagon, . . . she might ask herself, 'But who am I? The world is going on without me?' And I called it the problem that has no name.

"By putting a name to that problem, and by taking women seriously and their own experience seriously, I was able to free women to take their experience seriously. And women are still stopping me today and telling me it changed their life. I also see, as much as for women, that books like mine, and whatever meaning that comes out of them, will enable people over fifty to see their lives in new terms and possibilities.

"And you'll see, when younger people get it in their gut that there is life beyond youth and not to dread it. That there's a whole ever-changing, eighty-year life-span, it will enable you to make different decisions and explore different paths all the way along."

After the Mystique Is Gone

Jennifer Chapin Harris / 1997

First printed in *Off Our Backs* newsjournal,
(March 1997), v. 27, n. 9. Reprinted by
permission of *Off Our Backs*.

We owe a great deal to Betty Friedan, author of *The Feminine Mystique*, the
book which caused so many Americans to question the 1950s idealization of
the "Leave It to Beaver" family. Without her work, most American girls would
probably still grow up thinking they could only become housewives. By participating in founding such political organizations as the National Organization for Women (NOW) and the National Abortion Rights Action League
(NARAL), she pioneered the way for other major feminist victories in this half
of the twentieth century.

Yet her brand of feminism is not universally accepted. In the July/August
1995 issue of *Ms.*, Rita Mae Brown published an article entitled "Reflections of
a Lavender Menace: Remember when the movement tried to keep lesbians in
the closet?" There, Brown wrote, "The second wave of the women's movement
. . . shivered in mortal terror of lesbians. I told the truth about myself at one
of the early National Organization for Women (NOW) meetings in 1967,
which meant that women in Pucci dresses tore their hemlines squeezing one
another to get out the door. A short time thereafter Betty Friedan helped coin
the term 'Lavender Menace,' although I don't know if she wants to take credit
for it. And a short time after that, I was unceremoniously shown the door."
Indeed, when I listened to a lecture she gave in April at my school, St. Mary's
College of Maryland, I got the impression that Friedan prioritizes public opin-

ion as a means of gaining ground for feminism. Many of my feminist professors at school, however, played down any possible negativity about Friedan.

In the end, after reading Friedan's work, listening to her lecture, interviewing her, and speaking to other feminist scholars about her, I have a mixed image—both positive and negative—of her in my mind. I do not know how accurate or fair my idea of Friedan is, so I offer readers the transcript of my interview so that they can decide for themselves.

OOB: *How would you say feminism has changed since the publication of* The Feminine Mystique?

BF: When I wrote *The Feminine Mystique,* which was published in 1963, the whole previous century's battle for women's rights that began in 1848 with Seneca Falls, the first declaration of women's rights (it's about to be 150 years since then) had all been buried from the national consciousness and personal consciousness. We were in the era when there was only one image of woman: woman defined only in sexual relation to men—men's wife, mother, housewife, sex object, server of physical needs to husband, children, home. This was absolutely so prevailing that each woman thought there was something wrong with her. She was a freak, she was alone if, no matter how much she had wanted to marry that guy and get that house and appliances and all the things that were supposed to be woman's dream in the era of the idealization of the suburb after World War II, and no matter how much she had wanted the husband and two, three children, which were supposed to be the limit of women's fulfillment, if she had the feeling that something was missing, she needed to be or do something else, that the world was passing her by, she thought something was wrong with her. I called it the problem that has no name and *The Feminine Mystique,* the book, my book and others that followed it, broke through that obsolete definition of women that was limiting their vision of their own possibilities and necessities to move in society as a whole in the 80 year life span that is now American women's. The personhood of women—that's what it was all about, and we had to break through that feminine mystique, to say women are people, no more, no less, to demand our human and American birthright, equal opportunity to participate in the mainstream of society and our own voice in the major decisions of society, and we did that.

Feminism had become a dirty word in that era of the feminine mystique.

The movement for women's equality has been a very life-affirming, life-opening [one] and it has transformed the lives and the aspirations of women in this last quarter century. The Women's Movement for equality is what it's all about and was about as far as I'm concerned. It was also about going beyond the male model to put the value also on women's experience and not man as the measure of all things, but it's also a different kind of man.

Women are moving in society. Now women are half the labor force, and the great majority of women are working outside the home for most of the years of their lives. They are in every profession. It's gone from 4% or less than that in law school and medical school to 40%. Women are not just cooking the church supper anymore, but they are preaching the sermons. They are defining the rubrics in every profession on the basis of women's experience and not just men's. That's been an enormous creative thing for our society as a whole. Once we broke the feminine mystique and the male definitions and began to take seriously our own experience, there was new thinking in every field as far as modern feminism is concerned.

As far as I'm concerned, it is the women's movement for equality. It is not women against men. There were perversions of modern feminism. Women had suppressed anger (when you're completely dependent you can't express anger) that they had a right to feel if they were put down as they were. [For example,] there was the invisible woman in the office, even if she ran it practically as a secretary. Nurses had to stand up when the doctors came into the hospital. The girls didn't aspire to be doctors.

Women were put down even on the pedestal at home. There could well be anger, and there was anger, but the men were also victims of the obsolete narrow sex roles. Men are dying eight years younger than women in America. It wasn't women against men as far as I'm concerned. Women had to break through the male definitions; women had to demand and get equality. We are now in the next stage [of] what seems to me to be redefining all of our essential values and rubrics of every field on the basis of women's experience as well as men's. Men are becoming a different kind of men. The next big breakthrough has to be men, because they shouldn't be dying so young. They have to break through the obsolete machismo definition of masculinity.

Feminism . . . there are many different voices in feminism. There was, it seems to me, a perversion of feminism for a while that seemed to define it as "down with men, down with marriage, down with motherhood." You know, down with everything women had ever done to attract men, the brutes. Down with everything men had ever done in history, the male chauvinist pigs, the patriarchs, the brutes. There was a germ of truth in it, but basically it expressed the anger. But it was, it seems to me, ideologically and politically and actually fallacious. There wouldn't have been the life-opening, life-changing effect of the women's movement if that had been really its main message. The thrust was, for me, equal participation in society. And then that changes everything, including marriage, including children, motherhood. The other one of the two very important things the Women's Movement has done has been the movement for equality in every field and the movement of women into making the decisions and defining the terms, not just men, and the whole question of choice—those have been very important things.

OOB: *How should modern feminist deal with backlash from "angry white men?"*

BF: Well, I don't see that much backlash. I think that if this economy falls, then you will see backlash. Women are easily scapegoated for men's frustration. If there is increased violence against women, and I'm not sure there is, it may be that women are not accepting what they've passively had to accept and be victims of before. They didn't have a word for sex discrimination a few years ago, much less sexual harassment, so it may be just that women are not accepting what used to be considered man's right. It's no longer [a] man's right to beat [his] wife, not only in the United States, but as a result of Beijing and the whole Women's Movement worldwide, even in UN documents it's no longer a man's right to beat his wife. But if there is increased violence against women in the US now, I think it's because frustrations of men are being taken out on women. It is men, and college educated white men that have suffered nearly a 20% drop in income in the last six or seven years, not the upper two or ten percent of the very rich, but 80% have incomes that have stagnated or declined. The downsizing has hit mainly men and men can no longer count on that steady progression in [a] life-long career or profession, a job that used to define men's masculinity. I think that they may be taking this out on women, and women have often been the scapegoat of men's frustration in times of economic uncertainty.

OOB: *How do you see feminist values as different from "traditional family values" when the Republicans talk about them?*

BF: Well, I teach a course and run a symposium series at Mount Vernon [College], where I'm teaching now, on rethinking family values. The values of nurturing and responsibility and commitment and shared life . . . and affirmation and respect for each person's unique identity, are the family values, it seems to me, that are alive and well in many diverse forms of family today. When the right wing, religious right, reactionary Republican element goes on and on about the lack of "family values," they're using that term as a sort of a hype for their opposition to women's autonomy, to women's choice, to abortion, to divorce, to women's control over their own sexuality, to women's demand for equality. I would also use the term "family values," but I mean the mutual responsibility for nurturing, for caring, for shared life and commitment. I think you can find these today in many different forms. Very few Americans are living that traditional form of family. So that traditional form of family—mom as the housewife and papa the breadwinner and the two children who never seem to go beyond five or six [years old]—that is a dying form. Most people don't [live] that [way] in America now, although they may have for some years of their lives, or they may have had their childhood in such a form. But the two paycheck family, the single parent family, the his, hers, and theirs family—there are all these forms of family. The value is the mutual responsibility, commitment, the sharing, the nurturing.

OOB: *Where do you think feminism will go or should go in the future?*
BF: Well, I think feminism has opened life for women and therefore for children and men in this country. It has been enormously transformative. We are just beginning to see the creative aspects of it. The addition of as many as two women to a state legislature changes the agenda, not just in the direction of life, of the values of life, of priorities for life, whether it's the well or the sick, or the young, the old, children, the poor, the environment—these are the values that women would give priority to, not just the abstractions like balancing the budget. We're just beginning to see that in every field, as women come in and define the terms and not just men. But you're also beginning to see a new kind of man who also is getting that sensitivity to life as he carries the baby in the backpack.

Feminism's Matriarch

Robert Selle / 1998

From *World and I*, (May 1998), 50. Reprinted
by permission of *The World and I*.

Betty Friedan was brutalized by injustice early in life—but it had nothing
to do with bias against women. In her Peoria, Illinois, high school, Jews were
not welcome in sororities or fraternities, which played a big role at school.
And Betty Goldstein was very much a Jew.

Even though she was brilliant in her academics, shone as a writer poet, and
started a literary magazine, she was socially shunned because of her ethnicity.
To make matters worse, she was afflicted with asthma "and a big complex
about being unattractive," she said in an interview. But by focusing on her
studies and her writing, she got ahead dazzlingly, graduating first in her class
in 1942 from Smith College—where she also edited the college newspaper.
Then she did graduate work, becoming a fellow in psychology at the University of California at Berkeley.

Once she completed her stay at Berkeley, she moved to Greenwich Village
and married Carl Friedan, a World War II veteran. Her first child was born in
1949. But it was her second child that played a role, even while in the womb,
in her other jarring collision with injustice. "I didn't have so much concern
with women's issues as such," Friedan says, "till as a labor reporter I was fired
from my job on a leftist newspaper because I was pregnant." That awakened
her as never before to the second-class status of women in American society.
Following her dismissal, she free-lanced for magazines for years to augment
the family income.

For her fifteenth college reunion, she conducted a survey of her Smith classmates, and it was from this bit of research that her blockbuster 1963 book, *The Feminine Mystique*, came. It struck a chord in the hearts of millions of women across the world and helped get the 1964 Civil Rights Act passed. It also sparked the creating of the National Organization for Women in 1966. The fight for job and pay equity for women had begun in earnest.

By 1975, however, Friedan felt that NOW had gotten off course and had become largely irrelevant to basic women's issues. She lambasted the organization she founded for seemingly veering from the problems of mainsteam women and job equity to instead immersing itself in lesbian politics. The exasperated Friedan—who is now seventy-seven, divorced, the mother of three, and grandmother of seven—even once jokingly characterized the lesbian faction of the women's movement as the "lavender menace." She protested NOW's direction by forming her own network of moderate feminists.

Her 1981 book, *The Second Stage*, presented a withering analysis of what she saw as the extremes of the feminist movement. It lauded motherhood and other traditional feminist "whipping boys."

Friedan—who in recent years has been a visiting professor at the University of Southern California, New York University, George Mason University, and Florida International University, as well as Distinguished Professor of Social Evolution at Mount Vernon College—also spoke out boldly at the 1995 Beijing global women's conference, which tended to cold-shoulder conservative women's groups and other voices favoring women's traditional roles. She told fellow delegates that "the language of rage and sexual politics" was disaffecting large numbers of career- and family-oriented women.

"A significant number of the younger women say, 'I am not a feminist at heart, but I'm going to law school,' 'I'm going to come of age here,' 'I'm going to be an astronaut,' or whatever. But feminism has got the image of either anti-man, anti-sex victims or the image of super-ambitious, selfish career professionals ignoring realities of family life and the progress we've made," she said at the time. For all her vitriol towards NOW and other radicals, however, Friedan—who splits her time between Miami Beach; Sag Harbor, New York; and Washington, D.C.—has remained firmly planted within the greater feminist movement.

But today she discerns a turning point in U.S. and world history that she feels demands a reevaluation of feminist priorities—and that may presage a convergence of female and male interests. The convergence comes in the form of job and pay equity for women, and job and pay security for men. The corporate downsizing phenomenon—in which hundreds of thousands of workers and middle managers, predominantly males, lost their jobs over the past decade—has brought the issue poignantly home to men.

Friedan favors a shorter work week of perhaps thirty hours that would at one stroke widen employment opportunities, strengthen job security, and provide more free time for today's highly stressed two-earner and single-parent families.

"People's priorities—men's and women's alike—should be affirming life, enhancing life, not greed," she says, declaring that this is the wave of the future. "We're on the cusp of a paradigm shift: We're the richest, most powerful nation in the world, and nobody is addressing the larger philosophical question of what values we should have for the future," intones Friedan, who has never been a religious person but who says she only recently "recognized a dimension of religiousness" in her life.

"The way the women's movement has looked at men is how the Nazis looked at the Jews: that they had all the power, the money, etc.," she says. But now "the answer is not women against men. Instead, we have to have alternatives to downsizing. We need a broader definition of success, both in personal career terms and corporate terms. In reality, we have to move toward a new kind of family, a new kind of partnership," she says. "Men have to move to a new definition of masculinity. I think family values are very important, but we have to reframe them in terms of new economic and demographic realities. If you haven't been downsized, it might happen to someone you know."

friedan's new Agenda: fairness to Men, Too

Linda Myers / 1998

From the *Cornell Chronicle*, (3 December 1998).
Reprinted by permission of Linda Myers and
the *Cornell Chronicle*.

Betty Friedan would like to develop a quality of life measure—let's call it QOL—similar to economic measures like the Gross Domestic Product (GDP) that we've created to plumb our nation's economic health.

A QOL index would not only be used to measure success in individuals; Friedan would like to see it applied to companies and communities as well. "It's not impossible to do," said the woman who has made a career of making the difficult look easy. In the early 1960s, when she was fired from her job as a news reporter because she was pregnant, she used the free time to write a book, *The Feminine Mystique*, that launched a feminist revolution.

She has been going strong ever since. At seventy-seven the founder of the National Organization for Women has just returned from a whirlwind lecture tour of Europe, where she discovered a group of young women in Budapest who had been so inspired by her book that they began a feminist network in their native Hungary, despite opposition from the then-prevailing Communist regime. "I was very moved," Friedan said. "We really are living in a global village."

Friedan, a distinguished visiting professor at Cornell University's School of Industrial and Labor Relations who will be speaking on the university's Ithaca, N.Y., campus Dec. 2 and 3, credits the women's movement with playing a transformative role in American society. "I feel very lucky and almost awed to have been part of it. If we look back—although who has time?—we have to realize that we have changed the way women look at themselves and the way society looks at women, and that's been all to the good. Women's lives are no longer defined solely by marriage and children. These may be important to them, but they may only be part of the picture. Women now have choices."

It gratifies Friedan to see women working in every profession today and legislation in place prohibiting gender discrimination in the workplace. So what's next? Friedan's most-recent book, *Beyond Gender: The New Politics of Work and Family* (Woodrow Wilson Center Press, 1997), points the way to a new revolution. This time she aims to transform the world by using the feminist ideals of equality and justice to shape a broad societal and workplace agenda for men as well as women.

Now the director of "New Paradigm: Women, Men, Work, Family and Public Policy," a project sponsored by the Cornell ILR School's Institute for Women and Work, Friedan already has brought together policy-makers and researchers to talk. The Cornell sponsorship, plus a $1 million Ford Foundation grant, led her to develop monthly seminars and symposiums in Washington, D.C., on critical workplace issues.

"I'm trying to take the dialogue that I've helped shape and change the focus from women's rights to how jobs are structured for both men and women," explained Friedan. Although the workplace has changed radically since women began entering it in large numbers in the 1970s, jobs, career lines, training and professional advancement are all still based on the model of the employee with a non-working partner who takes care of life's details.

That model is out of step with reality, observed Friedan. "No one has moved to shorten the work week. In fact it's getting longer. That's ridiculous. We're co-opted by a culture of greed, as if the only measure of worth is how much someone earns."

New Paradigm's Oct. 28 symposium focused on men, with Friedan pointing out: "Men who play an active role in parenting live longer," a finding she saw as an incentive for them to achieve a better balance between work and life. The program's next symposium, Dec. 10, will look at trends among companies to contract out, rather than hire new staff, and its impact on working families. Friedan also co-teaches a course, "The New Paradigm: The Changing American Workplace and Family Life," with Francine Moccio, director of the ILR School's Institute for Women and Work and principal investigator for the New

Paradigm Project. The course gives Cornell students in Washington, D.C., an interdisciplinary look at such issues as the gender gap in wages and such workplace trends as privatization and downsizing, and features talks by practitioners as well as scholars.

Friedan has a strong response to biographer Daniel Horowitz's take on her life. In *Betty Friedan and the Making of The Feminine Mystique* (University of Massachusetts, 1998), the Smith College professor faulted her for portraying herself as merely a suburban housewife who discovered feminism while peeling potatoes at the kitchen table. He declared that she wasn't candid about her work as a reporter for union newspapers.

"He's got it so wrong it annoys me," she said. She made it clear that her feminism did not arise from exposure to left-wing ideologists during her reporting days. "They were every bit as male chauvinist as the rest of the world." She also turned on its head Horowitz's claim that she exaggerated her role as a housewife: "I was a suburban housewife. When I got fired from my newspaper job, my husband and I bought a big, old house overlooking the Hudson. I personally took off five coats of paint by hand and went to auctions hunting for furniture bargains. I enjoyed it." But she never presented herself as just a housewife. "That was the gestalt of the times."

While wheeling her first child in his stroller, she canvassed for Democratic candidates in Rockland County. And before writing her world-changing book, she wrote for such women's magazines as *Redbook* and *Ladies Home Journal* to help pay the grocery bills. That experience, as much as anything, helped shape her feminist consciousness. A former psychology student, she sensed a prevailing dissatisfaction among her female contemporaries that wasn't reflected in the magazines. "I realized I could use all my experience to challenge the ethos that I had been part of creating." She was recently named one of the hundred most important women in the 20th century in a book published under the *Ladies Home Journal's* name, and she enjoys the irony of that honor—she is unlikely to have made the list had she remained just a freelance writer for the magazine.

The self-described "American revolutionary" has three grown children, all in established careers, and seven grandchildren—but don't expect her to settle into grandmotherhood when the New Paradigm project ends in four years. "Maybe I'll write a whodunit," she said, "with a bumptious feminist sleuth" whose simplistic feminist values are challenged at every turn. "Life," Friedan said, "is more complex than that."

The New Frontier of Feminism: Busting the Masculine Mystique

Nathan Gardels / 1998

From *New Perspectives Quarterly*, (Winter 1998),
50 (3). Reprinted with permission of *New
Perspectives Quarterly*.

NPQ: *Over thirty years ago now, the publication of* The Feminine Mystique *gave birth to the movement for women's equality. The advance of women in the last half of the twentieth century is without doubt the deepest social transformation of our time. In your view, what have been the key successes of the women's movement? What have been its failures, shortcomings and diversions?*

BF: More than anything else, *The Feminine Mystique* brought about a paradigm shift in consciousness. In the United States, there had been more than a 100-year battle to win the vote for women. But, then, the movement for equality seemed to abort. Women's energies got diverted to issues like temperance—how to deal with drunken husbands—and other social-work causes. Women fighting for themselves as equal persons in society—not just as a man's wife, mother, sex object, daughter, housewife—reemerged with the publication of my book in 1963.

Once you broke through the feminine mystique by slamming the door, as Nora did in Henrik Ibsen's *Doll House*, and saying, "I am above all else a person, just as you are," could you see the barriers that stood in women's way.

Remember, also, this was the early 1960s, at the height of the civil rights movement and the beginning of the anti-Vietnam war movement. There was a feeling in the air that one could take action to change the conditions of society, to liberate those who were oppressed.

Now, nearly forty years later, the women's movement has succeeded, at least in the advanced countries, beyond my wildest dreams. The change is awesome. Women today are getting an equal number of professional degrees. In 1997, there is only a 26-cent differential in pay between women and men in mid-level jobs. Though the "glass ceiling" remains at the highest executive levels, it is only a matter of time before women break through. Women, who used to vote just like their husbands did, have become a potent force politically. In the United States, it was women who elected Bill Clinton as president. The "gender gap" in his election was around 20 percent.

Our daughters' and granddaughters' generation just can't imagine a time when women weren't taken seriously, when the political and social agenda was not defined by women's experience as well as by men's. So, at the end of the twentieth century in the advanced Western countries, women are in a state of very-near equality with men. This is a marvelous transformation from the days when I wrote *The Feminine Mystique*. The success of the women's movement has certainly been the most life-affirming experience of the twentieth century.

NPQ: *What about the failures and diversions of the women's movement?*
BF: I don't see any failures. Diversions, yes. The biggest diversion was the extremist personal sexual politics that drew a literal analogy between the oppression of women and race or class oppression. That deteriorated into a marginal politics that said, "down with men, down with marriage, down with motherhood." The perception this extremist politics created that the women's movement was just a bunch of lesbians did not help our cause. The media hyped this extremism, but, since the early 1980s, thankfully, it has faded.

My view then, as now, is that one's sexual preference is a private matter. The whole point of writing a book like *The Feminine Mystique* was to break through the definition of women solely in terms of their sexual relationship to men, as mother, housewife and servant. It would have been a big mistake to remystify women once again as sexual beings only and not as free persons in society.

NPQ: *What about the later backlash of the mid-1980s that blamed growing divorce rates and breakdown of the family on women who "abandoned" the home for work and, in the conservative critique, asserted their rights over their obligations to their husbands and children? The phrase that summed up this critique was "women can't have it all," meaning they can't have both kids and careers without doing damage to the family.*

BF: That is an absolutely stupid phrase. What it really means is that men can have it all, but women can't. Men can have love, sex, children and jobs, but women can't.

In fact, the women's movement made it possible for both parents to have more. Men also used to carry the sole burden of income. That stress made them fragile emotionally and vulnerable physically. They died too young, on the average of eight years younger than women. Now women carry half the burden. So, maybe men won't die so much younger. The point is, motherhood now comes as a choice. And a chosen motherhood is far better than the old motherhood as a prison.

NPQ: *Let us put the question another way: Can parents have it all without damaging the kids? If, together, both parents are working 80 hours a week to keep up the mortgage payments while the kids are shunted off to child care, is that a good thing? What conditions are necessary to make the family function?*

BF: Flexible time at work. A shorter workweek. Better, more affordable child care. Whatever criticism of child care there may be, the fact is that without child care there can be no equality for women. In short, we need to put the value of quality of life over material greed and status that seems to dictate all social relations today. When I look at American society now I sometimes see a big, stagnant pond covered by the green scum of materialism, but with small springs bubbling up from underneath. Those wellsprings of the common good, of the idea of a life that balances family and work, need to be encouraged. The women's movement, as a force for life, ought to concern itself with these issues.

NPQ: *Alva Myrdal, the late Swedish sociologist, once made the point that women could have it all, but in succession. Since women lived longer than men, they could have motherhood first, then a career. Of course, a woman's opportunity in such a society would then depend on the absence of age discrimination. Is there anything in this idea from your point of view?*

BF: As a society, we haven't yet come to terms with the extended life spans made possible by the creature comforts, nutrition and medical advances of modern times. Women's average life expectancy today is 80 years. For men it is seventy-two, and will be longer as they are released from the stressful burdens of being the sole income provider. People living into their eighties today are very vital, with few signs of deterioration. Hence, the whole notion that people ought to retire from active life at age sixty-five or less is entirely obsolete.

Increasingly, as Alva Myrdal foresaw, people are talking more and more of "my next career" or my "third career." If you start again in your sixties or later, you don't have to prove yourself. You don't have to support a family anymore or put the kids through college. So, you tend to do what interests you, not what you have to do. You revive dreams. I know a retired banker who became a nurse. I know people who have taken up composing music at seventy. The longer horizon of life also affects your choices earlier in life. It relieves the fear of having only one chance to make it and opens up life to more adventures and choices than was ever before possible in human history.

NPQ: *If the women's movement has reached most of its goals, what is next on the agenda?*
BF: Busting the masculine mystique. The unfinished business of the women's movement is changing the role of man. Equality will not have been achieved until the family is seen as much as a man's concern as a woman's. So far, family needs and family issues have been defined as the woman's domain. The next frontier is to make it the man's as well. Children ought to be seen as the equal responsibility of men and women.

NPQ: *How, then, do you see the recent efforts at placing the man, once again, front and center in the family? In the last two years, we've seen two big marches in Washington—Louis Farrakhan's Million Man March and, more recently, the Promise Keepers. Both were about men reaffirming their responsibilities to families.*
BF: It is almost ironic this movement should be interpreted as a backlash against women. In reality, there has to be a response by men to the fact that in over 50 percent of families women are earning half the family income. That means men must assume their share of responsibility. As women are now entitled to equal opportunity in the workplace, men should be considered equally responsible for the family.

A Conversation with Betty Friedan

Barbara Mantz Drake / 1999

From the *Peoria Journal Star*, (21 February 1999).
Reprinted by permission of Barbara Mantz
Drake and the *Peoria Journal Star*.

Q: *What did you take out of Peoria that's with you today?*
A: I think that there is a certain solidity, of rootedness, about America, about the United States. And second, I think it's in Peoria that I learned the power of community. In Peoria there really was a kind of can-do spirit of community organizing. If there was a problem, you could organize in the community to deal with the problem. And I think that I got a sense of that in Peoria even before I got all involved with the labor movement and progressive, left-wing politics.

Q: *When you look back on Peoria now, has your thinking about the community changed?*
A: Well, it's a good place to have come from and to have left. I think that the good thing that I got from Peoria was . . . a sense of a larger reality than the sophistication of New York and Los Angeles, which I think is a good part of my effectiveness politically.

What was bad about Peoria, certainly for someone like me probably, was that anti-Semitism which I experienced there. Peoria was not unique to that, but it was in that era. And the conformity. There is conformity in a small city like that. And I don't know about the ability to be truly different, you know. I got strength from growing up in Peoria, but I had to leave it to use it.

Q: *I read about you going back to Peoria for your twenty-five-year high school reunion just after writing* The Feminine Mystique *and feeling like you . . .*

A: Yeah! I think Peoria probably has changed in its attitude about me. If I recall correctly, that reunion I went back and I brought my husband and kids. It was right after *The Feminine Mystique* came out, so I was beginning to get a little famous, and I don't think everybody in Peoria was too happy about that.

Q: *How did you know that they weren't happy?*
A: I may not remember this right, but I think we were staying with Bobby Easton and we woke up one morning and someone had draped toilet paper in the trees. And when we went to the twenty-fifth reunion banquet, and I don't know what happened—some crack, some innuendo—my husband, who came from Boston, he was furious. He thought they were being insulting to me. And he said so loud and clear, "How dare they treat me this way!"

And I think that probably there were some people in Peoria that were just kind of annoyed, you know, that Betty, a Jewish girl from Peoria, was suddenly famous. I guess I am the most famous person that came out of Peoria. But some years later, I think they decided it was good for Peoria to have spawned someone like me. Because after all, the work I've done, my life's work, has made it much better for the women and girls that come from Peoria, as well as Los Angeles and New York.

Q: *What's your earliest memory from childhood?*
A: I loved school. I think my greatest joy was sort of make-up games. This was the era of Nancy Drew and the detectives, and so being a girl detective and making up with my friends, and there was this bridge and we'd hide under the bridge and spy on the smugglers. You know, imaginary things.

Q: *Good memories, friends, making up games. Bad memories?*
A: I had some bad memories when high school came along. I don't know if it's true today (but) life at the high school was sort of dominated by sororities and fraternities. And you know being Jewish . . . we didn't get into sororities or fraternities, and all of my other friends from grade school and high school were in. I really wasn't meant to be an Emily Dickinson reading poetry on her break. I did it, but I would have much rather been in a jalopy going down to Hunt's to have a hamburger with the rest of the kids.

But then, as I got further along in high school I made some new friends that weren't in the sorority and fraternity crowd, on the basis of shared abilities and interests. I really blossomed after I left and went to Smith, because I was very bright. That was not such a good thing to be for a girl in Peoria, but it was great at Smith.

Q: *Were there other favorite places to go?*
A: It was just below the hill, down on Farmington Road. I remember sledding the hills at Bradley (Park). And then I loved hiking and bicycle riding and stuff like that, things out in the country. In those days, I loved being in plays and I would get sort of the child actor parts you know in the Peoria Players. I won a prize in high school, a dramatic honor or something like that, for my five-minute walk-on as a madwoman in Jane Eyre. I would practice this maniacal laugh in the bathroom and would close the door, and my brother and sister were younger than I am; they would sort of listen outside the door and I'd practice this sort of maniacal laugh.

Q: *To what extent did the anti-Semitism you experienced affect your life and your perception of justice?*
A: I think it was so unjust that people should be barred from things or looked down on or whatever because of their race or their religion or any of that. So, I had that experience and that certainty sharpened my sensitivity and outrage of injustice of any sort.

Q: *Do you remember feeling injustice because you were a girl when you were growing up, or limitations on you?*
A: I really didn't. I'm sure that if I look back on it, I can give you ways. For instance, all my cousins, my boy cousins, knew from early on that they were going to be lawyers, go to Harvard Law School, blah, blah, blah. They did . . . and I should have. I had that kind of ability.

Q: *Did you assume when you were growing up that you would have both a career and a family?*
A: No. It was like when I graduated from college and I was thinking, what do I want to do? It was a real blank, because women weren't expected to have careers and I had no role model of a woman who had a career. And I also did want to marry and have children, but I knew that, I don't know how I knew this, but I absolutely knew that what was wrong with my mother was that she didn't have a real use for her ability.

Q: *Where did the words "feminine mystique," the title, come from?*

A: I was having lunch at Yale with Tom Mendenhall (then a Yale University administrator), who had just accepted an appointment to be president at Smith. . . . I wanted to check out if I was really seeing something that had to do with women. I thought, "I wonder if the Yale boys deteriorated like this." And somehow in discussing what I was finding and talking about, I kind of groped around and I said mystique of feminine fulfillment, and when he played it back to me he used the words "feminine mystique." And I said, "Hey wait a minute, that's mine!"

Q: *What were your expectations for the book?*
A: Something in my gut knew that it was important. Every time it would get turned down when I was trying to sell it to magazines, I would do more interviews. I knew I wasn't just talking about just overeducated Smith women. . . . I knew that it implied vast social change.

Q: *You said that writing* The Feminine Mystique *was the most important thing you had ever done. Was it more important than founding the National Organization for Women?*
A: No, the writing of *The Feminine Mystique* was what had made the change in consciousness, which made NOW and the women's movement possible.

Q: *When did you know that something extraordinary had happened in the book?*
A: I knew finishing it that it implied vast social change and it would be threatening to some. But I couldn't possibly have predicted the incredible impact it had. And it really did. And women come up to me, even today, even now all these years later, nearly forty years later, and they come up to me and they say, "It changed my life, changed my whole life," and remember where they were when they read it.

Q: *Do the daughters of those women who read your book when it was first published, do young women in their twenties, say anything to you?*
A: No, I think young women in their twenties take it all for granted. I really do. I mean, the women in their 20s today, they've grown up with expectations and with the kind of different consciousness and I think they think it's always been like that. They don't know what women had to break through.

Q: *Is there danger in that?*
A: There could be a little. The generations that fought or broke through or

very consciously experienced a change and had to fight some battles, they couldn't be pushed back again, but I don't know. Now it's only very reactionary groups that would say a woman's place is in the home, and they wouldn't even dare to say it quite so bluntly. If we had an economic downturn, there might be an attempt to turn women back again.

Q: The Feminine Mystique *was not the first book to reflect on the women's situation. . . .*
A: It was the first in America with any real impact.

Q: *Why, what was different about it?*
A: You have to read it. I think it was the first to really analyze the situation of women and conceptualize and define the feminine mystique instead of just accepting it as the conventional wisdom of the time. Now, Simone de Beauvoir in *The Second Sex*, she did a similar thing, but that work was very highly intellectual and did not somehow lead to action. It analyzed the situation of women in a very depressing way. I remember when I read it, which was some years before I wrote *The Feminine Mystique*, and it made me just want to go to bed for a week.

Q: *You said you wrote* The Second Stage *to help daughters break through the mystique you helped create. What were you referring to there?*
A: I don't know. I haven't read it recently. But *The Feminine Mystique* said no to something, to that way that women were expected to live solely in terms of husband, children and home. *The Second Stage* said it isn't enough for a woman just to sort of look in the mirror and say I am a person, I am going to think about my own life and do something for myself, if society isn't structured for her to be able to do it.

Q: *Is there a feminine mystique today? I mean like the myth of super woman.*
A: I get a little irritated by all of that. I don't think, oh poor women, they're so stressed, they have to be perfect mothers, perfect wives, have these brilliant careers. As far as I can see, and this is not just from my personal observation, but from research, women today don't have just one role. They're wives, they're mothers, they have professions. They're better off. They're not so highly stressed, for heaven's sake. If there's problems in one sphere, satisfaction in the other balances it out. That's another kind of a hype, a myth, about, oh, these poor women are so highly stressed. Nonsense!

Q: *And how about, I guess the question is, can women have it all?*
A: I just hate that question. Can men have it all?

Q: *That's the next question. Can men have it all?*
A: I mean, it's just a ridiculous question. Why shouldn't women have it all? I really just get furious at that question. To imply that women shouldn't have it all. It's an anti-women question. Women should be able to live the lives they want to live and have the opportunities to be in professions and careers and they have to have a choice, and they do now, of whether or not they want kids.

Q: *How do you respond to those who blame you and the women's movement for the decline of the family?*
A: Oh, bull——.

Q: *That's how you respond?*
A: In the first place, I don't think the family has declined. The family is no longer an operable term. Because there is an enormous diversity of families. That's only to be expected with the longer life span that women and men have today. Fifty percent of marriages end in divorce. . . . Not only are women participating in the outside world and sharing the earning burden, but you have men participating much more in the hands-on act of parenting. And that's just for the good.

Q: *Can you talk a little about the genesis of NOW?*
A: When it all started, we didn't have a word for sexual discrimination much less a law against it, because if women aren't people, then the concept of equality didn't apply to them. So there was an enormous change implied here. You begin to be aware of the barriers that kept women from participating equally in the mainstream of society, in the work, in the professions and the political sphere. History was ready for us in a way.

Q: *Is it true that you wrote the mission statement for NOW on a napkin over lunch?*
A: Oh that was just the first sentence. It was in the air, it wasn't original with me, it was in the air that we needed an NAACP for women. There were people in Washington and in the labor movement and in the government, women that had been thinking for much longer than me about women and the need for real equality and the need to break through and take a larger part in soci-

ety. And they kind of saw that I would be useful in that because I was now quite famous and really looked up to by women for *The Feminine Mystique.* And I had no job to lose. This was the end of the McCarthy era, where to organize for anything was suspect.

Q: *Has NOW met your expectations?*
A: I don't know what you mean by expectations. Basically I think NOW has been very good, very good. I lecture in other parts of the country, and always the NOW chapter people come to meet me, and they seem to be doing terrific work in their communities. I'm pretty proud of it.

Q: *You wrote once that it was easier to change society than to change your own personal life.*
A: Oh, well, that's true. I read somewhere that maybe Freud revolutionized our approach to sex but I don't know that it helped his own sex life that much.

Q: *How much of what was going on in your personal life, in your marriage and those difficulties affect what you wrote?*
A: Sometimes it was a little schizophrenic. Here I was Joan of Arc leading the women out of the wilderness and fighting for equality. In my personal life, and my marriage, I was pretty much of a. . . . Well, I wouldn't say I was a doormat; I wasn't a doormat, but I think I hadn't completely broken through the feminine mystique.

My own life, (the book) changed my life, too. I mean I got famous. That was a threat to my husband. I remember when I started being asked to lecture and I had three kids and Emily was still little. And I had it written into my lecture contract that if I went to give a lecture, I shouldn't be asked again for at least two weeks, because I didn't want to leave the kids that much and because my husband was pretty, kind of upset by my going off to lecture.

Q: *In* The Second Stage *you said by the year 2000, "I doubt there will be any need for the likes of Phyllis Schlafley or Gloria Steinem or Betty Friedan for that matter." You said that the argument for equal rights would be "nostalgic history."*
A: Well, I was a little over-optimistic. Certainly by the year 2000 I can say that the concept of equality for women is accepted in the United States and the idea that women will have their own voice and that women have to be taken seriously, not just as wives and mothers, but as people. That's here, that's in society now. And even the controversial part, like the right to choose when

and whether and how many times they have a child and, therefore, safe, legal access to abortion, there's even a consensus on that in society now. . . .

Q: *So where do we go from here?*
A: For one thing, women are only making 74 cents on the dollar for what men make, but when you analyze the discrepancy, it all begins in the child-bearing, child-rearing years. And women are not yet at the top, but that's getting to be there.

So obviously the next step is a much more focused attention—and priority attention—to a child-care program in terms of activism, in terms of legislation, in terms of innovations of child-care programs. It might be public and private, in other words a combination of corporate, city or state or national. Things like child-care programs (should) be given some priority in union negotiations, that sort of thing. That's on an activist policy level.

And then on the consciousness level, there must be a much more conscious push on parenting not being just the mother's responsibility. Two parents, not even just necessarily the father and mother, a recognition of diversity of family shape and structure today. And in all these weeks and years there has been such a focus on choice, and I think that has been right . . . OK, what about the choice to bear children? That has to be much more focused on the conditions that make it possible for a woman to advance in her career and not have to wait until she's 40 and needs maybe in-vitro fertilization to have a kid. So, there's more that needs to be done.

Q: *Is the women's movement still relevant?*
A: I think the women's movement is in society now. What had been the agenda of the radical of the women's movement, a revolutionary agenda, whatever you want to call it, it's in society now. There is a consensus.

Behind the Feminist Mystique

Michael Shelden / 1999

From the *London Daily Telegraph*, (9 August 1999). Reprinted with permission of Michael Shelden.

A new book paints Betty Friedan, the high priest of feminism, as a boozer and a bully. She sets the record straight to Michael Shelden.

The mother of the modern feminist movement peeks round the door of her quaint old house on Long Island, New York, and gives me a suspicious look. "Yeah, what is it?" Betty Friedan rasps. Though the sun is high overhead, she seems to have slept late and has come to the door wearing only a black nightie. I remind her that she agreed to be interviewed. "I did what?" she says, with a pained expression, and my heart sinks.

Having just put down a new biography that calls her "rude and nasty, self-serving and imperious," I have come to her door with, shall we say, low expectations. But not this low. And then, while I am silently counting the cost of a wasted journey to this remote part of New York State, her big eyes light up and she throws open the door. "Oh, of course, now I remember. I've had a few appointments canceled and I was confused. I thought the interview was another day. Come in and make yourself at home while I get dressed."

She saunters to the back of the house, the short nightie swaying from thigh to thigh, her bare soles smudged with dust from the exposed hardwood floors. I take a seat in the front room and wait. I see that Friedan has hung on the wall a framed woven cloth embroidered with the words: "A woman's place is in the world." On the other side of the room is a table cluttered with old newspapers, a mystery novel and a big box of poker chips. There cannot be many seventy-eight-year-old women who keep a ready supply of poker chips in the front room; but this is the author of the landmark work, *The Feminine Mystique,* a woman who has spent almost half a century urging members of her sex to be as independent and unconventional as she is.

At the conclusion of her book, she asks a generation: "Who knows what women can be when they are finally free to become themselves?" Yet her own battle for freedom has been so tumultuous that she has often found herself in conflict with both sexes. Her enemies have been given fresh—and potent—ammunition by the recent publication in America of Judith Hennessee's *Betty Friedan: Her Life.* The book argues that Friedan failed the feminist movement by attacking everyone she disagreed with and, worse, that she is too fond of men and does not even like most women. Hennessee paints a lurid picture of Betty's twenty-one-year marriage to Carl Friedan, alleging that it was a long ordeal of black eyes and broken mirrors. She claims that they drank too much, had bitter quarrels over money and sex, sometimes exchanged blows and that Carl would tell people at parties: "I'm the bitch's husband."

Yet, as this supposed Medusa enters the room, I see a peaceful expression on her large oval face and hear polite apologies for her tardiness. I hesitate before asking what she thinks of the new biography and brace myself for an explosion. There is a brief silence before Friedan remarks, calmly: "Oh, she can say what she wants and people can believe what they want. I can't stop that. If she's right, I thought to myself, what a terrible person I am. But she's wrong." She is? "Sure, even the reviewers have said she's wrong about me. They were critical of the book, but not of me."

You mean she's wrong when she says you're unhappy and combative? "Combative, absolutely, but not unhappy," she says—looking combative, but happy. "What's wrong with being passionate or angry? People are too namby-pamby these days. Anger, even righteous anger, may not be chic, but there is a lot in this world to be angry about. We need more passion. I was impressed when President Kennedy called for more passion in politics, but now the only passionate people are on the far Right. One thing I can say, though, is that I've had my share of passion. In politics and in life."

Yes, but your critics say that you're so passionate that you become . . .

"Bitchy?" She laughs loudly and wags her finger at me in mock reproof. "No, not bitchy, just spirited. That's the proper word. Though, years ago, I did tell a reporter from *Life* magazine that I may be bitchy, but I'm never boring. And then I got a letter from an aunt I hadn't heard from for years, who scolded me for using language that was not ladylike."

She shakes her head and laughs loudly again, amused by the thought that anyone would expect her to be ladylike. But there is another old-fashioned term that does seem right for her: bohemian. Colorful and casual in her dress, scornful of tradition and proudly defiant of polite society, she would be at home among the suffragettes of an earlier day, whose fight for equal justice she revived in the early Sixties.

"I'm at odds with the radical feminists because I'm not anti-marriage and anti-family. I always thought it was dangerous to go against the idea of family. I don't even like the phrase 'women's liberation,' because that idea of being set free from everything doesn't seem right to me. I like to think of the women's movement as a fight for equality."

That sort of thinking may seem reasonable, but her spirited defense of it has not always gone down well with some members of the feminist sisterhood. In particular, she has often feuded with Gloria Steinem, whom she once described as a female chauvinist boor. Hennessee quotes a feminist who says, "We all knew Betty hated Gloria's guts," and notes that Gloria used to remark that each time she held out a hand to Betty, she was left with "a bloody stump."

Betty rolls her eyes. "These biographers do like to exaggerate, don't they? But lots of people have made too much of my feud with Gloria. They can't seem to understand that every important movement is going to have a certain amount of fighting over turf. Men do it all the time in politics and nobody says that they're being cruel or pushy. It's just part of the nature of things. Am I supposed to be silent when Gloria says things I don't agree with? When she said marriage was a form of prostitution, I spoke up and criticized her. Her view had nothing to do with my kind of feminism, and I said so. And you notice that now you don't hear as much from Gloria or from the radical feminists. That extreme form of thinking tends to come from women who hate having to deal with the complexities of juggling a career and a family and so, almost literally, they want to throw the baby out with the bath water. It's just unrealistic to be a feminist who is anti-family."

She puts Germaine Greer in the same camp as Steinem, but insists that she doesn't have a grudge against her rivals. "We're still fighting for a lot of the same things. But they do have their problems. Germaine is such an exhibition-ist and I still get a kick out of hearing Gloria's followers object to make-up and beauty treatments. I mean, Gloria gets her hair streaked and is obviously a very good-looking babe who cares about her appearance and who has had lovers who are very rich men. I don't object to a woman trying to look her best. I always thought it was good to have a stylish woman like Gloria in the movement."

From the time that she was a young girl in the midwestern town of Peoria, Betty wanted to be a wife and a mother. She was close to her father, who was a prosperous jeweler, and was given a good education. But she couldn't help noticing that her male relatives were sent to better universities.

"All my male cousins went to Harvard Law School. I went to a woman's college and then did graduate work in California. I should have gone to Har-vard. I would have become a lawyer and, who knows, maybe I'd have a seat in the Supreme Court now. But I wasn't allowed that chance. When I was young, in the Thirties and Forties, a woman was not expected to have a family and a career. It was always either/or. If you look in *Who's Who* for those years, you will find that all the women who made it into the book were either married to famous men or didn't have a family of their own. I didn't want to settle for that."

So, at the age of twenty-six, she married a man in the advertising business and promptly began having babies. By the Fifties, she was a restless housewife with two sons and a daughter. Her one professional outlet was part-time work as a freelance writer for women's magazines. Frustrated by the lack of opportu-nity and the insipid views of womanhood espoused in the mainstream press, she began writing the 400-page declaration of independence that she would eventually call *The Feminine Mystique*. The book struck a chord with many women who, like Friedan, were suburban wives and mothers yearning for greater fulfillment. They were tormented by one great unspoken question and Betty was outspoken enough to put it into words. "Is this all?" she asked of her lot in life.

Hennessee's book suggests that Betty might never have been driven to speak out if her own marriage had not been so troubled. Long since divorced from Carl, Betty has never remarried and now contends that her relationship with her husband was not all bad. "Carl says that he wants to sue that Hennessee woman because she makes out that he was always abusing me. But he was very supportive of my efforts to write *The Feminine Mystique* and drove my publisher crazy by complaining that not enough copies were being printed to keep up with demand. We're friends today and still see each other. I spent last Christmas with him in Florida."

So there's not substance to the claims that the marriage was often painfully difficult? "I'd say it was stormy. Passionate. We fought and maybe we had a couple of drinks in the evenings and fought some more. Look, I'm not a doormat. We did have our battles, and when I became famous it was sometimes threatening to Carl. If someone wanted to introduce him as Betty Friedan's husband, he was not happy and wanted to knock the person down. But it was not all arguments and fighting. We had a lot of good times. We had good family holidays and we always had dinner together as a family every night. We love our kids and they've turned out great."

Indeed, their daughter Emily is a graduate of Harvard Medical School and a prominent physician in Boston. One son, Jonathan, is a partner in an engineering firm and Daniel is a renowned university physicist who has won several awards, including the so-called "genius grant" from the MacArthur Foundation. And Betty is now a proud grandmother. "What can I say?" she asks. "We must have been doing some things right."

Her sometimes abrasive and abrupt manner may not please everyone, but she has emerged with many of the things she once yearned for. She has fame, loving children, a decent amount of money and an interesting life that she divides between homes in Washington and Long Island. She still lectures and is said to have the ear of the Clinton administration when it comes to the appointment of women to senior positions.

In recent years, she has been treated for heart problems, but she is preparing to leave for a fortnight's holiday in Italy and is putting the finishing touches on a new book. "It's my memoir," she says. "It will set the record straight. I don't know how people will react, but all the important stuff is in there, and I tell it the way it is. So we'll see . . ."

One thing she knows for certain: despite the carping of her critics, she has won her place in history. "I have no complaints about the way I'm treated in the press or by my adversaries. Walk down the street with me in any big city and you'll see that I'm constantly stopped by women who want to thank me for my work." And if I have any doubts about her courage, they are put to rest when she tells me of a recent dinner invitation from her neighbor Thomas Harris, the reclusive creator of Hannibal "the cannibal" Lecter. Did you accept? I ask with a shudder. "Oh, sure, Tommy's a good cook."

Index